The
Global
Community

The
Global
Community:
Migration and the Making of the Modern World

W.M. SPELLMAN

SUTTON PUBLISHING

First published in the United Kingdom in 2002 by
Sutton Publishing Limited · Phoenix Mill
Thrupp · Stroud · Gloucestershire · GL5 2BU

British Library Cataloguing in Publication Data
A catalogue record for this book is available from the British Library.

ISBN 0-7509-2243-5

Typeset in 11/14.5pt Sabon.
Typesetting and origination by
Sutton Publishing Limited.
Printed and bound in England by
J.H. Haynes & Co. Ltd, Sparkford.

Contents

In Memory of
Edward G. Hartmann

Acknowledgements

A 2000 National Endowment for the Humanities Summer Institute on India, hosted by the University of Hawaii, enabled me to begin work on the South Asia section. A follow-on visit to India in 2001, with colleagues from the University of Georgia, afforded me additional time on this topic. Many thanks are due to Marc Gilbert of North Georgia College and State University and to Farley Richmond of the University of Georgia, Athens, for leading this academic project. A three-year term as Director of Interdisciplinary Humanities at my home institution, the University of North Carolina, Asheville, provided a reduced teaching load at a crucial period. I am grateful to Dr James Pitts, Vice-Chancellor of Academic Affairs, for appointing me to this post. As with earlier projects, Nancy Costello, Margaret Costello and Robert Burke contributed with support, and patience, throughout the process. The work is dedicated to the memory of a lifelong scholar of the immigration experience.

Acknowledgements

Introduction

Why do people remove themselves, and often their entire families, great distances to unfamiliar lands and uncertain futures? What combination of factors could be so compelling that one would forego the familiar for the foreign, the natal for the new, the attachment to a sedentary community for the incertitude of the wanderer? These are questions that our earliest forebears, given their everyday life experiences, would have found hardly worth asking. Indeed, the movement of groups of people from one locale to another has been a constant of the human experience at least since the appearance of *Homo sapiens* some 50–70,000 years ago. During the long period prior to the advent of agriculture around 10,000 BCE, humans typically organized themselves along kinship lines and pursued either a hunter-gatherer or pastoral form of existence, where cooperative labour and regular movement across the land were pre-requisites to survival. When plant and animal resources were exhausted in one area, whole companies of nomadic people would decamp and relocate to a more abundant environment, there to repeat the age-old process of maintenance without the burdens of accumulation.

Together with unpredictable shifts in climate, natural disasters and threats from hostile neighbours, a life of movement was the norm for most early people and, as a result, fixed notions of territory and resource appropriation, the material 'mine and thine', were largely absent from the collective assumptions of the group or kinship community.[1] Settled villages, towns and cities, with all of their attendant rules, social hierarchies and formal political institutions, were very much the exception for humans the world over until fairly recent millennia. In a manner that is all too

1

common in modern consumer cultures, we tend to overlook the newness and aberrational nature of our sedentary, civilized societies, our dogged defence of hearth and home. Roving, relocation, geographic change – these were the standard practices of early people, experiences as regular as the assurance of illness and the sting of death.

Prior to 1500 virtually all great migrations were land-based affairs, most often associated with warfare and the violent displacement of agricultural labourers by cruel, mobile strangers, but also involving the constant in-migration of rural populations to urban centres. It is not terribly difficult to identify a wide range of human migrations which have had a broad-based and lasting impact on world history. From the Bantu peoples, who over many centuries trekked from West to Central and then to south-east Africa, bringing their language and customs with them; to Turkish invaders who roamed from their traditional places of habitation in the steppes of south-central Asia to found the 'coastlands' Ottoman Empire in what is today Turkey, the Safavid Empire in Persia, and the Mughal Empire in India; to the Mongol nomads who traversed the Eurasian land mass during the thirteenth century, crushing all opponents with unremitting violence and threatening to occupy Western Europe – all of these large-scale movements of people and cultures are familiar to us. Many died in the wake of the important steppe nomad advances. The Turkish and Mongol peoples who swept out of their Central Asian homelands in recurring thrusts during the period 1000–1500 were indiscriminate invaders at the head of military plunder machines whose only innovation was to impose despotic and ramshackle Asian institutions on most Eurasian peoples unlucky enough to stand in their path.[2] And Europe's narrow escape from this nomadic aggression would be of enormous significance to the future political and economic development of the far western portion of the larger Eurasian land mass.

Significant overland migrations within each continent, together with country to city movement and the more recent phenomenon of temporary labour migration, are of course subjects worthy of study, and much detailed work has appeared on these subjects over the past few decades. But while the movement of very large numbers of people from one natural habitat to another was a common feature of pre-history, and certainly continued in many areas of the globe long after the advent of stationary civilizations, an unprecedented phase in the story of intercontinental migration began fewer than 500 years ago, and it is this extraordinary story that will be the focus of our attention in what follows. The new stage involved nothing less than a transoceanic transfer, and in not a few cases the forced dislocation, of millions of humans – largely from Europe and Africa, but including many from other global points of departure – and as such it must be identified as one of the more momentous developments in the history of humanity, both in terms of the numbers involved and in light of the overall impact of migrating peoples on the indigenous inhabitants of host territories. In an important sense, then, both intra-continental and temporary migrations represent a continuation of processes which began in the ancient world, whereas post-1500 oceanic intercontinental migration presents us with a number of unparalleled encounters between cultures and traditions which were fundamentally dissimilar. How these encounters were negotiated by both sides, how a single human space and new cultural boundaries were established on terms unforeseen at the outset of the process, and how a demographic transformation of whole continents took place – these issues in themselves constitute a pivotal moment in the history of human reformation.

The age of sail and, even more dramatically (after 1850), the advent of steam transport, forever altered basic migration patterns the world over. Now, for the first time in history, large numbers of women and men – as individuals, as family units, as whole communities – departed their countries and their continents for a variety of transoceanic destinations. The scale and diversity of the process had never been witnessed before. By the last decade of the nineteenth century, for example, two out of every five persons who had been born in British-controlled Ireland were living elsewhere, often an ocean away. Communities of North Indians were settling as indentured labourers in Caribbean sugar islands and on South

African plantations. Over 60,000 Japanese labourers and their families were relocating to independent Hawaii prior to the advent of American political supremacy over those strategic islands, while impoverished Chinese peasants assumed a variety of low-paid agricultural posts in California. Today more than 350 million people of African descent live outside Africa, compared with 540 million resident in that vast continent. Close to 30 million Chinese, and those of Chinese descent, live beyond the borders of mainland China. And almost 9 million South Asians reside elsewhere, separated from the land of their birth by larger political, economic and religious factors.[3]

Not surprisingly, international migrants over this 500-year period tended to be women and men in their most productive years, and their varied contributions to both the development and the destruction of new environments and indigenous peoples were enhanced by their physical, and in many cases, ideological, vigour. In the midst of this great transferral of human labour and spirit, new patterns of cultural diffusion, new encounters involving everything from disease patterns to religious systems, would help to redefine the contours of the global experience for every major civilization. No longer would major cultural traditions live in isolation from each other; thanks to transoceanic migration, the intermingling of faces and values, of preferences and traditions, of understanding and its opposite, would shrink the intellectual world to the point where knowledge of the 'other' culture often required no more than getting to know one's immediate neighbour.

The authors of an important recent study have identified four distinct eras of international migration over the past half millennium, and we will adopt this convenient periodization in what follows.[4] The role of Europeans in the overall process of global transformation was, for good or ill, absolutely central; even the involuntary and brutal transatlantic diaspora of 12–15 million African women and men between 1500 and 1808 cannot be accounted for without a reference to European ambitions, European problems and European priorities. Only after 1500 was the entire

4

globe brought into regular and sustained communication and trade contact, a network initiated and later dominated by ambitious Europeans. Again, only after 1500 did the inhabitants of one continent, Western Europe, begin the dynamic and often destructive process of overseas colonization which was to stamp the impress of a Christian and commercial civilization on to the varied templates of non-Western cultures. Without falling into the unedifying trap of Eurocentric history, there can be no denying the tremendous scale – demographic, intellectual, material and cultural – of European migration and resettlement after 1500, and especially over the past two dynamic and destructive centuries. The age of European imperialism may be at an end, but the descendants of Europe's migrants remain in political and cultural control of large parts of the habitable globe.

During the first era (1500–1800), European colonization and mercantilism transformed the Americas, Africa, Asia and Oceania. In the words of Immanuel Wallerstein, a European-defined 'modern world system' was inaugurated in which hundreds of thousands of indentured servants, African slaves, convict migrants, planters, religious dissenters and free farmers and artisans overspread lands inhabited by indigenous peoples whose numbers were decimated by European diseases.[5] Constituting over 20 per cent of non-indigenous inhabitants of the Americas in 1800, black Africans and their descendants struggled against enormous odds to secure personal freedom and individual advancement, a set of goals unlike those which obtained in so many of the stateless African societies from which they or their ancestors were abducted. In addition to African slaves, approximately half of the 2–3 million European transatlantic migrants during these three centuries travelled under some form of labour indenture. Indeed selling one's labour for a set term of years was, for most prospective European migrants, the only viable means of securing the cost of what was a slow and often dangerous passage under sail. During this 'Mercantile Era', plantation economies in the Americas provided the focus of most economic activity, with the profits realized through the labour of indentured and slave populations facilitating Europe's transition to the machine age.

The second or 'Industrial' period of international migration, which began in the early nineteenth century, again involved Europeans, but instead favoured free white labour seeking new opportunities outside of a continent experiencing both inordinate demographic growth and the hardships of an urban, manufacturing lifestyle. Only about 7 per cent of Europeans lived in cities at the start of this period, but with the advent of large-scale commercial agriculture, landless farmers relocated to towns and cities to form an industrial proletariat during the 1800s. By 1900 there were 135 European cities with populations larger than 100,000.[6] Larger families and a pattern of downward social mobility induced many industrial workers to seek opportunities overseas. If we examine global migration patterns over the entire 500-year period under consideration, it is obvious that the emergence and growth of capitalist, market economies greatly influenced both the scale and the direction of migration flows. While a confluence of disparate factors often informed decisions about transnational movement, the exigencies of the labour market played a pivotal, perhaps essential, role in the transfer of peoples throughout the world.

During the 125 years ending with 1925, between 50 and 60 million people left Europe's advanced industrial states, and 85 per cent of these migrants settled in just five countries: Argentina, Australia, Canada, New Zealand and the United States (which alone received 60 per cent of the total). By way of contrast, roughly 15 million Africans and Asians became intercontinental migrants during the entire 400-year period 1500–1900.[7] In the process of resettlement these nineteenth-century Europeans successfully superimposed key aspects of their culture on a variety of native peoples. The disparity had long-term consequences for the global community in the modern age. According to Alfred Crosby, 'None of the major groupings of humankind is as oddly distributed about the world as European, especially Western European, whites.' In both the north and south temperate zones (with the one exception of lands in Asia), people of European stock now form the majority population. Whereas Europeans and their overseas offspring constituted roughly 18 per cent of the human species in 1650, that percentage has now almost doubled; today a quarter of a billion of Europe's descendants inhabit lands around the globe, a model of diffusion made possible in no small respect by the scientific, technological and ideological resources available to the peoples of Western Europe throughout the second period covered by this book.[8]

The era of large-scale European migration ended with the fratricidal First World War. At the close of that terrible global conflict key receiving nations like the United States and Canada began passing restrictive immigration laws, and while these laws privileged migrants from Europe, the onset of the Great Depression followed by another disastrous global conflagration (1939–45) effectively brought an end to voluntary European resettlement. Forced removal, however, especially in the form of millions of war refugees, continued to define Europe as a sending area during the war. Finally, an age of post-industrial 'Global Migration' began in the 1960s and involved a much wider array of sending and receiving countries. The preceding era had witnessed the transfer of people from densely settled, industrialized regions to sparsely settled industrializing areas. In more recent decades, the model has shifted to the movement of peoples from densely settled countries experiencing the earliest stages of industrialization and entry into the global economy to areas which are already highly urbanized, industrialized and densely settled.[9] The advent of plural sending areas, instead of ameliorating the economic and political challenges faced by sending nations, has in many cases actually exacerbated the problem of development, as receiving nations tend to favour admission of skilled professionals, men and women who otherwise might serve as catalysts for change in their talent-depleted home states.

As a field of inquiry, migration has attracted the interest of social scientists from a number of disciplines, and specialized studies continue to enrich our understanding of this prominent component of the human experience. The literature on international migration is enormous, and includes contributions from political scientists, economists, sociologists, statisticians, historians, anthropologists and demographers. The reason for the heightened interest is transparent; in a world where capital and information flow instantaneously across international borders, the movement of people, while anything but instantaneous, is nonetheless at unprecedented levels in terms of volume and diversity.[10] Talk of an emerging 'global village' may be difficult to accept in light of regional conflicts which have claimed the lives of over 25 million people since the end of the Second World War, but the strength of the migratory impulse has doubtless enhanced the creation of culturally diverse societies in a number of developed countries.

In each of the academic disciplines, scholars typically refer to 'push' and 'pull' factors when seeking to explain the phenomenon of human passage from one's place of origin to another home. 'Push' simply refers to internal incentives, usually hardships experienced by individuals and often whole communities in the place of their birth. Including both man-made (war, religious intolerance, political, ethnic and economic oppression) and natural variables (famine, exhaustion of resources, climate change), internal incentives have over the centuries proved to be the most potent factors in the process of human relocation. On the other hand, 'pull' catalysts include the perceived attractions of life opportunities in a new and distant land. Ancient peoples followed a migratory lifestyle due to modes of production suited to low population numbers, and cultural priorities which placed the communal good of the kinship unit before the satisfaction of the individual member. Migrants over the last five centuries, by contrast, took their leave in unprecedented numbers for reasons both spiritual and mundane, but in almost all cases the goal of individual self-betterment was paramount. The chance for an improved work environment, property ownership, religious and/or political freedom, greater opportunity for one's children, social mobility and personal dignity all combined, especially over the last two centuries, in drawing the prospective migrant to leave the accustomed and embrace the unacquainted.

Of course push and pull factors were rarely, if ever, mutually exclusive in the decision-making process. The choices made by millions of nineteenth-century migrants to the Caribbean, to East and South Africa, to Australasia, and to North and South America were often informed by both ingredients. We now live in a world of over 100 million immigrants, and the global transfer of skilled and unskilled human labour which the phenomenon of intercontinental migration has made possible over the past 500 years has had a dramatic impact on the development of particular civilizations – typically in the West – while the emigrant's native land – often less developed in terms of economic benchmarks – has been handicapped in the quest for material advancement by the departure of so many talented women and men.

The subject of intercontinental migration can be treated on a number of levels: state sponsorship, economic imperatives, cultural diffusion and the preservation of ancestral ways, the impact of migrants on native peoples, the personal and psychological consequences of dislocation and relocation, the consequence of mass migration on the natural environment, intermarriage and genetic mingling, contrasts between free and unfree, legal and illegal, voluntary and forced, migrants. These are but a few of the many variables in what can best be described as a rich and multi-layered story. In a brief survey like this, however, much has by necessity been omitted. The nominal hope is that some of the leading contours of the process and its overall global impact can be suggested in a manner in which both state concerns and personal experiences have their legitimate place. For at every juncture in the story both the political/economic and the personal were (and remain) in play – the ambitions of great powers and the dreams of humble farmers and factory hands; the exigencies of cash-crop plantation owners who thought in terms of global markets and the sufferings of the enslaved and the semi-free whose labour made those markets possible; twentieth-century state restrictions on immigrants fuelled by xenophobia and racism, and the ongoing desire of humans for a better quality of life in more prosperous lands.

We will attempt to address the phenomenon of global migration from both perspectives, always keeping in mind the irreducible if unhappy fact that the companion to migration is some measure of dislocation, and with dislocation in any form comes suffering. The world's 20 million international refugees know something of this, surely. But even those free migrants who eagerly boarded the crowded steamers and took their place in steerage at the turn of the twentieth century knew in their hearts that there would be no turning back, that something of individual and collective identity would be sacrificed or at the very least transformed in a new setting beyond the great oceans. How that happened, how place was redefined by travellers from afar, how differences were treated and how one civilization on the far north-west corner of the much larger Eurasian land mass came to play such an influential role in making the modern world – these are issues of not insignificant moment at the start of the twenty-first century.

PART ONE

The Mercantile Era,
1500–1800

Before 1450 and the age of European exploration, the world's major races were largely segregated, its civilizations mainly isolated and autonomous. Caucasoids dominated in Europe, North Africa, South-west Asia and Northern India, while Negroids held population hegemony in sub-Saharan Africa. Mongoloids occupied Asia and the Americas, and Australoids inhabited Australia and Southern India. This relative isolation came to an abrupt end during the course of the next 300 years, as European Caucasoids spread into Central Asia, the Americas and Oceania, and finally into Southern Africa during the closing decades of the nineteenth century. This expansion also led to new demographic trends, as world population, which stood at approximately 425 million in the year 1500, expanded to almost 650 million in 1700, and then rose rapidly to just under 900 million in 1800.

Whatever else might be said respecting the global expansion of select European kingdoms after 1500, the role of state-based power politics in the decision to sponsor and support voyages of exploration must be situated at the centre of any treatment of international migration. From the age of Athenian presumption and aggression against its city-state neighbours in the fifth century BCE, to the Aztec expropriation of property and person in sixteenth-century Central America, to the late twentieth-century Chinese communist occupation of Tibet, the irreducible penchant for power, resources and territory has been a brutal constant of sovereign state policy, either implicitly or more directly. In Europe, feudal particularism and Christian universalism were undermined by a form of nascent nationalism made more strident by the Protestant–Catholic divide. The autonomy of Europe's Christian kingdoms was first signalled by the success of the Protestant Reformation. Luther's revolt put an end to a millennium during which the universal Catholic Church, under the leadership of the papacy, asserted its primacy over every territorial monarch, and instead inaugurated a new age, more familiar to us, in which individual identity was increasingly linked to one's status as either subject or citizen. Even in kingdoms which remained loyal to the Catholic Church, aggrandizing monarchs began to wield unfettered authority over their respective lands. Organized force prepared the way for the eventual European peopling of three continents, and peremptory 'reasons of state' facilitated the subsequent pace of occupation by European kingdoms that were deeply at odds with one another. The religious wars of the sixteenth and seventeenth centuries were as much about the political integrity of the respective kingdoms as they were about the eradication of misguided religious tenets.

Moral considerations had rarely guided political action in state-based societies prior to 1500, and the discovery of the 'New World' by the Genoese seafarer Columbus (in the employ of the Spanish crown) offered a novel and heretofore 'unplayed' field of action for divided and ambitious European crowned heads.[1] After 1500 the West began to transform the global community on a scale previously unimagined, but that work of change was not animated by a sustained consideration for the cultural or religious priorities of non-Western peoples. The proselytizing energy of early modern Christianity was doubtless an ingredient associated with the project of initial conquest in the Americas and Africa, just as it had been for Charlemagne's armies in the wilds of Saxon Germany during the late eighth century, but nowhere did the spiritual itinerary trump the blueprint of the more prosaic material agenda. Columbus observed that the indigenous peoples might 'become Christians very easily', but he was also convinced that they 'should be good and intelligent servants'.[2] If anything, religious factors reinforced the strong sense of propriety which Europeans felt about their physical takeover in the Americas and Australasia, and about their economic domination in almost every other area of the globe by 1800.

And factors associated with political control were rarely to be found disengaged from those involving economic might. Both at the state and private levels, early modern Europeans accepted a mercantilist model of economic development where the material well-being of the home kingdom and its subjects was based upon control over and exclusive appropriation of colonial goods, where prospective colonies and colonists served as the source of strategic precious metals, raw materials, cash crops and labour. The discovery of these metals and materials would be left to free subjects of the crown; the extraction of these resources, on the other hand, together with the cultivation of agricultural products, would be reserved for natives, for bonded labour, and in the end for Europe's poor and dispossessed.

Power and coercion in the service of nation-state priorities had always been at the heart of political life; now after 1500 the fiscal imperatives of merchants and businessmen would increasingly direct the robust exercise of coercive state authority. The ancient Chinese legalist maxim that men of commerce should not be upheld, that 'an enlightened ruler will administer his state in such a way as to decrease the number of merchants, artisans, and other men who make their living by wandering from place to place, and will see to it that such men are looked down upon' – a view that was mirrored in much medieval Christian teaching – was after 1500 notable only by its absence in the West.[3] Getting, keeping and accumulating were for the early modern West the new keys to the city of man, now rehabilitated and declared worthy of humankind's principal desires after centuries of Augustinian neglect.

ONE

Conquerors and Indentures

The world after 1500 became more economically and in some respects more ideologically integrated than at any previous time in the human experience. And it was largely due to the efforts and ambitions of Western Europeans that this forced convergence took place.[1] Civilizations which for centuries had developed in a relatively autonomous fashion were, after 1500, regularly exposed to the influence of the West, and the innovation and anti-authoritarianism which marked sections of Europe after the voyages of Columbus and the challenge of Luther undergirded the rapid spread of Western ideas and approaches to life. What had been for centuries a tradition-bound, subsistence-based and insular medieval Christian culture suddenly thrust itself on the world in a brash, reckless and often callous manner under the consolidating leadership of rival monarchs who were constantly seeking an ever-elusive hegemony over their neighbours. In the wake of this momentous advance, European settlers migrated in fairly significant numbers to exploit the natural resources, and the peoples, of newly discovered lands.

Of course it was all quite unexpected. In the year 1500, the likelihood that Christian Western Europe would soon have a profound material, religious, intellectual and demographic impact on the rest of the known world was quite small. Indeed even if we discount the debilitating consequences of religious division triggered by the Lutheran Reformation of the 1520s, the prospects for European global expansion looked very unpropitious. At the start of the sixteenth century the quarrelsome inhabitants of Christendom faced an immediate mortal danger at home from the potent Ottoman Turks, as the startled Habsburg rulers of the Holy Roman Empire – Europe's south-east flank – were thrown on the defensive in a contest for the very survival of Christian culture. Under the decisive leadership of Suleiman 'the Magnificent' (r. 1520–60), Muslim armies swept across large sections of the Balkans and Hungary, and in 1529 – just as Pizarro was completing his destruction of the enormous Incan Empire – the Habsburg capital at Vienna itself was subject to a protracted siege. The Turks were narrowly rebuffed at this point, but their formidable presence in the lands of eastern Europe continued to stand as a serious threat to the security of the continent for another full century. And Ottoman control over strategic points throughout the eastern Mediterranean effectively vetoed sustained European land contact with the peoples and riches of the Asian world.

Together with the Shi'ite Safavid Persian Empire and the neighbouring Mughal Empire in India, Muslims monopolized land-based trade and effectively dictated terms under which the Christian kingdoms of the West might realize the full potential of commercial relations with South Asia and China. This was true even in North Africa, where the Almoravid rulers of Morocco posed a very serious threat to the continued flow of gold from the sub-Saharan region into Europe. It has been argued that one of the principal motives for Portuguese exploratory voyages along the west coast of Africa during the late fifteenth century was well-placed fear of Almoravid power.[2] Avoiding the Muslim middleman became an important strategic objective, indeed a preoccupation, of European crowned heads and their merchant subjects alike, as trade with the East and with Africa's West Coast kingdoms in a mercantilist economic setting was equated with the enhancement of state power and long-term political survival.

In an important sense the overriding goal of Europe's competing and pugnacious monarchies was exclusive access to global sources of wealth, which in turn would translate into greater domestic and international political power. And vast, concentrated, and known wealth, at least as far as sixteenth-century Europe was concerned, really meant China. Links with China, sustained economic dialogue with the great Middle Kingdom, regular and predictable trade routes – this was the great entreaty, the unparalleled ambition of Western political and commercial elites. Nor was China, despite being aware of the extent of its material superiority over its distant neighbours, devoid of comparable ambitions with respect to the rest of the world. During the first two decades of the fifteenth century, long before the Portuguese and the Spanish gave serious consideration to underwriting overseas exploration, the Ming Emperor Yongle had outfitted a series of remarkable naval flotillas designed for long-distance trade and discovery. Under the command of the Muslim eunuch Zheng He, seven voyages were undertaken between 1405 and 1433, carrying Chinese explorers as far west as Arabia and the east coast of Africa. The first expedition included sixty large treasure ships with a combined crew of 28,000 men, a dramatic contrast to Columbus's later inaugural voyage featuring three small vessels and ninety sailors. Boasting construction technology at a level simply unavailable in the West, including multiple-masted ships with stern-post rudders and watertight bulkheads, Chinese explorers returned with little that was of interest to their imperial masters in the Middle Kingdom.[3] The great ships came back to port for good in 1433, as the Ming emperors were obliged to devote state resources to more pressing economic and political difficulties. Mongol threats from the north necessitated the costly bolstering of land-based defences, and with Confucian scholars gainsaying the value of overseas expeditions, the subsidies previously dedicated to outfitting an enormous oceanic fleet were reallocated to less exotic obligations.

China could afford such deliberate insularity in 1500, but the less stable and far less prosperous European monarchies could not. Early modern Europeans were by no means stay-at-homes. Especially in the western portion of the European promontory, free labourers moved regularly from rural to urban settings, from countryside to portside, from areas of seasonal agricultural work to temporary contracts in more heavily populated areas. And, as Peter Musgrave has recently written, most of this internal migration 'was not caused by crisis but was part of the normal operation of the economic and social system'.[4] One might plausibly argue that Westerners had been on the move internationally since the tenth and eleventh centuries, when Viking raiders voyaged across the north Atlantic, reaching Newfoundland from bases in Greenland, or a little later when Crusaders drove to the East with the sanction of the Church, forcing themselves upon the Muslim 'infidel' and in the process established new and profitable trade links with Asia.[5] Those contacts were sporadic, however, and just as the mercenary crusader states were retaken by the armies of Islam at the start of the fourteenth century, so too Christian Europe lacked the skill and the will to replicate the bold navigational feats of the pagan Northmen.

The first step to sustained oceanic transport involved the accumulation of reliable geographical information. For aspirant European explorers in the late 1400s, knowledge of the world's great oceans was still in its infancy. Although Western scholars had been familiar with the concept of a spherical earth as early as the thirteenth century, the size of that sphere was unknown. In 1450 Europeans understood little more than their ancient Roman predecessors had about the earth's surface, and for most informed observers the earth itself still resided at the centre of God's creation, blanketed by the sun and planets which travelled around humankind's habitat on crystalline spheres. For contemporaries, Jerusalem stood at the centre of the known world, the whole of which consisted of three continents: Asia, Africa and Europe. And the land-locked Mediterranean (whose eastern shore had been the birthplace of the one true religion) was the principal highway linking all three.[6] The riches of Cathay and the splendour of the East in general were both known and much commented upon by envious travellers and would-be traders, and something of northern and West Africa was familiar to Portuguese seamen. But the variety and scale of what lay beyond this horizon was to prove both enormously energizing and unsettling to those who reflected on the import of the larger and increasingly interconnected planet.

Another key prerequisite to sustained transport across the Atlantic, what the Spaniards referred to as the 'Ocean Sea', involved the accumulation and employment of new maritime technology. A host of borrowings and breakthroughs enabled Europeans first to secure and subsequently maintain their dominance of the oceans.

For centuries, the ship of choice in Mediterranean waters was the open galley, propelled by slave and convict oarsmen and defended by soldiers on deck. Military engagements normally involved close combat as ships came directly alongside one another in open water. While adequate for the relatively calm conditions of the Mediterranean, a new, sturdier design was necessary on the stormy Atlantic.

The stern-post rudder, pioneered by the Chinese, was adopted by Spanish shipbuilders in the 1280s and gradually replaced the much less stable steering post. Together with new rigging techniques, in particular the adoption of the triangular lateen sail, which improved the agility and speed of vessels, Europeans could construct larger ships with multiple masts and sails of varying size, all of which enhanced the manoeuvreability of the vessel in open water. New instruments of navigation also facilitated long-distance ocean travel. The magnetic compass, again most likely a Chinese invention, was initially employed by Mediterranean navigators at the close of the twelfth century. By the early 1400s, these innovations were coupled with a new, shallow-draft, strong-hulled ship design which came to be known as the caravel. A modest crew size of twenty could manage such a vessel of 30–50 tons, and while the ship was of moderate overall size, its hull was large enough to carry provisions for a long ocean voyage. Thanks to the addition of double planking, this stoutly constructed, all-weather and long distance craft was also able to accommodate the fire and recoil of heavy cannon, a weapon that would give the Europeans an enormous advantage over other sea-faring peoples the world over. Employing such ships, sea-borne Europeans quickly transformed the world's oceans into commercial, military – and migration – highways. So significant were these engineering and building changes that the basic design of ships at the outset of the age of exploration remained steady until the advent of steam propulsion in the late nineteenth century. According to J.M. Roberts, 'Columbus' ships would have been perfectly comprehensible machines to a nineteenth-century clipper captain.'[7]

With the new knowledge, technology and firepower, and sustained by the financial support of competing sovereign monarchs, a handful of daring explorers quickly made three new continents part of Europe's global equation. Asia's size and population were discovered to be much greater than previously assumed, but Europe would have little impact here in terms of future human migration. Whatever the extent of Europe's overland commercial contacts with the Far East during the Mercantile period, there would be no significant Western population incursion into that area of the world, or into sub-Saharan Africa. This is hardly surprising given that the population of Asia has steadily represented over 60 per cent of humanity from around the year 1000 – and by 1800 this figure actually increased to almost 70 per cent. Europeans confronted strong established monarchies in China, South Asia, and parts of West Africa, while climate and disease contributed mightily to the failure of settlement plans in these regions. For example, an estimated 995,000 Europeans departed on ships owned by the Dutch East India Company for points in Africa and Asia between 1602 and 1795, but fewer than 400,000 of these adventurers returned. Of the majority who occupied forts and factories in places like Manila, Macao or Surat, most succumbed to sickness and disease in these unfamiliar tropical environs.[8] In eighteenth-century Africa alone, a European death rate of 250 per 1,000 was ordinary. Those hardy Europeans who did reside in coastal footholds in these zones were largely missionaries, merchants and soldiers. No permanent agricultural settlements were ever successfully developed; independent yeoman farmers and indentured labourers from Europe never made an impact upon the local African economy.[9]

Elsewhere around the globe, and especially in areas where indigenous political institutions were weak or where the native population was either sparse or vulnerable to European diseases, or both, the influence of European peoples, institutions and ideologies since 1500 has been extraordinary. The sheer geographic sweep of the European enterprise, the demographic takeover of Europeans in three major continents, the catastrophic die-off of indigenous peoples, the momentous transfer of plants and animals into new environments – nothing comparable can be identified in the history of the world. And the takeover is all the more significant in light of original intentions, which were limited from the point of view of political leaders and commercial investors to exploitative trade contacts and a bit of religious proselytizing.

A NEW CONTINENT

During the first three centuries of European presence in the Americas, the governments of Spain, Portugal, England and France were not especially eager to encourage free migration to the New World. While embracing the view that the retention of population, especially skilled personnel, was integral to political strength and state building in a mercantile age, European monarchs and their ministers were loathe to facilitate widespread transatlantic relocation. As late as 1773 the English Parliament was considering a bill which would have prohibited further English settlement in the American colonies. Until the middle of the eighteenth century, population increase across Europe, while incontestable, was fairly slow, and certainly not in the accelerated range apt to alarm the political elite and give them pause regarding the problem of maintaining social order. There were roughly 80 million inhabitants in Europe at the start of our period, and by 1800 this total had grown to around 200 million. Modest growth after 1500 was viewed as an asset to the centralizing state, but only if the increases could be sustained. Mortality rates were of course still very high, with infants remaining the most susceptible to illness and death, while fairly few people were able to survive much beyond their forties. In 1800 Europe's 200 million represented about one-quarter of the earth's inhabitants, up from one-fifth in the middle of the eighteenth century. Migration to the Americas, while an option for some religious dissenters in England, was not freely permitted by authorities in the other Atlantic world powers. If for no other reason, national security mandated that government maintain an unfriendly attitude toward overseas migration.

The total number of European migrants to all of North and South America from 1500 until 1700 was approximately 2 million. Estimates are anything but exact, but one figure places the entire

British migrant population to North America at only 750,000 before 1780. French migration to Canada by this date was less than 15,000, while somewhere close to 1 million white Europeans (mostly Spanish and Portuguese) had settled in Latin America and the Caribbean.[10] After more than three centuries of direct political control in Central and South America, then, there were relatively few migrants from Spain and Portugal living in the colonies. Compared to the 7.8 million Africans who were brought to the Americas in chains during the same period, the limited nature of free and indentured white migration is placed in stronger relief.[11]

A higher birth rate in Europe during the second half of the eighteenth century, however, coupled with the emergence of *laissez-faire* economic theory, led to a relaxation of initial emigration restrictions. Agricultural output began to increase in selected regions west of the Elbe River as early as the sixteenth century, and surpluses meant that towns and cities, which were small in comparison to urban centres in the Islamic world or in China, could now support more inhabitants and thus further opportunities in trade and commerce. There were only 120,000 Londoners in 1500, but more than 700,000 residents in the city 200 years later. Similar growth occurred in French and German cities.[12] Overseas migration, while still costly under sail, had become a viable option for those seeking a new start in life, and official opposition to permanent departure was apt to be muted by favourable demographic trends.

The Americas offered a unique combination of climate suitable for the cultivation of cash crops (most of Old World origin) such as sugar, tobacco, coffee, cocoa and cotton, and an enormous labour shortage brought about largely by inadvertent bacteriological warfare. Writing at the conclusion of his famous *Beagle* voyage, the nineteenth-century scientist Charles Darwin observed that 'Wherever the European has trod, death seems to pursue the aboriginal.'[13] When a significant need for labour power emerged in the Americas, where climatic conditions were largely similar to those of Western Europe, where good arable and pasture land was plentiful and imperial governance provided a modicum of political stability, where official fears of overpopulation and unrest at home acted as a catalyst for promoting relocation, and where indenture mechanisms were developed in order to ease the cost of transport, the potential for oceanic relocation became significant.

During the first three centuries of European intercontinental migration, four basic groups of settlers made up the constituent elements of Europe's first effort to create a global economy. Administrators, contract (usually indentured) agrarian labourers from Europe, slaves from Africa, and a sprinkling of convicts all took transport for the Americas. Only a small fraction of the total (roughly 10 million) number of emigrants from both Europe and Africa during the 300-year period 1500–1800 were military men, missionaries, bureaucrats, merchants or property-owning farmers. Most of the non-Africans were peasants living on the margins of economic subsistence in Europe, and now destined for work on tropical and subtropical plantations under conditions every bit as arduous as those left behind in the Old World setting. Indeed, more than 30 per cent of all European migrants before 1800 were bonded labourers of some type, with most in this category serving terms of indenture in an agricultural setting. Fully one-half of all European migrants to Britain's colonies in North America during the seventeenth and eighteenth centuries were under some form of indenture; in seventeenth-century Virginia colony alone, for example, almost three-quarters of the settlers were indentured.[14] While in practice their living conditions were better than the regimen experienced by African slaves, the legal position of indentured whites was not significantly different from black bondsmen. Migration during the Mercantile Age, both in terms of sending and receiving areas, involved an acute paucity of personal freedom in the service of cash-crop and extractive economies.

THE IBERIAN PRECEDENT

The resettlement of Spanish subjects in America represents the first stage in what was to become a great mass migration of Europeans across the Atlantic. And the success of the political takeover which occurred in the early sixteenth century must be attributed not to

Spanish military prowess but instead to the weakness and disunity of their indigenous opponents. It would be a pattern replicated by other European powers in North America, South Asia and the East Indies in subsequent decades. From the four expeditions of Columbus until the middle of the seventeenth century, some 438,000 Spaniards emigrated to the Americas or the 'Indies' as these lands were collectively named, and roughly another quarter of a million (including about 60,000 soldiers) arrived between 1650 and the end of empire at the start of the nineteenth century.[15] Most of these took transport and settled before 1700, as estimates of the migrant population for the entire eighteenth century place the total at no more than 53,000.[16] The full estimate for the colonial period represents about 3,000 emigrants from Spain per year, a figure which is neither terribly large in terms of the kingdom's overall population (around 7 million in 1540), nor representative in terms of regional cultures and traditions within Spain.

By definition all migration from Spain to the New World was voluntary and involved only free subjects of the crown. No Spaniard was ever forced to relocate to the American colonies, but there were restrictions on who could cross the Atlantic. In staunchly Catholic Spain, transatlantic migration definitely did not mean open-access travel and resettlement. Religious minorities (Jews, Muslims, and later Protestants), together with gypsies and foreigners, were forbidden to travel to the New World. And unlike the situation in Portuguese Brazil and later in the British colonies to the north, criminals and other undesirables were never 'dumped' on Spain's American settlements. Virtually all migrants to America were Roman Catholics drawn from lands under the control of the crown of Castile. About one-third of these emigrants were natives of the southern province of Andalusia, whose capital of Seville was *the* major overseas departure point, while another 28 per cent hailed from New Castile and Extremadura.

The most favoured migration destination points for Spaniards throughout the 300-year colonial period included the centrally located, salubrious, and mineral- and agriculturally rich areas of New Spain (Mexico) and Peru.[17] During the decades following the conquest of the Incas and the discovery in 1545 of silver at Potosi in the Bolivian Andes, 37 per cent of all known immigrants from Spain sought out this location for settlement.[18] If at all possible, migrants tended to avoid the Caribbean and lowland areas due to the extreme mortality rates associated with a much higher incidence of disease. Death rates of 100 per 1,000 in the West Indies were common throughout the colonial period, with mortality escalating sharply during yellow fever epidemics.[19]

Not surprisingly, the overwhelming majority of travellers were young single males, and this sex imbalance remained constant over the entire course of the colonial period. The crown required that married men travelling alone to the colonies prove that their wives consented to their decision, but it is unlikely that many complied with this directive.[20] During the era of the conquest (1520–9) only about 6 per cent of migrants were female, while at its high point in the late sixteenth century, roughly 28 per cent of all migrants from Spain were women, and most of these were married before departing for the colonies. For those Iberian women who did resettle in the colonies, the goal of a better life was very often an elusive one, and migration levels seem to have declined after 1600, just as the first generation of American-born *creole* or *mestiza* women matured.[21]

One important result of this sexual imbalance was a very high rate of racial intermixing between Spanish male settlers and native women, and subsequently between black Africans and Native Americans, and in some cases between Spanish and Africans. New mixed races of *mulattos* (black and Spanish), *zambos* (black and Indian) and *mestizos* (Indian and Spanish) emerged over the course of the first century of settlement, and as their numbers increased, settlers and colonial authorities struggled to first create and then maintain a rigid social hierarchy centred on the category of race. At the top of that hierarchy, not surprisingly, were the Iberian white settlers, a group who thought of themselves as the true nobility of the New World. Free from the obligatory head tax or *pecho* imposed on commoners in Spain, and without any genuinely titled nobility in the colonies (with the exception of the Viceroys, whose tenure in the

Americas was transitory), the white settler who had braved the Atlantic crossing claimed a type of privileged status which could not be contested. The Native Americans, who in general had lost their traditional leaders in military clashes with the newcomers or as a result of disease, took the place of a common 'estate' or *estamento*, but race mixing obviously complicated any convenient lines of division here. Still, the obligation that male natives pay tribute to colonial authorities, together with the fact that native peoples were forced to provide labour services in all lands under Spanish control, created the conditions whereby social distinctions could be institutionalized. With natives treated as minors before the law and excluded from all access to political power within the colonial administration, Spanish migrants from a wide spectrum of backgrounds took comfort in the establishment of their alleged superiority over indigenous inhabitants.[22]

The largest percentage of Spanish-speaking migrants to the colonies was drawn from the middling sectors of Iberian urban society; aristocrats, on the other hand, had little interest in emigration unless it was viewed in terms of a temporary administrative commission. Since passage to America required some financial resources, it is not surprising that most emigrants were urban dwellers of at least modest means, and for them the recreation of a familiar urban lifestyle in the colonies was a priority. The expanding body of clergy and crown officials, most of whom were educated at university level, also preferred to live and conduct their affairs from an urban base. Thirty-one Spanish cities provided almost half of the total number of overseas migrants to America before 1580, and two cities in particular, Seville and Toledo, contributed over 20 per cent of this figure.[23] In the year 1600 an estimated one of every five male emigrants, and two of every five females, came from the city of Seville alone.[24] Toledo was a city which grew rapidly during the sixteenth century, and for some inhabitants the opportunity to create new urban centres presented by resettlement outweighed the chances for economic improvement at home. By 1574 some 121 towns had been founded in Spanish America, and by 1628 this figure had expanded to over 300. The urban centres were often built in areas already densely populated by the indigenous peoples, and this choice tended to exacerbate the epidemiological impact of European disease on the surrounding native populations. By and large the landless and impoverished Spanish peasantry did not travel to the New World prior to 1800, and those few who did migrate without the requisite cost of passage were almost always men called *criados*, servants in the personal employ of an important official.[25] With the advent of the profitable African slave trade immediately in the wake of the catastrophic mortality of native peoples, the need for indentured plantation labour from Iberian sources was absent.

In Portuguese-controlled Brazil the total number of early emigrants is difficult to determine due to the fact that no general or regional statistics were gathered prior to the mid-eighteenth century. This is aggravated by the fact that many of the central government's official records were destroyed during the Lisbon earthquake of 1755. Estimates suggest that there were no more than 3–4,000 European settlers in Brazil by the year 1649, and that this presence had increased to about 30,000 whites during the second half of the century. Sugar production and mining were the main 'pull' factors here, with some 4,000 people leaving for the mining regions each year in the early eighteenth century.[26] For the entire eighteenth century, approximately 400,000 Portuguese, out of a total peninsular population of 2 million, left their homeland for Brazil in hopes of quick riches.

The Portuguese crown even encouraged the migration of entire families from the overpopulated Azores, hoping to settle these newcomers in strategically vulnerable areas in Brazil, in an effort to pre-empt settlement by other European powers. Villages and towns sprang up in new, and previously uninhabited, mining areas and riverbanks, and with the removal of the Portuguese royal court to Rio de Janeiro in the aftermath of Napoleon's invasion, another 300,000 white settlers arrived by 1818.[27] In an effort to secure labour resources for mining and agricultural enterprises, early residents mounted a series of military expeditions into the interior of the colony in hopes of obtaining Indian slaves. These raids intensified during the course of the seventeenth century, but succeeded only in further reducing the native population through exposure to disease and brutal work regimes.[28] By 1819, the native population of Brazil stood at roughly 800,000, one-third of its total before the arrival of the first Europeans. By way of contrast, by 1810 the slave population of Brazil numbered more than 2.5 million Africans.[29]

NATIVE PEOPLES

Contrary to earlier assumptions, some scholars now believe that the population of the Americas at the moment of Spanish arrival in 1492 was approximately the same as Europe's – between 60 and 80 million.[30] In 1500 there were over 350 major tribal groups living in what became Latin America, some nomadic, others sedentary agriculturalists living at or near subsistence level, and a third category living in advanced urban civilizations where specialized political and religious systems allowed for the widespread organization of labour.[31] When the Spanish *conquistadores* made initial contact with the advanced civilizations of the Aztecs and Incas, they were deeply impressed by the high level of political and economic organization achieved by these 'uncivilized' (that is, non-Christian) peoples. In 1520 Hernan Cortez confided to his master, the Emperor Charles V, that the Aztecs 'live almost like those in Spain, and in as much harmony and order as there, and considering that they are barbarous and so far from knowledge of God and cut off from all civilized nations, it is truly remarkable to see what they have achieved in all things'.[32]

No one among that first generation of *conquistadores* expected to discover indigenous empires and urban cultures which rivalled in size and sophistication the domains of the king of Spain. Nor, it should be noted, did many of those early sailors, soldiers, bureaucrats or priests intend to remain in the Americas on a permanent basis.[33] The Iberians (and subsequently all European colonizers) who did commit to settlement certainly did not wish to destroy native peoples; instead they very much hoped to exploit them for commercial purposes, to extract labour and tribute from the inhabitants of the New World, and to further the economic interests of the metropolitan power back in Spain and Portugal. In Peru, for example, the conquistadors sought to continue the Incan *mita* system of forced communal labour which had been in place long before the arrival of the Europeans.[34] Although African slaves were already present in large numbers in the Iberian cities of Lisbon and Seville, the enslavement of Amerindians by early settlers in America was forcefully decried by Catholic Church leaders.[35]

As an alternative solution to the problem of labour recruitment, Spanish authorities established a system known as *encomienda*, where influential migrants received grants of rights to the labour and tribute of Amerindian peoples resident on the land, and this quickly became the preferred model of economic organization until the close of the sixteenth century. Cortez, for example, was granted *encomiendas* with over 100,000 natives. On the island of Hispaniola, natives were moved by compulsion to the gold fields, where they worked in conditions so harsh that King Ferdinand was moved to issue the so-called 'Laws of Burgos' which were designed to regulate the treatment of indigenous peoples. The tribute demands and regular maltreatment of native peoples contributed not a little to the rapid decline in overall population, especially in the Caribbean islands.[36] During the seventeenth century, *encomienda* was replaced by the *hacienda* system, whereby nominally free labourers were assigned to large landed estates owned by *peninsulares* (persons born in Spain) or by *creoles* (persons of Spanish descent born in America). The hacienda would become a central feature of Spanish colonial life, with agricultural workers essentially denied the option of moving to alternative estates in pursuit of better economic arrangements. A form of debt peonage emerged where persons who were forced to purchase goods from their landowners found themselves hopelessly indebted in a cycle of ever-declining material expectations.

A forced labour regime also became the norm in other mineral-rich areas like the Potosi silver mine in Bolivia, where the Spanish extracted great wealth over the course of two centuries. By the start of the seventeenth century some 40,000 Indians miners worked at Potosi, and together with smaller mines in Mexico, by 1700 these labourers produced 80 per cent of the world's silver. All of the plans to exploit native labour were undermined, however, by the inadvertent introduction of European pathogens into a previously isolated environment, micro-organisms that led to the outbreak of a number of deadly epidemics against which the Amerindian peoples had no defences. Smallpox, measles, typhus, chicken pox, whooping cough, yellow fever, diphtheria and influenza all swiftly overwhelmed the native populations, resulting in death rates that easily exceeded the demographic catastrophe of Europe's fourteenth-century Black Death. Mortality figures above 90 per cent were common in some areas. When Columbus made first landfall on Hispaniola in 1493, there were an estimated 100,000 inhabitants living on the island; 80 years later only about 300 indigenous residents were still alive. On a larger scale, when Hernan Cortez arrived in the Aztec Empire in 1516, the population of the Mexican heartland was an estimated 25–28 million. Fifty years after first contact only 3–6 million were left alive, and by 1620 that number had been reduced to a mere 750,000.[37] Native population levels began a modest rebound after this point, but irreparable damage had already been done.

The stark results of this 150-year demographic downfall were twofold. In the first place the high mortality rates created an acute dearth of manpower throughout most of the lands under the control of Spain and Portugal, a shortage which now made the purchase and transportation costs involved in the brutal transatlantic slave trade seem less prohibitive. The profits already realized through the extraction of precious metals portended even greater returns in the cash-crop agricultural sector if only the requisite supply of labour could be found. As early as the 1520s, almost 100 ships each year made the voyage between Spain and the Americas, and the yearly average by the late sixteenth century was between 150 and 200 ships.[38] A world market system centred in Europe, if it were to encompass the commodities of the newly discovered American continents, demanded the muscle-power of the African continent.

Secondly, the deaths of millions of Amerindians, coupled with the destruction of the two most politically advanced civilizations in the Americas, convinced many indigenous peoples of their own inferiority. Their priests and their native gods had proven impotent before the mysterious sicknesses brought by the white travellers from afar. In the Spanish and Portuguese-controlled colonies, Roman Catholic religious orders, church establishments, educational institutions and general missionary activity followed close on the downfall of indigenous religious forms, and conversions proceeded apace. A vigorous building programme was undertaken by the Church thanks to income derived from large landed estates, and recent converts were provided with a modicum of religious instruction. Mission activity on the frontiers brought many of the native peoples into a brand of Catholicism 'ranging from superstitious piety to scarcely veiled paganism or curious combinations of Christian and indigenous usage.'[39] The Church also played a pivotal role in the advancement of white settlers. Non-Indian children received their primary training in schools sponsored by monastic institutions, while secondary training for the elite took place in Jesuit-controlled schools located in towns and cities.

By the close of the eighteenth century, the total population of Spain's empire in the Americas was just over 14 million. Half of this number was non-Indian and 20 per cent was *mestizo* or *pardo (mulatto)*. As we have noted, the highest levels of Iberian immigration occurred during the century of Spain's imperial hegemony, roughly 1500–1600. By the early seventeenth century, after decades of demographic disaster, the native population began to rebound, and some of this expansion was due to the introduction of European livestock, including cattle, sheep, pigs, goats and horses, to the Americas. Together with the products of domesticated livestock – milk, meat, skins, manure for fertilizer – and the introduction of European wheat, important improvements were made to the diet of indigenous and mixed race peoples. In exchange American crops like the potato, sweet potato and maize became important staples in the European, African and Asian spheres, helping to swell global population from 500 million in 1500 to almost 6 billion in the year 2000. Little of this increase would be enjoyed by the Indian population of the Americas, however. The increase in overall population was almost entirely restricted to the European occupiers and their descendants. Transatlantic migration and epidemic pestilence had forever altered the demographic, cultural and religious landscape of the continent. If we are correct in assuming that humans first arrived in the Americas via a land bridge across the Bering Straits into Alaska some 20,000 years ago, then the arrival of the Westerners was a fairly late development in the history of these separate civilizations. Still, the divergence precipitated by what has come to be known as the 'Columbian exchange' was sweeping in its impact across the vast continent.

NEW FRONTIERS IN NORTH AMERICA

There was a rapid acceleration of European and African migration to the New World during the seventeenth century, as mortality rates declined and as the economic stability of the American colonies improved thanks to the advent of a sustained global trade. The overwhelming majority of settlers in North America before 1800 were of British stock. It is estimated that between 1629 and 1640 more than 80,000 people migrated to America from England, and that during the course of the entire seventeenth century about 250,000 Britons, some indentured but most free, opted to emigrate.[40] For Englishmen and women who found themselves lodged at the bottom of the social and economic ladder at home, the attractions of the mainland colonies were many: comparatively easy access to land and to land ownership, reduced incidence of disease (especially during the course of the eighteenth century), the opportunity for social and political advancement, and a culture of religious toleration. Anglicans, Congregationalists, Baptists, Quakers, Presbyterians and Roman Catholics alike had access to property and the promise of social mobility. And the appeal of new land accelerated significantly after the French threat west of the Appalachian range was removed in 1763. In little more than a decade between the end of the French and Indian (Seven Years) War and the start of hostilities between Britain and America in 1775, around 125,000 Britons – Scots, Irish and English – took their leave of the realm for a new beginning in the thirteen colonies. Recently analysed data from the customs service reveals that bonded labour, single young men who had made an individual decision to travel, remained the typical migrant from the south of England and particularly from the region around London. Migrants from the north of the country and from Scotland were more likely to be independent farmers travelling with their families, unencumbered by indenture obligations, and eager to take advantage of inexpensive and plentiful land in the western reaches of each colony.[41]

In addition to the English, a small number of Dutch, Swedes, Germans and French Huguenots were resident in England's mainland colonies at the start of the eighteenth century, and in the main these newcomers were able to carry on their lives comfortably as distinct communities. During the 1800s, additional contingents of Irish, German, Huguenot and African migrants were transported to America by ever more efficient recruiting and shipping networks.[42] A handful of Frenchmen had settled in Canada before this vast territory was usurped by Britain, and approximately 200,000 Germans had taken passage for America, settling largely in the middle colonies of Pennsylvania, Delaware and New Jersey.[43] More than 70,000 German migrants, most of whom arrived as part of an organized contingent from either the Rhineland or the Palatinate, settled as established communities in and around the city of Philadelphia between the years 1727 and 1776.[44] The arrival of German speakers appeared threatening to some. 'Why should the Palatine Boors be suffered to swarm into our settlements,' asked Benjamin Franklin, 'and by herding together establish their language and manners to the exclusion of ours?'[45] Despite such alarmist hostility, however, the newcomers were able to adjust and to flourish. According to one recent estimate, about 10 per cent of the entire pre-revolutionary population of the colonies was German speaking.

Early European colonial history can usefully be framed within the context of international labour history, especially since the overwhelming majority of emigrants to Spanish, Portuguese, Dutch,

British and French-controlled lands during the colonial period were either slaves, convicts or bonded servants. In this respect the transatlantic movement of people from Europe and Africa westward to the Americas can be viewed as an integrated whole, a process where, despite regional variations, European political and economic elites defined the shape of the exodus which took place after 1500. Still, there were important regional and national differences to be observed in the wider European drive for wealth, land and labour, and nowhere is this more the case than in England's North American empire. The settlements which were founded along the eastern seaboard of North America were among the least valuable territorial assets secured by England during the course of the seventeenth and eighteenth centuries, and it was by no means clear after the first half-century of settlement that these lands would over time become prosperous and populated. In the absence of easily extracted precious metals or valuable commodities like spices, the value of exports from the mainland colonies paled before the productive capacity of the much smaller Caribbean islands, while the total late eighteenth century population of about 3 million was far smaller than the number of Spanish settlers and their offspring in Central and South America.

Inauspicious beginnings aside, these same North American colonies were destined to become the host lands for unprecedented numbers of European emigrants in the two centuries after American independence, and important political, social and cultural patterns were established early on in the colonial settlement process. The economic and social structures which emerged in England's migrant communities during the first century of settlement, for example, were fundamentally different from those at home. This was mainly due to the fact that the recruitment of labour quickly emerged as the biggest challenge facing colonists and their financial supporters, a situation which contributed greatly to the peopling of the new lands by marginalized, outcast or enslaved women and men. Outside of New England, for example, between one-half and two-thirds of all white migrants to the mainland were either indentured servants or convicts whose sentences had been commuted to transportation.

One recent study places the number of white labourers who were imported into North America between 1580 and 1775 at 350,000, while an additional 50,000 convicts and political prisoners were forcibly relocated.[46] Normally working as labourers for four years or more in return for passage and the promise of a small parcel of land at the conclusion of their term of service, the estimated 100,000 youthful indentured migrants who arrived before 1700 had a reasonable chance of someday establishing themselves as independent farmers or tradesmen. There were no institutional or legal barriers to relocation in the English colonies, and since many transatlantic migrants had already experienced labour dislocation and movement while living in England, the thought of resettlement once in America was not unfamiliar.

No members of the English titled nobility relocated to America. Few representatives of the land-owning gentry had any incentive to strike out anew either, and those who did had no intention of performing manual labour on the land themselves. Most often it was humble farmers, tradesmen, artisans – and their families – who left Holland and England for the colonies in the capacity of servile labourers. A large percentage of those who arrived as bonded labourers would live to become small landowners in their own right, a goal that was virtually impossible to realize back in England. Unlike Spain and France, the English crown did not restrict emigration to members of the established Church. Thus many of the free white males who defined the political culture of the colonies came from a variety of religious communities. Protestant dissenters had already developed a strong tradition of self-government within their respective churches, and this preference quickly informed the temper and form of colonial politics. A vibrant political self-reliance and the demand for accountability would play an important part in precipitating the imperial conflict with Britain after 1763, and it would later stand at the core of American politics during the centuries after independence, providing a powerful pull factor for aspirant migrants the world over.

The significance of these variables can be highlighted by looking further north into the less hospitable lands controlled by the French.

Efforts at settlement in Canada were derisory in comparison to the English relocation. By the mid-eighteenth century there were fewer than 15,000 Frenchmen living in small forts and outposts along the St Lawrence River and further west in the Great Lakes region. The first permanent French settlement had been established at Quebec in 1608, but the area known as New France would never become a home to religious dissidents or those seeking greater political freedoms. The crown government ruled over New France directly, appointing royal governors and making no effort to encourage the emigration of subjects, even those in the category of paupers, criminals and dissidents. Hunters and trappers, not entire communities or land-hungry agriculturalists, made their way to the frigid north.

England's entry into the Americas had to wait for the conclusion of the dynastic and religious instability occasioned by the Tudor-inspired Reformation of the sixteenth century. The first Tudor monarch, Henry VII, had sponsored an exploratory voyage to North America by the Venetian seaman John Cabot in the late fifteenth century, a venture animated by the hope that a North-west passage to Asia might be discovered, and subsequent adventurers like Sir Humphrey Gilbert and his half-brother, Sir Walter Raleigh, were willing to stake their private resources in efforts to establish permanent settlements, but these inaugural efforts were both costly and unsuccessful. Early ambitions of replicating the Spanish appropriation of Native American gold and silver resources were frustrated at each North American landing site, while the inability of the Tudor state to underwrite colonial enterprises placed would-be explorers at a serious resource disadvantage when confronting hostile Spanish and Portuguese competitors. During most of the sixteenth century, aspirant Dutch, French and English colonists were reduced to parasitic raids on Spanish shipping, reckless attacks against Caribbean ports, and buccaneer smuggling operations on both sides of the Atlantic. As late as 1617, an aged Raleigh was still calling for yet another expedition in search of a new El Dorado, supposedly located somewhere in the interior of Guyana, but it was clear to most by this date that the fortuitous Spanish experience was not to be replicated in North America.[47]

The situation would change significantly after the death of Queen Elizabeth I in 1603. England's principal enemy throughout much of the sixteenth century had been Catholic Spain, and the Iberian monarchs claimed sovereignty over all of the Americas both on the basis of prior discovery and, more importantly, on the strength of the 1494 Treaty of Tordesillas with Portugal. This rather immodest papal grant allowed the King of Spain exclusive rights to all new territories west of an imaginary line 360 leagues from the Cape Verde Islands, while the Portuguese crown enjoyed sovereignty east of the line. Spain refused to accept the legitimacy of the nascent English position, which claimed that 'effective occupation' was the only compelling measure of rightful ownership, and the superiority of Spanish naval power during the 1500s effectively prevented Elizabeth's Protestant kingdom from breaking the Iberian monopoly. The Elizabethan promoter Richard Hakluyt had called for the establishment of permanent colonies in North America not only in order to 'keep the Spanish King from flowing all over the face of America', but also due to the abundance of strategic resources to be found there, in particular 'plenty of excellent trees for masts, of good timber to build ships and to make great navies . . .'. But not until the reign of James I (1603–25) did England's domestic and international situation improve. The new monarch concluded an unpopular but prudent peace with Spain in 1600, thereby officially ending almost a quarter century of debilitating hot and cold war, while on the continent Spain's military power began to crack, especially after the outbreak of the devastating Thirty Years' War in 1618.

England now enjoyed the benefit of relative internal stability, at least until the outbreak of civil war in 1642, and it was under these conditions that the government, still unable to finance large-scale overseas colonizing schemes unilaterally, encouraged the evolution of new financial mechanisms whereby subjects of the crown might invest in privately organized migration and settlement projects whose main attraction was the concept of limited liability. Whereas economic opportunities in the Spanish and Portuguese New World empires were restricted to a small percentage of the Iberian population, where monopolies and royal patronage networks defined the process of extraction, production, and transportation of commodities, the English, together with their Dutch and French rivals, encouraged the formation of 'joint-stock' overseas enterprises focused on trade and colonization. The crown sold the privilege of rights to settlement to organized groups of powerful investors, and more humble investors were then attracted to the projects due to the fact that in the event of failure, liability would not exceed the level of one's initial modest contribution. Large sums were raised in this manner, and the resources were then put at the disposal of ambitious men committed to ending the Iberian stranglehold on the New World.

Still, the beginnings were not especially propitious. When the first permanent English colony was established at Jamestown in 1607, the settler-employees of the joint-stock Virginia Company busied themselves with the search for quick mineral wealth, playing distinctly less attention to the more mundane matter of securing adequate provisions for the winter months. The crown-chartered Virginia Company had sent out three tiny ships bound for America in December 1606. Of the 144 passengers, only 105 survived the winter crossing and arrived in the Chesapeake Bay region in April. And although the colony would survive, the whole enterprise was a near disaster throughout the entire term of the Company's existence (1606–24). In 1609, after it had become obvious to the settlers that Spanish successes in Mexico were unlikely to be repeated here, a new publicity campaign was launched in London designed to recruit fresh subscribers to the joint-stock enterprise. The sale of shares now included the innovative option of pledging personal service in the colony as payment for one's investment. The details of the scheme were preached enthusiastically from the London pulpits and new recruits eagerly signed on. Five hundred men and 100 women were sent out to Jamestown in that year, but after a gruelling passage, much on-board sickness, and general physical debilitation upon arrival, sufficient crops were not planted and by spring of 1610 barely sixty inhabitants remained alive. New leaders arrived at this critical juncture and quickly imposed military-style compulsory service. The export of small quantities of fur and timber did little to satisfy disappointed investors in London, but after 1620 the cultivation and sale of tobacco back in Europe assisted in the creation of a small cash-crop economy.

In order to induce more migrants to settle after these initial misfortunes, Company leaders established a 'headright' system whereby prospective colonists would receive the right to locate, survey and own 50 acres of land in Virginia. Together with the establishment in 1619 of America's first representative assembly, the dual lure of land and political rights proved attractive to about 4,500 additional English women and men. Tragically, intermittent clashes with the native peoples culminated in a full-scale attack against Jamestown and its outlying farms in 1622. The settlers neglected their planting and harvesting and took up arms in revenge attacks, and the result was widespread crop failure in 1623. The government of King James I had seen enough by this point; the Company's charter was revoked and when Virginia became a royal colony in 1624 fewer than 1,300 settlers remained alive out of a total emigrant population of 8,500. The first numerically significant English migration enterprise to the New World was in tatters.

Misplaced expectations and poor planning and execution aside, the initial migration to Virginia did set important foundations for what would become the broader economic and political pattern of settlement life in the southern region for the duration of the colonial period. Those who survived the early 'seasoning' times could count on material success only if they jettisoned the pretences of class and dedicated themselves first to clearing and then to cultivating the land. As in South America, the biggest impediment to economic development during the seventeenth century was a severe shortage of labour. Indentured servitude was introduced almost immediately, and during the 1600s approximately 1,500 indentured workers arrived annually in the Chesapeake region. But such numbers were hardly adequate to the challenges at hand, and within four to seven years of their arrival these labourers were free to establish their own farming operations. Not surprisingly, African slaves first arrived in Jamestown courtesy of Dutch traders in 1619, just as tobacco, what the English king James I referred to as 'that noxious weed', was becoming commercially viable as a cash crop. A total of 350,000 African slaves were brought to Britain's North American mainland colonies before 1820, a modest number when compared to the Caribbean islands and to Brazil, but significant enough to give the southern economy a distinct character.[48] With a plantation economy centred on the production of tobacco, indigo and (later) cotton, the cash-crop culture took strongest root south of the Chesapeake. Plantation agriculture driven by slave labour would become one the cornerstones of economic life in the southern colonies, a fact which over time would have a powerful adverse impact on the recruitment and retention of free English settlers. For those whites of modest means who did live in the South, the establishment of representative institutions of government in Jamestown some twelve years after the founding of the colony served as a benchmark in the political development of all of the subsequent English colonies, and where political rights for white males were combined with access to land, as was largely the case in the middle and northern colonies, the potential for population growth through migration, despite the presence of slavery, was still significant.

THE RELIGIOUS FACTOR

Early migration to the New England colonies is probably one of the more familiar stories in the history of migration, if not the most difficult for the modern mind to appreciate. For when humans set aside the primacy of material considerations in calculating important life decisions, when they forego relative economic and political security in their place of birth for the uncertainties of a new and distant environment, the entire migratory endeavour takes on a special, almost transcendent dimension. There are few examples of this phenomenon over the past 500 years, and the New England project is doubtless one of the most compelling. No other important European power was willing to condone (albeit grudgingly) the establishment of dissenter communities overseas. Of the two separate settlements founded in Massachusetts during the third decade of the seventeenth century, the first at Plymouth in 1620 and the second at Boston in 1629, it was the latter effort which flourished and eventually subsumed the smaller neighbouring enterprise, but both settlements placed the religious imperative at the core of their founding ideology, and both were characterized by enviable survival instincts in a less than ideal climate.

Given that the Pilgrims at Plymouth under the direction of Governor William Bradford were deeply committed to a final and permanent separation from the Elizabethan Church of England, whereas the initial migrants to Boston led by John Winthrop viewed their settlement as but a temporary exile, a 'city upon the hill' whose charge was to set an example to wayward Protestants back in England, the success of the Boston colony in establishing a permanent foothold in the harsh New England climate is not a little surprising. For Winthrop, Boston was undertaken as a grand didactic exercise; once the misguided churchmen and advisors to King Charles I had realized the error of their Catholicizing ways, once the Church of England was truly purified and reformed, then the Massachusetts sojourners could return to their native land.[49]

In retrospect these founding hopes seem terribly naive and misplaced. The Pilgrims at Plymouth certainly shared none of this remedial mentality. Three thousand miles separated the Protestants of Boston and Plymouth from the Court of St James in London. Entire families had been uprooted, properties sold, careers forfeited, educations abbreviated. These first migrants were by no means England's desperate, rootless, or landless. Indeed many of the approximately 40,000 who came to Governor Winthrop's Massachusetts Bay colony before the outbreak of the English Civil War in 1642 were successful yeoman farmers, lawyers, preachers, and leaders in their respective communities back in East Anglia. Massachusetts was no get-rich-quick scheme along Virginia colony lines, no haven for the aspirant cash-crop planter where in 1625 almost three-quarters of the settlers were men; rather, these were largely true believers, covenanted family units and communities which were willing to relocate, if perhaps temporarily, for reasons of the spirit, for a particular view of orthodoxy. If initially intolerant of other religious perspectives, the Puritans were nevertheless faithful to a spiritual imperative conspicuously absent from most other migratory schemes in the Americas.

The initial Plymouth adventurers were few, and they had already relocated first to Amsterdam and then to Leyden before making the decision to abandon Europe altogether. In September 1620, after long negotiations with the Virginia Company, a small group of 101 men, women and children departed from Southampton on the 180-ton *Mayflower*; six weeks into the voyage Cape Cod was sighted, and by early December the malnourished group began constructing simple shelters on a slope of land near Plymouth harbour. Although that first winter was mild by New England standards, and while the native peoples assisted the newcomers with crucial foodstuffs, almost half of the original party was dead by springtime. Still, the migrants, animated by the lure of religious autonomy outside the effective coercive control of the crown, continued to make the difficult Atlantic crossing. By the time of Governor Bradford's death in 1657, eleven towns had been established and the population of the little colony stood at 1,300. And when a new charter was issued by the crown consolidating both Massachusetts colonies in 1691, the economic viability of these modest fur, fish and timber producing communities was firmly established. Never would this area of the British Empire in America, dotted by small farms and imbued by the spirit and practice of congregational self-government, become the economic peer of the Caribbean settlements, but its model of civil organization, where political rights were extended first to male church members and later to all male property holders, set a powerful precedent for all subsequent English colonization.

The organizational priorities, the strong commitment to education, the tenacious drive to transform the landscape and dot the countryside with family-owned small farms, the self-confidence informed by religious conviction – all of these qualities helped to shape the culture of the migrant communities in New England. Between 1630 and 1643, as England slid towards fratricidal civil conflict, some 20,000 dissenters had been dispatched across the stormy North Atlantic. A few hardy souls returned to fight on the Puritan side during the English civil wars (1642–9) but the overwhelming majority of those who left their motherland would never make the return crossing. In time, small towns radiated out from around the Boston coastal centre – some as far as 100 miles away along the banks of the Connecticut River, where another colony was established in 1636. Each of these communities was organized around congregational churches which doubled as political bodies and land corporations. Towns sent representatives to the General Court and distributed land to individual families. By the end of the seventeenth century over 90,000 settlers and their descendants were living in the New England colonies of Massachusetts, Connecticut and Rhode Island.[50] They were almost exclusively of European stock; the land and the climate did not lend themselves to the sort of agriculture where slave or bonded labour might be profitably employed. Rather, self-employed small farmers, tenant farmers who either rented land or worked for wages in the employ of small farmers, and independent craftsmen made up a large proportion of the workforce in these colonies. Family units, complemented by the occasional hired agricultural worker or apprentice, normally provided the requisite labour pool and enabled most agricultural communities to realize a modest profit.

CROWN AND COMMERCE

After the restoration of the Stuart monarchy in 1660, the crown took a much more serious interest in colonial projects. Indeed it can be said that during the first half of the century there had been no English imperial policy, no general supervision from the motherland.[51] Comparatively speaking, not many seventeenth-century Englishmen and women chose the American colonies as places to begin life anew. In 1660 there were only approximately 60–70,000 settlers along the entire length of the eastern seaboard.[52] As seventeenth-century Europe reached the limits of its ability to support a growing population (Britain, France and the Netherlands had a combined population of roughly 30 million), few inhabitants of these three states opted for life in the colonial setting. Some viewed the colonies as best suited to serve as convenient receptacles for paupers, criminals, political subversives and religious troublemakers, especially dissident Protestants who refused to conform to the established Church of England.

This casual outlook changed dramatically after 1660.[53] King Charles II (r. 1660–85) granted proprietary charters to a number of his political backers, and by the start of the eighteenth century all of the colonies came under direct royal charters with crown-appointed governors. The 1681 Pennsylvania grant, for example, was in part repayment to William Penn's father for personal debts incurred by the crown. The younger Penn viewed his colony not only as a refuge for the much-persecuted Quakers in England, but also as a shrewd investment in land and as an opportunity to profit from the fur trade. His insistence upon religious toleration in the colony, while certainly not applauded by the crown, did serve to encourage diverse settlement. The first migrants to Pennsylvania arrived in 1682; by 1700 there were over 18,000 inhabitants in the proprietary colony.[54] For English imperial strategists like James, Duke of York (the future King James II), promoting colonization along the eastern seaboard was part of a larger strategy designed to drive out Dutch and French rivals. New Netherlands colony was wrested from the Dutch in 1664 and renamed New York, while new colonies were created in Delaware and New Jersey. By 1700 the entire eastern seaboard of North America was enveloped by twelve separate royal colonies; in 1732 Georgia, originally conceived as a gigantic convict station, would be added to the list.

White settlement was restricted largely to a narrow band along the coast and adjacent to rivers, but with the removal of Dutch and French commercial and military rivalry, English settlers began to push for additional expansion west of the Appalachian range. The authorities in London, however, were loath to risk potential confrontations with Native Americans, and instead urged movement into the recently acquired lands of eastern Canada. The American Revolution would settle the issue in favour of further westward occupation and development, in effect confirming the triumph of European emigration over Native American claims to the land.

The real colonial prize in terms of return on investment involved the expropriation of Spanish assets in the Caribbean, and by the middle of the seventeenth century a number of smaller islands in the sugar-producing West Indies were in the hands of the English and French respectively. During the 1620s the English had established 'plantations' at St Christopher in the Leeward Isles, and in Barbados. Ten years later, and thanks largely to the cultivation of tobacco products, the combined English population reached 10,000. By the mid-1640s it had expanded to over 50,000 white settlers, with another 7,000 French inhabitants on islands claimed by the Bourbon monarchs. But migration to these tropical venues began to abate as tobacco cultivation, which could be carried out at a profit on smallholdings, was replaced by intensive cultivation of sugar, a cash crop which was best cultivated on large units of production where labour could be organized in a systematic and highly disciplined fashion. Worker recruitment now began to focus heavily on enslaved Africans supplied mainly by Dutch traders; after mid-century few Europeans opted for the unfamiliar climatic conditions of the steamy islands. By 1660 there were over 60,000 black Africans in Barbados, up from 6,000 seventeen years earlier; never again would whites constitute a majority in the West Indies.[55] Beginning with the second half of the seventeenth century, as the French islands of Martinique and Guadeloupe began, like their English competitors, to focus on intensive sugar production, the market for slaves expanded exponentially. The overwhelming majority of African slaves imported into the English colonies lived and worked in the sugar islands of Jamaica, Barbados, Antigua and the Leeward Islands. By 1700 these valuable islands were producing 12 per cent of England's total recorded imports.[56]

From an economic standpoint, the North American colonies could not generate the sort of wealth associated with the sugar islands of the Caribbean, but the fish, grain and meat products from the mainland colonies did play an increasingly important role in the provisioning of the island plantations and their slave populations. In addition, New Englanders engaged in a robust shipbuilding industry, distilled molasses and grain spirits, and produced foodstuffs for an ever-expanding Atlantic export market. Ships from New England enjoyed a sizeable portion of the carrying trade with the West Indies and with Africa, especially after 1700.

NATIVE PEOPLES IN NORTH AMERICA

By the beginning of the eighteenth century, then, the eastern seaboard of North America was inhabited by approximately 250,000 Europeans and their descendants, together with roughly 10–20,000 African and African-American slaves. While numerically small when placed into the larger context of 100 years of English, Dutch and French settlement, and certainly modest when patterns established over the succeeding two centuries are taken into account, the European migrants to North America nevertheless had transformed the centuries-old relationship between humans and their environment in this part of the New World. In terms of its overall impact on native peoples, migration to French, Dutch and British North America involved the same compound of cruelty and callousness found in the lands controlled by Spain and Portugal. Recent estimates suggest that half a million Amerindians may have resided east of the Allegheny Mountains in 1600 (including the Chesapeake region), while another 150,000 lived in what was to become New England.[57] Conservative estimates for total North American Indian population in 1500 range around the 2 million figure. In the New England area epidemics had already struck the Abenakis, Pawtucket, Massachusetts and Wampanoag Indians prior to the arrival of the Pilgrims in 1620. French, Dutch and English transient trade contacts with native peoples in this area and north to Quebec City after 1600 contributed to an overall death rate of almost 90 per cent of the native populations by 1619.[58] And as infected populations fled, disease was spread quickly to other populations. According to Francis Jennings, the European settlement of North America was in fact a 'resettlement, a reoccupation of land made waste by the diseases and demoralization introduced by the newcomers'.[59]

Hunting and horticulture, mostly of the 'slash and burn' variety which necessitated removal to new locations every decade or so, provided the main sources of Native American sustenance prior to the arrival of the Europeans. The native peoples who had inhabited the land for centuries lived in a series of communal cultures where hunting, fishing and farming (especially the cultivation of maize) provided nutritional levels sufficient to maintain social relationships where European notions of property as personal possession were entirely absent. Land was a communal resource to be used for common needs and to be preserved by leaders in the interests of subsequent generations. Population density was light, with most groups concentrated along rivers and coastal locations. Indeed the overwhelming majority of the land east of the Appalachian range was covered by forest, and some estimates suggest that less than one per cent of the arable land was under cultivation at the start of the eighteenth century. By 1700, however, many of the Amerindians who had lived east of the Appalachians had died either from disease or in clashes with white settlers. Those who survived moved across the mountains in hopes of preserving their culture and identity, but even they were eventually enmeshed in the imperial struggles between Britain and France during the course of the eighteenth century. Native peoples found themselves allied, often unwillingly, to French and British sponsors in a debilitating series of colonial wars. The loss of land, the removals in the wake of military defeats, and the economic and legal restrictions imposed on surviving native communities redefined the texture of Amerindian life.

The dramatic decline in Indian population, while lamented by Roman Catholic authorities in Spain's colonies, was often interpreted by New England Puritans as the constructive work of God. As early as 1631, Increase Mather justified the appropriation of Indian land when he observed 'about this time the Indians began to be quarrelsome touching the Bounds of the Land which they had sold to the English, but God ended the Controversy by sending the Smallpox among the Indians of Saugust, who were before that time exceeding numerous'. The Boston minister John Cotton, writing soon after his arrival in Massachusetts, found Old Testament support for the fate of the indigenous population. In Genesis 1:28, God had told Adam and Noah to 'come and inhabit . . . where there is a vacant place'. Governor Winthrop argued that 'for our purposes here, God hath consumed the natives with a great plague in those parts, so as there be few inhabitants left'. According to Winthrop, 'If God were not pleased with our inheriting these parts, why did he drive out the natives before us? And why dothe he still make roome for us, by deminishinge them as we increase?'[60] Without the germ theory for the spread of infectious disease, providence stood as a dynamic force justifying the Europeanization of the North American continent. The first two centuries of contact had prepared the way for a new occupation by peoples from across the Atlantic. And the first to make a great demographic impact were unfree Africans.

Smallpox remained the principal killer well into the eighteenth century. The disease had reduced the Huron Indian population of Canada from 35,000 to 10,000 in the 1640s. One century later, in the wake of a 1763 revolt against British authority, the commander in chief of British forces in the colonies, Sir Jeffrey Amherst, went so far as to recommend that blankets used by victims of smallpox be sent to Indians in order 'to extirpate this exorable race'.[61] The directive was never carried out, but the overall work had been completed by that date. In the aftermath of the American Revolution, most of the states had restricted their Native American populations to small reservations. The first federal census of 1790 revealed that in a nation of 4 million persons, just over 3 million were white while three-quarters of a million were black. Indians 'not taxed' (meaning most Indians) were not included in that first census, but we know that there were but a few hundred living in Massachusetts, while only about 3 per cent of the population of the south-eastern states were indigenous.

Europeans reproduced in great numbers in North America; black African slaves would do the same during the eighteenth and nineteenth centuries. For native peoples, on the other hand, the future promised no redemption. The Powhatan Indians of Virginia had witnessed a mortality rate of 80 per cent among the first group of white settlers to Virginia. No one at the time of that first contact would have anticipated that whites would outnumber Indians twenty to one less than a century later. European indentured labourers, farmers, craftsmen and merchants sought material, and in some cases spiritual betterment in the Americas. Many would realize their mercantile, capitalist, and evangelical ambitions, but at a very high cost for those who had long preceded them in the Americas.[62]

TWO

African Diasporas

Human mobility over broad geographical areas was for many centuries one of the salient features of sub-Saharan African life and culture. Indeed, it is thought by many scholars that all of humankind originated in a single centre somewhere in the lower half of Africa.[1] The closely related languages of the southern reaches of that continent, referred to by linguists as Bantu, most likely originated in the Niger-Congo region, suggesting a widespread movement of peoples in ancient times.[2] In the pre-colonial period, the majority of Africans south of the Sahara lived within lineage-based communities where hunting and gathering, together with herding, served as the focus of economic life, and in which communal models of social organization best fitted a lifestyle devoid of notions of territory as possession. Even with the advent of so-called 'slash and burn' agriculture, where communities would become sedentary for a few years until weeds crowded out grain seeds, periodic relocation was an accepted convention in the search for food. Africa's tropical and subtropical soils did not lend themselves to the sort of regularized and intensive cultivation familiar to European peasants.[3] Movements which would today be defined as international migration were understood in the long sweep of African human experience prior to the arrival of the Europeans as nothing more than natural transitions to more fruitful ecological niches. Traditional territorial borders, familiar to Europeans, Chinese, and most Muslims by the year 1500, were simply non-existent for the majority of African peoples whose lives were shaped by regular relocation.

Even as states began to emerge in portions of sub-Saharan Africa over 1,300 years ago, pastoralists, cultivators and traders continued to move across shifting boundaries with relative impunity. The introduction of Islam into the Savanna regions south of the great Sahara desert during the course of the eighth century, while facilitating the emergence of tributary states, also promoted the movement of men (often slaves) and resources northward across the desert into Mediterranean markets. But it was mobility within the continent that distinguished most pre-colonial African migration. While some east coast states developed seaborne commercial relations with Arabs to the north, indigenous west coast kingdoms did not exhibit the least interest in oceanic travel. Unfortunately, our knowledge concerning those who left these kingdoms is fairly limited. Since the overwhelming majority of black Africans who lived outside the continent before the twentieth century were non-literate bondsmen, it is especially difficult to recapture their experiences without relying heavily on the evidence of non-blacks who more often than not were in a position of dominance over the expatriate Africans. And because slavery was a normal part of Muslim and European Christian culture, the experiences of those who were enslaved did not merit a great deal of attention. Still, it is possible to say something about the breadth of the African diaspora over the past 500 years, a forced removal which represents perhaps the most significant global migration in terms of human productive capacity put to service of other, non-African cultures.

ISLAM AND SLAVERY

European involvement in the horrific African slave trade was a rather late development. The movement of black slaves across the Sahara desert under the auspices of Muslim entrepreneurs had been in place for well over 500 years before the start of the European-dominated transatlantic project. In the words of David Brian Davis, 'The Arabs and their light-skinned converts from Morocco to Iran were the first modern people to create a continuing demand for a large number of foreign slaves, a demand that persisted from the seventh century well into the twentieth.'[4] The source of supply for these traders centred on African rulers, some recently converted to

Islam, who had enslaved prisoners of war.[5] Slaves sent north to serve as concubines, eunuchs and domestic servants in Muslim-controlled North Africa were the key exchange commodity for Sudanic monarchs hoping to maintain the strength of their cavalry units. Indeed, the connection between horses and the trade in human chattel is central to understanding the impetus behind trans-Saharan commerce. South of the great desert horses were used almost exclusively for military purposes, in particular raiding expeditions against neighbouring tribes. Securing a sufficient supply of horses for cavalry operations was thought to be imperative to the security of aspiring African rulers. According to the sixteenth-century Muslim author Leo Africanus, 'the ruler of Borneo derived his wealth exclusively from selling prisoners his men had captured to North African merchants. This ruler had 3,000 mounted troops for slave raids, their horses obtained from the North Africans in exchange for slaves.'[6] And the exchange rates were not favourable to Africans. When the Portuguese first began trading along the west coast of Africa in the 1450s, for example, a horse could be traded for twenty-five to thirty slaves. The well-known medieval Sudanic kingdoms centred in Ghana, Mali and Songhai were deeply implicated in the transfer of war captives to the north across the great Sahara.[7] During the 400-year period beginning in 1100, millions of people who had lost their freedom were forced to trek across the desert in conditions almost as harsh as those subsequently faced by Africans on the Middle Passage to the Americas.[8]

Islam prohibited the enslavement of co-religionists, but non-believers could become the absolute property of the faithful so long as the slave's human capabilities were recognized – but very basic humanity only. The fourteenth-century Arab historian Ibn Khaldun, who was born in Tunis and lived in Egypt, expressed an Arab commonplace when he observed that 'the only people who accept slavery are the Negroes [Sudan] owing to their low degree of humanity and their proximity to the animal stage'. One recent estimate places the number of black slaves exported via the trans-Saharan and Muslim-dominated trade at 1.7 million persons over the 200-year period 900–1100. When including the Red Sea and

Indian Ocean trade, the rough estimates for the period 1100–1200 near 1.4 million.[9] Once in a Mediterranean setting, the slave frequently was accorded a modicum of domestic autonomy, including the opportunity to marry, while the offspring of unions between masters and their concubines were generally accorded status as free subjects.[10] Africans who served as slaves in the Muslim world always faced a considerable level of social discrimination due to their status and race, but some attained high positions by virtue of the fact that their mothers were concubines in the households of influential political figures. Not a few of the Abbasid caliphs were the sons of slave concubines.[11] Whereas black slaves in the Americas were valued almost exclusively for their labour value, in the Islamic world a wider range of functions was evident. Domestic service, concubinage, advisory roles, traders – unfree blacks could be found in a wide range of activities. The Islamic kings of Mali, for example, employed royal slaves as provincial governors, a practice which was not unfamiliar in African societies after 1500.[12]

Much later, during the course of the nineteenth century, an extensive slave network was organized and conducted by Muslim traders linking East Africa with the Middle East and South Asia. Most African slaves who resided in the Arab-dominated Middle East worked in a domestic capacity, but others were assigned to agricultural tasks. In India, by way of contrast, the majority of African slaves engaged in menial tasks – forbidden to Indians due to the caste system – while princely leaders held bondsmen from Africa as a measure of social status. It is likely that most of the Africans living in the Indian subcontinent before the nineteenth century were natives of Ethiopia, but others came from Somalia, Madagascar and Mozambique. Some were the descendants of Africans who themselves had been resident in Islamic lands as slaves. It is impossible to provide statistics on the total population of blacks in India, but by the late fifteenth century there were some 8,000 slave soldiers in the Muslim sultanate of Bengal alone. Most served as palace guards and minor government functionaries. During the course of the sixteenth century, the Portuguese were rebuffed in India more than once by armies led by black slave commanders whose service under Muslim leaders placed them at the centre of Indian military life.[13] Once the British presence in India began to predominate in the late eighteenth century, slaves could be found working in military service and in building trades associated with military fortifications. The number of bondsmen was small in terms of Africa's overall population, but this does not discount the important fact that the diaspora was much wider than the transatlantic paradigm suggests.

AFRICA AND EUROPE

Still, without any question, the abominable slave trade to the Americas stands as the catalyst for the single largest demographic movement within and beyond the African continent. In total, more than 22 million people were forcibly removed from sub-Saharan Africa during the period 1500–1890, with almost 4 million sent north across the Sahara, nearly 3 million transported from East Africa to destinations bordering the Red Sea and in South Asia, and an estimated 12–15 million dispatched by white Europeans across the Atlantic to plantations in the Americas.[14] The unforeseen arrival of the ambitious Europeans in the mid-fifteenth century represented the first sustained contact between black Africans and a larger global community via the oceans, and this initial communication would set the foundation for centuries of unimaginable suffering.

Most Africans taken during this early period of involuntary servitude were deposited in Europe, and resided mainly in urban centres, particularly port towns. Here they were afforded opportunities to build incipient community organizations, normally associated with the church. Between 1450 and 1500 Portugal imported between 700 and 900 slaves each year, with these vicious actions in West Africa 'legitimized' as crusading enterprises by papal bulls issued in 1454 and again in 1456.[15] The unfolding of relations between the two peoples would have an enormous impact on the nature of the migratory process starting in the sixteenth century, fostering both an intensification of involuntary internal migration and external slave migration. Portugal was Europe's largest receiving country for African slaves at the start of our period, with the Portuguese crown collecting dues under the supervision of a royal official. By 1530 the annual intake of slaves reached as high as 2,000 per year, with black Africans constituting 2–3 per cent of the entire Portuguese population of 1.2 million in the mid-sixteenth century.[16]

In addition to service as domestics in aristocratic households, African slaves worked in Portuguese hospitals as launderers and cleaners, on the docks as general labourers and boatsmen, and in the construction trades. In general, blacks were treated better than their Muslim counterparts, largely due to the fact that Muslims were considered the infidel enemy, while many black slaves were quick to convert to Christianity. About 10 per cent of the black population in Portugal had secured their freedom through manumission by the mid-sixteenth century.

Spain was also home to modest numbers of African slaves after 1500. In the port city of Seville – the point of departure for thousands of white migrants to the Americas – there were equal numbers of Muslim and black African slaves at the start of the sixteenth century. Most of the Muslims were prisoners taken during the protracted *reconquista* of the southern provinces. The city's 1565 census revealed that there were 6,327 slaves in a population of just over 85,000, and it is likely that blacks constituted the majority of those held in bondage by this date.[17] As in the Portuguese case, slave occupations varied considerably, from assistants working under shopkeepers to porters and longshoremen, and residency was normally within the master's urban household. Blacks slaves were baptized, and a number of urban parishes were established to serve the African population.

When Spain ceded to its Dutch possessions the exclusive right to transport African slaves to the Americas in 1600, a small number of slaves were employed – as chattels – in the Low Countries. The same was true for England, especially after 1713 when the monopoly right of supply to Spain's extensive empire was awarded to British carriers. Early in her reign, Elizabeth I complained that there were too many 'blackmoores' in her kingdom, and she urged that they be returned to Africa without delay.[18] The directive was ignored, however, and by the late eighteenth century an estimated 15,000 black Africans were living in England.[19] Many of these men and women had entered the kingdom via the American colonies, where they had served as domestic slave labourers for many years before accompanying their masters back to England. In any event, there were certainly more black Africans living in Europe by the eighteenth century than Europeans residing in all of Africa before the 1850s.[20]

AFRICA AND AMERICA

As an augury of things to come, slaves were also employed in plantation agriculture on Atlantic islands such as Madeira and the Canaries off the coast of West Africa. Both the Portuguese and the Spanish established sugar plantations here, and these undertakings served as models for the later, more extensive cultivation of sugar in America's tropical zone. Large plantations, unfree labour, and a European market for a single commodity: these characteristics of the later American economy could be found within two groups of small islands – the Canaries and the Madeiras – where previously mixed agriculture and grazing had been the norm. By 1500 there were some 2,000 slaves working on Madeira, up from a total slave population of around 800 persons 50 years earlier.[21]

The enslavement of Amerindians in Spanish-controlled lands was forbidden by royal decree in 1542, and eight years later the abusive *encomienda* system, where groups of native peoples were ordered to work for specific colonists in return for exposure to Christian instruction, was ended by officials in the colonies. The Spanish crown, keen to regulate the entry of persons into the New World colonies, began licensing slave traders as early as 1513, setting quotas and fees due to the monarch. Smuggling remained a problem for authorities throughout the long period of Spanish rule, while the potential profits involved in a 'successful' voyage guaranteed that official regulations would be circumvented. Direct shipment of slaves to the Americas commenced in 1532, after a range of European diseases began to wreak havoc on the indigenous

Amerindian population. Many of Spain's early military expeditions in the New World included slaves who accompanied their Iberian masters, and some became skilled fighters in the service of the crown. Indeed the Native Americans most commonly associated blacks with the invading European culture.[22]

Philip Curtin has estimated the number of blacks captured in Africa and transported to Spanish America during the sixteenth century at 75,000, while another 50,000 landed in Portuguese Brazil. During the seventeenth century the total number of human imports for all of Latin America and the Caribbean was 1,316,000, and for the entire 350-year period of the transatlantic slave trade, Curtin estimates that 9.5 million African slaves disembarked from the reeking holds of European ships for a life of unremitting labour in unfamiliar Central and South American surroundings. The sugar plantations of Brazil and the sugar islands of the Caribbean were the principal destinations, but the Spanish mainland colonies received almost 13 per cent of the total before 1820.[23]

Three distinct types of society emerged in the Americas prior to the start of the industrial revolution in the nineteenth century, and each area was distinguished by unique ecological features. In the highlands of central Mexico and Peru, white Europeans dominated the countryside and engaged in pastoral agriculture and mining activities. Amerindians provided much of the unskilled labour force in this environment despite the high mortality rates accompanying the arrival of the white population. But black Africans also came to play an important role in the economies of these areas. In mid-seventeenth-century Peru, for instance, the number of slaves had reached almost 100,000 by 1650, and this constituted between 10 and 15 per cent of the entire population. In the city of Lima, slaves could be found in the metalworking, clothing and construction trades, and every urban construction site included semi- and unskilled African slaves working alongside Indian labourers and their white masters. Overall, the experiences of slaves in Mexico, Argentina and Chile differed greatly from those in the plantation economies of the Caribbean and Brazil.[24]

As their numbers increased, the Roman Catholic Church took steps to assimilate urban slaves into the culture of the Church and to lessen the many hardships which they faced. Slaves were baptized and marriages were recognized in both civil and canon law, while Church authorities struggled incessantly to curb the penchant of owners to split families by selling the offspring in violation of the law. The sexual imbalance among the slave population made it extremely difficult for male slaves to find and secure a marriage with an African female, but where such unions did occur the Church worked to protect the conjugal rights of the couple. Inevitably, however, unions between white males and black slave females produced a significant population of *mulatto* children. Like the *mestizo* offspring of whites and Native Americans, many *mulattos* were spared the indignity of slave status but were clearly situated at the lower end of the colonial social hierarchy. Manumission was much more common in Latin America when compared to the later situation in the English colonies, and this was particularly true of blacks living in urban settings.

In North America, Argentina and parts of Chile, white settler societies developed with the newcomers successfully introducing many facets of Old World society, including seaboard towns and cities, widespread land ownership and market-driven agriculture. Slavery would become a central feature of economic enterprise in the southern colonies of Britain's North American empire by the early eighteenth century (roughly 1.5 million Africans transported here by 1700), but, more generally, settlers themselves provided the bulk of labour in these three colonial regions.

It is important to remember that while North America was the principal destination of Europeans involved in transatlantic migrations over the past 500 years, it was but a minor receiving area for black African slaves, largely due to climatic conditions which were unsuitable for sugar cultivation. According to Philip Curtin's estimates, 42 per cent of all African slaves landed in the sugar-producing islands of the Caribbean, 38 per cent engaged in plantation agriculture in Brazil, while only 5 per cent went to North America.[25]

The final ecological and social model was established on the Caribbean islands and lowland Central and South America. It was in these areas that the highest concentration of African slaves could be found producing sugar in a large plantation setting, for it was here that the native population had been virtually extinguished through disease. Most of those slaves who survived the horrors of the 'middle passage' across the Atlantic in what was 'the greatest long-distance migration by water or land before the nineteenth century' were forced into this difficult environment.[26] Their task was to produce cash crops – sugar, cotton, indigo, coffee, rice – for a European and global market. The profits, of course, were reserved for the inhabitants of the imperial metropolis, absentee landowner and investor alike. The wealth generated by the harvesting and sale of sugar for a European market easily outstripped the profitability of the other two zones combined; thus the initial expense involved in the purchase of African bondsmen was easily recouped in this tropical environment.

The conditions experienced by plantation slaves were extremely harsh. Long working days in difficult tropical conditions, with little prospect for improved material conditions, led to a serious runaway problem by the end of the sixteenth century. By the 1670s the runaway population in Brazil alone hovered around 20,000, with half of these forming free communities away from colonial control. In colonial Brazil such villages or *mocambos*, once discovered were often successful in fending off assaults. One such community in the Brazilian province of Pernambuco numbered upwards of 1,500 male and female inhabitants, all of whom were led by a king for nearly twenty-five years before their eventual defeat at the hands of Portuguese colonial authorities in 1694. Similar communities of escaped slaves emerged in the Spanish mainland colonies.[27]

With the establishment of sugar plantations in Portuguese-controlled Brazil in the 1540s (the Europeans had learned sugar cultivation from the Muslims during the era of the Crusades), the principal role of West Africans in the New World was firmly defined. The Atlantic slave trade remained comparatively small during the first 150 years of its operation, and trade in humans did not replace gold as Africa's chief export commodity until around

1700.[28] The Portuguese were the main carriers to the New World until the middle of the seventeenth century, when Dutch merchants began to intrude upon Portuguese operations both in Africa and in the Caribbean. By 1672 the English crown had chartered the Royal African Company, and by the start of the eighteenth century private traders based in Liverpool and Nantes expanded English and French involvement. Almost 2 million people were transferred to the Americas over the course of the seventeenth century, while another 6 million were involved during Europe's purported 'Age of Enlightenment'. The 1780s was the decade of greatest activity, as just under 90,000 slaves arrived in the Americas each year. Another 3.3 million were captured and sent across the Atlantic before the end of the trade in the late nineteenth century, by which time Africans and their descendants had contributed mightily to the agricultural and commercial success of the Americas.[29]

LEAVING AFRICA

Most of those who experienced slavery in the Americas had already lost their freedom in Africa, as victims of war, kidnap or some sort of judicial conviction on a variety of (often specious) charges. Normally, stateless peoples were terribly vulnerable when assaulted by well-organized and armed neighbours. Europeans offered African rulers cloth, alchohol, firearms, tobacco and a variety of beads in return for their cargo, and traders who dealt with powerful African middlemen normally followed one of two collection models. Some established 'factories' or collection points where the unfortunate would be kept until a full ship's complement had been reached, while others cruised the coastline, purchasing slaves along the way and heading west for the average eight-week voyage across the Atlantic once the hold was full. Mortality rates were very high both during initial capture and incarceration along the coast, while during the Atlantic passage, mutinies, gastrointestinal disease, smallpox, scurvy and suicide were the harsh constants. Conditions below deck were both brutal and physically debilitating, as slave traders regularly overloaded their ships in anticipation of a high mortality during the crossing.

The slave sending areas evolved over three centuries to include most regions along the West coast of Africa, beginning in the 1450s in Senegambia and moving southwards to Angola. During the 1740s, the Gold Coast supplied 20 per cent of all human exports, but this figure was reduced to about 9 per cent by 1790 as other areas were exploited: demand remained constant, but slave origins shifted.[30] By the start of the nineteenth century, almost 80 per cent of all British and French slaves originated in Angola, the Bight of Biafra and Mozambique. Not surprisingly, two-thirds of all bondsmen exported to the Americas were young men, who normally cost 20–30 per cent more than women. The numbers of children captured and exported increased during the course of the eighteenth century due to the fact that European regulations permitted more children to be packed aboard slave ships for the horrific transatlantic passage.

The enormous reservoir of black African labour contributed much to the rapid emergence of the Americas as a dominant region in a variety of productive enterprises. Blacks served as explorers and as soldiers in the Spanish armies stationed in the New World, and they assisted in the building of major cities like Havana, Mexico City, Lima, Buenos Aires and Rio de Janeiro. Further to the north their skills were employed in the creation of port cities like Philadelphia, Boston, Charleston and New York. But the bulk of black African contributions to the economic development of the Americas involved large-scale plantation labour, and the harsh conditions experienced in this setting are reflected in fact that the estimated 8.5 million African-American population in 1800 was less than the total number of slaves brought to the Americas since 1600.[31] Until the second half of the nineteenth century the migration of blacks to the Americas was numerically much more significant than white settlement. Approximately 8 million blacks, virtually all of them slaves, entered the two continents before 1820, while white settlement numbered no more than 2.5 million.[32] Return migration was rarely a viable option for black Africans once breakthroughs in transport made the prospect realistic for white Europeans. For slaves and their descendants, the possibility of identifying one's roots in the vast African continent were very remote indeed.

When the Europeans first began to intrude upon what had previously been a Muslim monopoly of the transcontinental slave trade, the population of sub-Saharan Africa was small in relation to available agricultural land. In fact prior to the late twentieth century, Africa was an underpopulated continent: only the introduction of European medical advances over the last century has altered this demographic profile. Due to poor soils, fickle rainfall and a surfeit of insects, Africa's agriculture was highly mobile, with farmers generally working to adapt themselves to a given environment instead of seeking to transform it. Pre-capitalist modes of production were the norm, with modest levels of interregional trade engaging a few elites, and a subsistence economy remaining at the heart of production. While it is difficult to estimate the demographic consequences of the slave trade on West Africa, the economic and social impact of the trade on indigenous peoples is undeniable. The Atlantic trade continued for over 300 years, but despite the fact that Europeans were obliged to pay for their cargo, very little economic development took place in West Africa during these centuries. The scale of the Atlantic slave trade weakened the ability of African states to begin the process of sustained economic development and entry into a global trading network. Slave related depopulation struck at the heart of West and East Africa's efforts to manage labour for the enhancement of commercial, market-oriented agriculture and the manufacture of cloth.

The Arab-dominated slave system involved a disproportionate number of females destined for concubinage, while in the transatlantic trade roughly 30 per cent of all slaves were female. The overall impact was doubtless a diminution of reproductive capacity in sub-Saharan Africa, leading to an overall population decline from the mid-seventeenth century until 1850. Chronic warfare between black rulers, animated largely by the desire to sell war captives to European merchants, stunted the development of commercial agriculture and intra-African commerce. Handicraft production never evolved into manufacture for export, while subsistence economies remained the norm in Africa until the middle of the nineteenth century.[33] Europeans were loath to encourage the development of African textiles, while artisans who worked with iron and brass found few outlets for their skilled products beyond their own region. Most poignantly, not a single West African kingdom became a cash-crop exporting area comparable to the West Indies, where African labour made possible the creation and operation of lucrative sugar plantations. Sadly, the main agricultural export was food for slave ships, often produced by slave labourers along the coast of West Africa.

Unlike communities of indentured labourers, who most often originated in the same country and spoke a common language, African slaves often found themselves living and working with other blacks who shared neither a common language, culture or set of organizing principles. One contemporary estimated that the 1657 population of the English-controlled island of Barbados included 50,000 whites and over 100,000 black slaves. The bondsmen were 'fetch'd from severall parts of Africa, who speake severall languages, and by that means, one of them understands not another', making the master's task of maintaining control over large slave populations less difficult.[34] This situation certainly frustrated early attempts at unified resistance to white oppression, but nonetheless there were frequent revolts against the slave system. And when they did take place, slave rebellions were put down with excessive violence. Describing the process of retribution on the island of Jamaica in the early eighteenth century, Hans Sloane observed that rebel leaders were burned, 'by nailing them down on the ground with crooked sticks on every Limb, and then applying the Fire by degrees from the Feet and Hands, burning them gradually up to the Head, whereby their pains are extravagant'.[35]

RETURN TO AFRICA?

Slavery was finally proscribed within England and Ireland in 1772, and by 1807, after years of struggle in Parliament, opponents of the slave trade, led by William Wilberforce, secured a parliamentary statute outlawing the transport of bondsmen. By 1834 the institution of slavery itself was abolished throughout the Empire, the result of a combination of humanitarian and material forces, not the least of which was Britain's transition from a mercantile economy based largely on cash-crop plantation agriculture to a *laissez-faire* system centred on manufacture and free labour.[36] Adam Smith's conviction that slaves were more costly than free workers may not have impressed opponents of slavery who condemned the institution on moral grounds, but his position was borne out in the midst of the world's first industrial revolution. In an effort to address the growing problem of poverty among London's expanding black population, philanthropists led by Granville Sharp, Henry Thornton and James Stephen had proposed a 'repatriation' scheme in the 1780s, and in 1787, with nominal financial support from the British government, a group of about 400 blacks set sail for Sierra Leone in West Africa.

Sharp drew up a constitution for the settlement which included the principle of self-government, but despite initial high hopes, a combination of inexperience, disease and hostility from local inhabitants almost doomed the colony during those first years. A treaty was concluded with the local ruler (who was not literate) which included an unprecedented clause granting permanent sovereignty to the settlers. After four years of economic setbacks, however, in 1791 the settlement was reorganized as a joint-stock company under the direction of a white governor (Zachary Macaulay) who was appointed in London and who was to rule without the consent of the migrants. The goal was to create a haven for ex-slaves, a beachhead for Christian missionaries, and an agricultural export centre for the London investors. The next year some 1,200 blacks from Nova Scotia, former slaves who had been liberated by the British army during the American war for independence, arrived in the fledgling community to begin their lives anew, and in 1795 an additional 500 ex-slaves from Jamaica were allowed to make the return crossing.[37]

In the year that the slave trade was abolished, Sierra Leone became a crown colony and was designated as the reception area of choice for Africans who were later rescued from slavery by British naval patrols located in West African waters.[38] During the early nineteenth century, Freetown harbour became a leading point of reception where recently liberated blacks from a wide range of African cultures were encouraged by Christian missionaries to learn English as a common language and develop an economy based on staple agriculture and trade with industrial Britain. The anti-slave trade campaign provided a significant boost to the free population of Sierra Leone. There were approximately 2,000 inhabitants in the colony in 1808, and the number doubled by 1811.[39] Timber exports to British dockyards began in 1816, under the direction of a Irish entrepreneur, while vegetable oils met a growing industrial demand for lubricants. Products developed for export were closely tied to European demand, making the crown colony a dependent economy where all manufactured goods were imported from mature European producer economies. It was a troubling anticipation of Africa's twentieth-century post-colonial relationship with the West.

Just 200 miles south-west of Freetown, another experiment in repatriation was undertaken, this time by Americans, in an area named Liberia for the freedom which it ostensibly signified. Some 250,000 American free blacks were resident in the United States at the start of the nineteenth century. But all of these women and men suffered from a variety of social, political and economic handicaps which essentially denied them opportunities for meaningful advancement. According to the influential Congressman Henry Clay, ex-slaves might be protected by the laws, 'but prejudices more powerful than laws deny them the privileges of freemen'.[40] Thomas Jefferson, for his part, could not foresee a time when blacks and whites could live together on equal terms in the same society. Free blacks in the southern states appeared as a menace to the majority white population, constant reminders of the injustices associated with the slave system, while in the North they were viewed with deep suspicion by independent white farmers and urban (especially unskilled) tradesmen.

The idea of repatriating such freed black Americans to West Africa led to the establishment of the American Colonization Society in 1816. As early as the revolutionary period, prominent white leaders like Jefferson and later James Monroe had called for the creation of 'black territories' in the Pacific North-west or in the lands of the Louisiana Purchase. The number of freed blacks reached 60,000 by 1790 and by the start of the Civil War in 1860 almost half a million resided in states both North and South. Southern planters who supported colonization viewed the West African venue as an opportunity to remove persons who set an unwelcome example in slave society, while influential supporters from a variety of Protestant churches anticipated the formation of a West African missionary beachhead. Others of a more secular and humanitarian inclination saw the prospective state in terms of the black man's potential for self-government and economic improvement, goals accepted as largely unattainable in a society where racial prejudice denied free blacks equal opportunities in the United States.[41]

The enterprise enjoyed the support of a number of powerful political figures, including Henry Clay, Andrew Jackson and Daniel Webster. The United States Congress appropriated $100,000 in the first of a series of grants designed to purchase land in West Africa, while the navy assisted in transporting the initial eighty-eight settlers in 1821–2. African tribal leaders were induced to 'sell' their land in return for clothing, muskets, gunpowder, tobacco and alcohol, while settlers worked to impose American standards of speech, law and rules of commerce on their reluctant hosts and neighbours. The returnees, who numbered some 2,600 by the early 1830s, really came to Africa as settlers since none had been born in Africa, and most refused to learn the local languages, adopting instead the airs of a social elite and monopolizing the American-style political institutions of the country. Despite the backing of major political leaders, public support for Liberia turned out to be derisory, as less than $5 million was subscribed privately and publicly before the Civil War. And most of this money was dedicated to transportation costs.

In 1847 the American blacks who had settled the region issued a 'Declaration of Independence' from the American Colonization Society and inaugurated the first republic in black Africa, a republic that was not recognized by the United States until 1862. In terms of the repatriation project, Liberia was a failure. Fewer than 20,000 freed blacks had departed from the United States and British-controlled Caribbean islands by 1867, and with emancipation achieved at the end of the Civil War there were few incentives linked to the pioneer enterprise in West Africa. In the 1930s, a League of Nations investigation confirmed that some powerful Americo-Liberians had even re-instituted slavery, repeating the very social practices which had been so roundly condemned by the founders of the Liberian state over a century earlier.[42]

Thus, the two early nineteenth-century settlements established in West Africa by Europeans and Americans did little to advance the interests of indigenous black Africans, nor did they truly address the material needs of blacks who had been born and raised in England and the United States. Understandably, the prospect of settlement in Africa had little appeal for blacks from North America who had never lived in the land of their ancestors. The product of mixed motives on the part of white philanthropists, investors and Christian missionaries, these new receiving areas succeeded in appropriating land held by native blacks, but settlers offered little in return. With close economic ties to European markets, these sponsored homelands, troubled from the outset, set the stage for the subsequent era of European territorial expansion and economic domination throughout Africa.

In the late nineteenth century, the political carve-up of the African continent by European imperialists involved the arbitrary establishment of new boundaries, territorial divisions erected in a manner which often separated ethnically related peoples. The colonial powers were interested primarily in the economic potential of their respective domains, and this resulted in the establishment of export-driven plantation economies and the relocation of mostly male workers within colonial frontiers. Forced labour and compulsory cropping systems shattered the pattern of shared production which had focused the lives of African hunters and pastoralists for centuries. From the cultivation of cocoa in the Gold Coast (now Ghana) to mining operations in Southern Africa, thousands of black Africans were subject first to European taxation and then recruited into market-related enterprises in order to pay those taxes to the imperial authorities. Colonialism altered African migration patterns in fundamental ways, and this relocation was always related to the influence of global capital and world markets. Areas where goods were produced for an export market became destination points for male migrants, while women were obliged to maintain agricultural output in the sending areas. This pattern of exploitation would continue down to the era of independence, and we will examine the repercussions of the legacy in Chapter 6 under the heading of the global refugee crisis. In the decades since independence, many educated Africans who face unemployment or political repression at home have sought opportunities outside the continent. And much of this migration reflects the previous colonial connection, with leavers seeking to settle in the old colonial metropolis. One estimate from 1987 placed the number of migrants from sub-Saharan Africa to Europe at 70,000, or about 30 per cent of the continent's indigenous skilled professionals. The nation of Ghana, for example, lost 60 per cent of its physicians in the 1980s, while half a million Sudanese and 2 million Egyptians worked abroad in 1985.[43] Ninety per cent of the Sudanese international migrants were literate, coming from a country where more than 60 per cent of the overall population was illiterate.

Clearly the diaspora, begun under slavery and the imperatives of the mercantile economy, continues in a post-colonial, capitalist setting. Black Africans have a very strong claim over their white European counterparts to making both the Americas and Europe central to the global economy which emerged after 1500. Obviously the latter alone reaped the profits of this new model of exchange, but even in their unfree status, persons from Africa were instrumental in shrinking the world dramatically after 1500; no longer were separate and divergent civilizations the norm in the human community. Muscle power from West Africa had become the essential precursor to industrial power in Birmingham, while unfree labour in Virginia provided the material underpinnings of political democracy for property-owning white males in Washington.

PART TWO

The Industrial Era, 1800–1945

Three substantial developments occurred in international migration patterns between 1800 and the conclusion of the Second World War. First and foremost, free labour became a much larger, indeed the predominant, source of human productive capacity both in sending and receiving countries. The institution of slavery was effectively challenged and repudiated by the 1880s in the West, and while abolition proceeded at a slower pace in the Muslim world, forced migration of unfree labour no longer played a significant part in the world's nascent industrial economies.

The second, and related, development involved the introduction of indentured labour from previously untapped sending areas around the globe, and especially from Europe's colonial empires. With the collapse of slavery, contract labour was aggressively recruited from South and East Asia in order to maintain the physically intensive cash-crop enterprises previously reserved for bondsmen of African descent. Indentures were also involved in Western infrastructure projects for the building of rail lines and roads to mining and construction sites. Thus a new, and this time semi-free labour pool from underdeveloped regions of the world was recruited by advanced Western powers to assist in the ongoing work of building modern capitalist economies.

69

The third salient development concerns the massive departure of Europeans from their homelands. Thanks in large measure to a series of technological breakthroughs in oceanic transport, Europeans departed for the Americas and Australasia in numbers never before witnessed in the history of migration. Between the start of the sixteenth century and the outbreak of the First World War in 1914, it is estimated that between 60 and 65 million Europeans left their homes for new settlements around the world, but the vast bulk of this migration took place only after 1800.

While borders generally remained open during the 1800s (China and Japan constituted the major exceptions), migration took on greater importance for policy makers. In the West, some leaders continued to be guided by the mercantilist argument that labour was a national resource and that national wealth would be impaired by the departure of youthful subjects and their families. Other political elites and social critics championed emigration as a solution to troubling social problems at home. Vagrancy, criminal conduct, overpopulation and attendant poverty – these and many other social ills could be effectively addressed, it was thought, through the vigorous promotion and sponsorship of overseas settlement: Britain's Georgia colony, for example, was originally conceived as a penal settlement, while Canada later became a major repository for abandoned and orphaned children. Indeed 11 per cent of Canada's present population consists of the descendants of destitute British youngsters.[1] As the population of Europe continued to grow even in the midst of the migration streams, the majority of political leaders, especially those in democratic states, were loath to interfere with the process.

The concept of the autonomous nation state, already present in the sixteenth century, expanded across most of Europe in the wake of Napoleon Bonaparte's wars of 'liberation' and subsequent occupation, and this principle of state sovereignty later took hold throughout the respective empires controlled by the European powers. At one level, then, strong nationalist movements of the nineteenth century were inherently opposed to the movement and mixing of peoples. It is one of the paradoxes of European migration

70

to the Americas that it reached its height just as Social Darwinist thought was emphasizing the alleged value of 'racialist' identities, and the supposed dangers of the intermingling of peoples for the long-term well-being of the nation state. But while the majority population in major receiving areas was not indifferent to the appeals of exclusionists, the abundance of work opportunities helped to secure the continuation of open borders policies.

These three factors – the end of slavery, the expansion of indenture systems, and the escalation of Caucasoid or European voluntarist migration around the world – were each closely connected to the industrialization of the West. The material transformation of the landscape, particularly in the United States of America, was brought about in large measure by the ability of vast numbers of people to leave their place of birth at a young age and to devote a large part of their productive labour to agriculture, commerce and manufacture in a new global setting.

Towards the end of this period, in the shadow of two World Wars, developed nations in the West begin to impose extraordinary immigration restrictions. War-time conditions understandably inhibited the movement of any but refugees, but more central to the advent of immigration regulation was the dramatic intensification of racist ideologies which decried cultural mixing. Not surprisingly, much of the emergent Western xenophobia was related to unfavourable developments on the economic front. The global depression of the 1930s effectively put a stop to all recruitment of overseas labour, and significant international migration did not resume again until the end of another global conflagration in 1945.

THREE

Free Labour and the 'Great Migration'

International migration patterns changed dramatically after 1800, both numerically and geographically. During the greater part of the nineteenth century and continuing into the first two decades of the twentieth, the main story involved the movement of youthful Europeans, some 50 million of them by 1914, to North and South America. On a lesser scale, other Europeans headed east to Australasia, and in that same area of the world Chinese migrants, albeit with the sharp disapproval of Beijing authorities, began a significant relocation into South-East Asia. In South Asia, particularly India, Hindu and Sikh subjects of the expansive British imperium fanned out as unskilled workers in a variety of locales from East Africa to the Caribbean – all lands similarly controlled from London. And in the powerful Russian Empire, a great eastward push across the vast stretches of the sparsely populated Siberian landscape brought the largest portion of mineral-rich central Asia under the direct control of imperial authorities in Moscow.

Variety of sending and receiving areas notwithstanding, the largest outflow of human enterprise and intellect was clearly from western, southern and eastern Europe. During the course of the nineteenth century, 'the population of areas of European settlement (in Europe and the world) . . . increased from 24 to 36 per cent of world population'.[1] Europe certainly seemed to have the requisite surplus inhabitants to make such figures possible. Even during the peak years of emigration, when hundreds of thousands were leaving the continent, Europe's population continued to grow at a rapid pace. In the period 1750–1850 alone, the total figure had nearly doubled, expanding from 270 to just over 460 million persons. And unprecedented numbers were crowding into Europe's new industrial centres, creating at least the potential for serious social and political upheaval. The level of urbanization (defined as the proportion of the population living in settlements of over 5,000) was at 12 per cent in 1800, reflecting little change over the previous century. By 1850, however, the number of urban dwellers had reached almost 19 per cent of the total population and in 1900 it was just under 40 per cent.[2] Many of these migrants from the countryside to the city would constitute the core of subsequent travellers overseas, as the initial promise of city life in Europe, the hoped-for economic opportunities, failed to materialize in the face of harsh factory conditions, low wages, inadequate housing, sickness and infectious disease, and massive poverty associated with an over-supply of urban labour. When the opportunity for a new start overseas (especially in colonial lands) presented itself, and when transport costs plummeted thanks to the advent of steam power, Europe's major ports began to fill with candidates for relocation.

During the West's first 'Industrial period' (*c.* 1800–1914), over 85 per cent of some 50 million emigrants settled in just five destinations: Argentina, Australia, New Zealand, Canada and the United States. The most popular receiving nation was the United States, which alone admitted 33 million people. But it is important to remind ourselves that two out of every five Europeans who emigrated to the Americas after 1800 did *not* disembark in the United States. Around 6 million arrived in Argentina, 5 million in Canada, and 3.8 million entered Brazil. In fact, in the other major American receiving countries, Canada, Argentina and Brazil, 'the relative incidence of immigrants in the population was higher than in the United States'. During the first decade of the twentieth century, the rate of immigration to the US was a little more than 1,000 per 100,000, while in Canada it was 1,500 per 100,000 and 3,000 for Argentina.[3]

With respect to sending nations, the majority of migrants, almost 18 million, came from the comparatively small British-Irish archipelago. The most intensive period of migration, 1870–1914, not surprisingly overlapped with a period of British economic and

74

military dominance around the world. The German states sent over 5 million before 1914, Italy accounted for 10 million, and Spain and Portugal sent a combined 5.5 million. The remainder of migrants came from Russia, eastern Europe, Scandinavia and the Low Countries.[4] In 1800 only 4 per cent of ethnic Europeans were living outside their homelands, but this number would increase to 21 per cent by the start of the First World War.[5] The hegemony of Western cultural forms would follow as the twentieth century unfolded.

SOJOURNERS

One of the more remarkable characteristics of international migration during the industrial era was the high degree of transiency among travellers, and in particular the remarkable rate at which migrants, especially those of European origin, would return to their homeland after a brief period in the Americas. Recent studies have indicated that the many leavers, especially from sending countries in southern and eastern Europe, were young single males who had no intention of remaining overseas. One estimate places European return migration at one quarter of the total for the entire nineteenth century. If accurate, then Europeans were no different from their Chinese counterparts, who returned to their place of birth in the Middle Kingdom at the rate of about 50 per cent during the course of the late nineteenth century (and who were much criticized by citizens of America's western states for this proclivity!).

Perhaps we should not be surprised by these back and forth perambulations, for when we think of Europe's growing population during the years of intense overseas migration in the late nineteenth century, it is helpful to recognize that an enormous volume of internal, intercontinental traffic was also under way. Nine million Italians may have travelled to the Americas between 1876 and 1926, but an additional 7.5 million departed for points throughout Europe and in North Africa. Normally this movement across borders was associated either with seasonal agricultural work or, more significantly, from rural to urban centres.[6] Walter Nugent has written that 43 per cent of all European migrants to Argentina returned to Europe between 1857 and 1914, while during the years 1899–1912 almost 66 per cent of those who landed in Brazil subsequently retraced their steps to the land of their birth. And in the United States, a noteworthy 52 per cent of those who arrived eventually returned to Europe during the period 1908–14.[7]

Italians were the most remarkable of the sojourners in terms of distances travelled for employment. Thousands would regularly take ship to Argentina in the autumn of each year in order to harvest wheat and flax on the pampas before returning home for spring planting. Seasonal shifts were common across international borders within Europe during the late nineteenth century, but the transatlantic sweep of temporary labour movement was something new altogether. At least 10 per cent of Italians entering the United States in 1904 were doing so for the second time, indicating that even repeated stays abroad were not uncommon at this period.

This very high number of sojourners was one of the more signal results of rapid and inexpensive rail and steamship transport systems linked to a new set of expectations for youthful males seeking long-term economic security at home.[8] The advent of efficient steam propulsion and the founding of large shipping lines meant that itinerant labour migrants could rely upon regular, timetable passage to American destinations. In addition to taking advantage of low costs, nomadic workers could now plan both their departure and return in a fairly efficient manner. Most of the peripatetic Europeans found temporary work in urban settings, especially in the United States, after the 1880s. Return migrants were much less likely to toil in a rural, agricultural environment, for if they did the propensity to remain was much greater. For the sojourner, saving for the purpose of purchasing land in traditional locales, together with remitting funds for family members and loved ones left behind, explained the frequency of travel for work overseas. Remittances were an important part of the domestic local economy where land was scarce and partible inheritance the norm, as was the case in Southern Italy, for example. Remittances were also used for maintaining 'chain migration' networks, enabling the overseas worker to pay for the transatlantic passage of indigent kinsmen. During the period 1908–14, about one-third of all arrivals in the United States boarded ships on tickets purchased by previous immigrants. For Swedish migrants, close to one-half of travellers to North America had pre-paid passages.[9]

NORTH AMERICAN DESTINATIONS

The character of European migration to North America, and especially to the United States, changed dramatically during the course of the 1800s. In the earlier part of the century, before the introduction of regular steam transport and the start of industrialization, migrants normally travelled as family units. The cost of transatlantic passage from Liverpool to New York under sail during the early nineteenth century equalled about a month's income for a skilled artisan and two month's wages for an unskilled agricultural worker. The passage itself took between three and ten weeks (with the average being forty-four days), and when combined with the fact that additional time might be spent travelling overland in the United States once the migrant arrived, as was the case for Norwegian and Swedish immigrants who settled in the wheat belt of the north-central states, a typical worker would normally forego at least two and sometimes three month's wages before engaging again in work for remuneration.[10] Sex ratios were roughly even, and families would normally engage in agricultural pursuits, often seeking land well away from coastal towns and cities.

By the end of the century the profile was much altered. The typical migrant was now a young, single male whose first language was not English, who resided in an urban area along the eastern seaboard and worked in the industrial or service sector, and who often had ambitions of returning to Europe. During the peak years of immigration to the United States at the turn of the twentieth century, two out of every three entrants were male, most either youths or young single men. Not surprisingly, for those groups within which a roughly equal number of men and women migrated – the Irish, Jews, Germans – there was a higher likelihood that settlement in the New World would become permanent.[11] By 1900 there were twice as many foreign-born workers employed in manufacturing over agricultural pursuits in the United States, although some 37 per cent of the total US population continued to engage in work related to agriculture. The potential for land ownership throughout the Americas had diminished after 1900, but the convenience of working close to port cities facilitated the possibility of returning to Europe some day.

One unique feature of emigration to the United States during the industrial era is the sheer diversity of sending areas that contributed to the whole. Dozens of countries added to the mosaic, and while Britons and their descendants continued to dominate the political, economic and cultural life of the nation, new inroads were being made, especially on the local and urban political fronts, and most pointedly by Irish and German Americans. From 1861 until 1920 the percentage of foreign-born Americans remained remarkably consistent, remarkable because these were the decades of the greatest influx of new Europeans. One in every seven, or 14 per cent of all Americans, was born outside the United States throughout this period. The figure remained constant due to the fact that the American-born population was burgeoning from 10 to 100 million in the century ending in 1920.[12] Marked change did occur, however, in the ethnic composition of the United States during the sixty years before the start of the First World War. In 1860 over 80 per cent of all foreigners were British, Irish, or German. Thirty years later this majority had shrunk to 63.9 per cent of the total, and in the 1920 census that majority had become a minority of 25 per cent. In the interim they had been overtaken by new arrivals from Italy, eastern and south-eastern Europe and Russia.

The United States maintained a largely porous immigration policy throughout the nineteenth and early part of the twentieth century, and as the nation expanded its borders westward during these decades, large tracts of open land were occupied by newcomers at a rapid pace. The same generalization can be made with respect to Canada. Some western states in the US even accorded immigrants the right to vote and to hold public office before they had secured citizenship. The entire naturalization process was eclectic and haphazard throughout much of the century, with federal, state and local courts alternately awarding certificates of citizenship to recent migrants, and (more troubling) with large-city political machines holding mass citizenship ceremonies, normally just before important election dates.[13]

When federal authorities finally opened an immigrant reception centre for steerage-class migrants on Ellis Island in New York in 1892 (those who could pay for cabin passage were normally excluded from this experience), the first concrete and visible steps toward exclusion of European 'undesirables' were taken. Federal laws had been adopted in 1887 prohibiting contract labour or indenture (treated in Chapter 5) as a concession to organized unions in the United States, while an 1891 statute denied admission to felons, polygamists, or anyone with a mental condition or who was otherwise likely 'to become a public charge'. Even with these statutory encumbrances, however, few were actually denied admission. Steamship companies began pre-embarkation checks after they were made financially responsible for the return of rejected applicants, and this procedure helped to alleviate the problem of rejection in New York. In 1905, admissions topped 1 million people for the first time, while only 1 per cent, or just under 13,000 were denied entry into the United States.[14]

American hospitality was not unalloyed, however. Waves of anti-Catholic nativism were directed against Irish and German immigrants during the course of the nineteenth century, but prejudice in this area did not translate into legislative proscription. The few formal restrictions which did emerge were directed against Chinese nationals who, as we shall see in Chapter 5, were generally unwelcome along the country's west coast, unwelcome at least until transcontinental railroad companies faced acute labour shortages. Subsequent anti-Japanese and anti-Filipino sentiment, when combined with a heightened antipathy toward non-English speakers from southern and eastern Europe at the beginning of the twentieth century, resulted in the passage of the highly restrictionist Immigration Act of 1924, but by this date the United States had already become a genuinely multicultural society. While the 'melting pot' metaphor is much disparaged today, the United States on the eve of the First World War was doubtless the most ethnically diverse of the major receiving nations in the Americas.

German-speaking migrants represented nearly one-quarter of all foreign residents in the United States between the 1830s and the 1880s. By the latter date, a unified German nation had been forged under the direction of Otto von Bismarck, but still the relocation across the Atlantic continued. A few of the migrants were political exiles, losers in earlier struggles to unify all Germans under one national flag, but for most migrants the economic imperative stood as the key motivating factor. Catholics (one-third of the total), majority Protestants, Jews (about 250,000), farmers, skilled tradesmen and factory operatives – a wide variety of Germans departed their homeland just as it was emerging as a dynamic world leader on the military and economic fronts. Germany's rapid modernization programme during the second half of the century, and especially its proficiency in port construction together with rail and ocean transport facilities, contributed to the brisk pace of overseas transport. About 10 per cent of those who migrated at the international level settled as far afield as South Africa, Argentina and Brazil, but the choice of the overwhelming majority was the United States. Once admitted, the newcomers engaged in a diverse set of occupations, skilled and unskilled, with about one-quarter engaged in farming. Unlike the Irish in America, Germans were by and large intensely proud of their European background and applauded German unification when it was achieved in 1871.

Scandinavian migrants (Danes, Norwegians and Swedes) to the Americas numbered just over 2 million during the six decades between 1865 and the start of the First World War, but when considered in relation to the sparse populations of these countries, the total outflow was quite significant. More than 95 per cent of all leavers settled in the United States. Population pressure on the land served as the principal 'push' factor behind much of the migration. Thanks to a better diet made possible by the widespread cultivation of the potato, together with the start of vaccination for smallpox,

Sweden's population of 5.1 million in 1900, for example, represented a doubling over the previous fifty years.[15] Partible inheritance laws meant that farms could not be preserved as integral units, and this served as an additional incentive for prospective migrants. It is not surprising that most Scandinavians re-established themselves as farmers in the northern portion of America's Midwest, for it was here that the rhythm of traditional Old World work patterns could be most closely replicated. Like their German counterparts, Scandinavian migrants were quick to establish educational and cultural institutions which preserved their religious and intellectual traditions. Chain or stream migration to the Midwest became a strong part of the overall process, even in the case of those few who settled in urban centres like Chicago. On the whole the decision to leave had been one devoid of political factors, something that can not be said of another group from Europe's northerly climes: the Irish.

IRISH EXODUS

Perhaps more than any other single experience, the Irish migrations of the nineteenth century have captured the modern popular imagination as the most disturbing, indeed by some accounts the most tragic, chapter in the recent history of human relocation. Forever linked to the mid-century potato famine and the alleged British incompetence or malice in addressing the crisis, the estimated 3 million women, children and men who were emitted from their ancestral homeland between 1845 and 1870 did so in an act of sheer desperation. Over the course of the nineteenth century a strong nationalist ideology developed within the ranks of the Catholic majority in Ireland. At its core was the angry conviction that all Irish migrants, irrespective of personal circumstances, were involuntary exiles, victims at the hands of British expropriators and landlord oppressors. More than anything else, the self-perception of impoverished refugees was framed by the belief that they had been obliged to avoid the fate of their landless and luckless neighbours, tenant farmers who continued to produce cash crops for export even as starvation gripped the countryside.[16]

Over 8 million people have emigrated from Ireland since the start of the eighteenth century, and more than 5 million of these departed during the period 1800–70. Remarkably, by the year 1890 almost 40 per cent of all women and men born in Ireland were living elsewhere.[17] The great hunger was of course a major catalyst to removal, but we must not forget that mass emigration from Britain's 'other island' began decades before the terrible famine years of 1845–7. It has been estimated, for example, that between 50,000 and 100,000 Irish sailed to North America during the seventeenth century. Several thousand of these were unsuccessful rebels against the Puritan government during the English civil wars. For their disloyalty they had been banished to Barbados, Jamaica and the mainland colonies by the military government of Oliver Cromwell. Beginning with Cromwell's depredations, the Irish comprised 'the largest single flow of white immigrants to the seventeenth-century West Indies'.[18]

Over the course of the next century, between 250,000 and 400,000 Irish men, women and children left their ancestral homes. Given the fact that the total population of Ireland was around 2.3 million in 1754, this represents a significant exodus.[19] Some left for military service in the employ of other European heads of state but, paradoxically, most of these eighteenth-century travellers were members of the Protestant community. During the 1800s they outnumbered Catholic migrants three to one, this despite the fact that the latter comprised 70 to 80 per cent of the population and that opportunities for indentured service in America were available to the Irish and English alike. These Presbyterian dissenters from Ulster, the majority of whom were responding to the 'push' factor of religious intolerance visited upon them by the official Church of Ireland, turned to America as their final religious refuge. While clearly interpreting their departure from Ireland as involuntary, Protestants were also quick to embrace their American resettlement as an escape from oppressive conditions. Many settled as far south as the Carolinas, but later, in the wake of the mid-nineteenth-century famine and the arrival of large numbers of Roman Catholic countrymen, they began disembarking in large numbers to the north, in Canada.[20]

For the Roman Catholic majority, on the other hand, religious intolerance had little role to play in the decision to migrate. A burgeoning population, periodic bad harvests, poor soil and disappointing return were the key factors in leading landless Catholics to depart. During the course of the eighteenth century, most of the impecunious who left did so as indentured servants. A very small number of Catholics paid their own passage across the Atlantic before 1800, and they were truly the exception. For those who did own a small piece of land in Ireland, a deep-seated desire to preserve the family farm, no matter how marginal its productive capacity, led to a situation whereby younger unmarried children were more apt to leave, either for industrial work in Britain, or for the prospect of new land and social advancement upon completion of a term of indenture in America.

As we have noted, the cost of an Atlantic passage was high before the advent of steam; thus it is no surprise to learn that more Irish crossed the Irish Sea than the Atlantic. Still, recent estimates suggest that between 1815 to 1845 'Ireland may have provided over one-tenth of all those who had voluntarily crossed the Atlantic since Columbus'.[21] Estimates of total permanent departures during the period 1800 and 1845 run as high as 1.5 million, with just over one-third of these living in Britain by the latter date and contributing greatly to the seemingly insatiable labour demands of British industry. And the reservoir of unskilled labour seemed limitless. Population growth in Ireland during the century between 1750 and 1850 easily outpaced every other European country with the possible exception of Finland. The 8,500,000 inhabitants on the eve of the famine represented a quadrupling of the total from 1750. But whereas in the rest of Europe growth was accompanied by important demographic shifts to urban centres, this was not the case in Ireland. By the early 1840s only one-eighth of the population lived in towns or cities with a minimum population of 1,500. Irish urbanization involved movement to places like Manchester and Glasgow, not Dublin or Cork.[22]

Migration to Britain always carried with it the possibility of returning home should better times unfold, but in the light of

England's expansionist factory-based economy and Ireland's continued agrarian stagnation, British statesmen and economists stood in favour of the migration process. Here at last was a solid, long-term solution to Ireland's chronic underemployment and overpopulation.[23] The response was robust, and it was not until 1851 that the Irish-born population of the United States overtook its British counterpart. By 1901 there were approximately 600,000 Irish living in Britain, and if we include first and second generation offspring, the total increases to over two million.[24] This permanent migration was complemented by a wide-scale seasonal transfer, especially to Scotland where temporary work could be found in the shipyards, to help support small farms back in Ireland. Famine conditions simply accelerated a process, accepted as a stage in life by most of the Irish, already well under way.

Nineteenth-century migrants to Britain invariably faced a host of prejudices not uncommon when new faces appear in a quickly changing economic environment. Images of the immigrant as strike-breaker, blackleg, clannish criminal and violent inebriate were combined with a residual disdain for the Irish prompted by ongoing political unrest and calls for home rule in Ireland itself. The early Cromwellian view of the Catholic Irish as unbridled savages was now replaced by two separate and distinct caricatures: the first highlighted the sins of the ignorant 'Paddy', the feckless and fatalistic slum dweller who undercut the economic position of the sturdy British labourer. The second and more menacing image linked the Irish community with the violence of the late nineteenth-century Fenian movement, a numerically small but influential political cell not averse to the use of terror in the drive for national independence. The English view of the emigrant community was reflective of Protestant views of the Catholic majority in Ireland. Largely excluded from the skilled trades, the Irish – most of whom could be found in large communities in Liverpool, Manchester, Lancaster and London – worked as factory operatives, day labourers and artisans. Over 55,000 served in the British army and navy by the mid-nineteenth century, while in Scotland almost 7 per cent of the entire population was Irish-born in 1851.[25] Despite this influx, the Irish communities in

Britain still thought of Ireland as 'home'. Proximity, resentment towards colonial status, family ties and association with the land – not to mention English and Scottish xenophobia – all made the assimilation process both difficult and protracted.

By the late nineteenth century, the United States clearly had become the destination of choice for most Irish emigrants. Prior to the famine, the British government sought to discourage emigration to the former colonies and instead directed the migrant ships to Canada. As early as the 1820s, small government schemes to subsidize relocation to Canada were undertaken. Wilmot Horton, who was Under-Secretary of State at the Colonial Office between 1821 and 1828, moved hundreds of landless families from in and around Cork to Ontario. In all, about 3,000 migrants were afforded some form of government assistance during these years. During the famine period itself, Canadian officials expressed shock at the condition of the newly arrived exiles. By the end of 1847, 30 per cent (roughly 20,000) of the victims of famine had completed the difficult crossing only to perish shortly after disembarking in their adopted homeland.[26]

Whereas Canada had been the main North American recipient of Irish emigrants during the first half of the 1800s, the overwhelming majority of those who survived the overcrowding and disease of the coffin ships during those harrowing mid-century famine years began their lives anew in the United States, the pre-eminent anti-English nation after Ireland itself and the locale of rough-and-tumble Jacksonian democracy. The famine exiles, the majority of whom had been farm labourers or servants in some capacity, expressed their strident disdain for Britain by embracing the land of successful revolutionaries against the crown. Between 1876 and 1921 this one country was the host nation for 84 per cent of all persons leaving Ireland, whereas only 7 per cent chose Australia and 8 per cent settled in Britain.[27]

Interestingly, upon securing admittance, most of the migrants to the United States quickly rejected their rural roots and turned instead to factory work and (especially in the case of women) urban domestic pursuits. Boston, New York and Philadelphia emerged as centres of Irish settlement along the eastern seaboard, and they retain this designation even today. Work was comparatively easy to find for newly arrived unskilled labourers, not a few of whom spoke little English. The overwhelming majority of those who landed in America financed their passage privately. Families pooled meagre resources in order to send one member across the Atlantic, and remittances to Ireland from those who had saved their wages played a very big part in facilitating the movement of relatives. Between 1848 and 1867 over £30,000 was sent back to Ireland in the form of pre-paid tickets for family members.[28]

Once in the United States, the Irish-speaking population was often subject to very sharp prejudice, but this did not prevent the fairly rapid rise of a powerful political elite in a number of big cities by the close of the nineteenth century. The Roman Catholic Church in the United States made important strides, thanks in no small measure to Irish immigrants, while Irish religious orders recruited priests and nuns for service in the major cities. Unlike so many migrant populations to the Americas, the Irish were particular in their adamant attachment to the fiction that emigration was exclusively the product of imperial oppression at home. As early as 1847, priests, editorialists and nationalist politicians in Ireland were loudly denouncing emigration as forced exile. Initial interpretations of the famine as the product of divine providence or punishment for sin were now discredited.[29] The myth of systemic British malevolence served to politicize the Irish immigrant to America in a very concrete and enduring manner. In its refusal to forget the situation 'at home', the dominant culture of the post-famine Irish in America was one of deep sympathy with and support for those who continued the struggle against the imperial oppressor.

Historians have disagreed over the impact of mass emigration upon those who stayed. Between 1841 and 1901, the population of Ireland decreased by almost a half, from 8 million to just over 4 million. Nowhere else in Europe was this pattern repeated; indeed the opposite was the case in most countries, thanks to better diet, improved medicine, and lower infant mortality. While one result of the famine was the consolidation of many marginal farms into more economically sustainable holdings where dairy and cattle products replaced grain production, R.F. Foster has argued that the outflow from Ireland of so many of the young and able-bodied during the nineteenth century served to protract archaic patterns of rural life, in effect discouraging innovation on the land and placing the entire economy of the island in the hands of its least creative elements. Young and vigorous Irish migrated at a much higher rate than their English counterparts, with the result that Ireland's most capable source of labour was absent – many in factory centres like Manchester and Birmingham – at the very moment when England was becoming a mature industrial powerhouse. And unlike other European migration patterns, in which men predominated, equal numbers of Irish males and females left their homeland for overseas destinations. Most were single and youthful, fuelling the contemporary fear that those who remained behind were among the least productive members of the population.

After the First World War, Britain once again became the principal destination for the Irish migrant. Despite securing independence in 1921, the economic problems facing the Irish governments of the 1920s almost guaranteed that movement overseas would continue. During that decade a further 250,000 decided to leave, 'at an estimated economic cost in lost wealth to the country of between £125,000 and £200,000'.[30] The worldwide economic depression of the 1930s slowed the outflow to an average of 14,000 per year, but the numbers rose again during and after the Second World War. Roughly 200,000 Irish went to work in British factories during the six-year conflict, and another 30,000 enlisted in the British armed forces. The outflow accelerated after the defeat of Germany. The 24,000 England-bound migrants of 1945 swelled to 40,000 in 1948. In that year an alarmed Roman Catholic hierarchy declared that 'our young are leaving Ireland to take up employment in circumstances, and under conditions, which, in many cases, are full of danger to their religious and moral well-being'. Such protests were to little effect; beginning in 1947, Irish migrants to the United Kingdom were no longer required to hold a visa, and the Irish government took the position that 'the denial to individuals of the opportunity to seek a livelihood or a career abroad would . . . be the restriction of a fundamental human right which could only be justified in circumstances of great national emergency'.[31]

From an estimated 187,000 emigrants in the decade of Depression and the Second World War (1936–46), over 400,000 left Ireland for new homes overseas (again mostly in Britain) during the 1950s. Indeed for every five children born in Ireland in the 1930s, four emigrated overseas in the 1950s. While lamenting this trend, the government recognized publicly that official intervention to halt the outflow would be disastrous. In a 1954 report, a government Commission on Emigration and Other Population Problems concluded that restrictions on emigration 'would lead to heavy unemployment, a lowering of wage rates and a reduction of the average standard of living'.[32] Meanwhile, population in Ireland continued to decline, signalling in certain respects a failure of the traditional agrarian way of life endorsed by the government of Prime Minister Eamon de Valera.[33] Ireland remained an overwhelmingly rural nation in the postwar period, a new nation whose leaders were seemingly incapable of adjusting to the dominant small farm culture. Well into the 1980s the young continued to depart in significant numbers, again mostly to the land which nineteenth-century Irish nationalists had vilified as the root of Ireland's problems. The migrants, less able to place nationalist rhetoric above economic advancement, continued to vote with their feet. At home, economic innovation and the application of industrial techniques to the production of foodstuffs and manufactured goods had to await the Irish entry into the European common market. And even then, the more salutary effects of European integration have only been felt in a substantive way in recent years.

THE AUSTRALIAN ANOMALY

May 1788 marked the date of the first British settlement in Australia, a colony consisting not of religious minorities seeking to practise their faith unhindered, nor of indentured servants and their masters hoping for a new start in a land where material resources seemed limitless, but instead a colony of outcasts, of pariahs, dangerous undesirables who had violated the norms of British imperial order and the sanctity of property. Australia was an unprecedented crown-sponsored human refuse zone, a distant penal facility where malefactors might never again trouble the march of British domestic progress as it entered the industrial era. The 'criminal class', including petty pickpockets, extortionists and forgers, would be excised body and soul, banished from the heart of the world's greatest workshop and Empire, and left to languish for their myriad sins in the most remote and unloved portion of the globe. 15,000 miles and eight months transport away, it was truly a land of no return for the criminal class. The founder of British Utilitarianism, the indomitable Jeremy Bentham, observed that the new colony was ideally fit to host 'a sort of excrementitious mass, that could be projected, and accordingly was projected – projected, and as it should seem purposely – as far out of sight as possible'. When the period of convict transportation to South-eastern Australia came to an end in the early 1840s, a total of some 160,000 people, male and female, adult and child, and mostly Londoners, had been condemned to exile on the other side of the world.[34]

But dominion over, and involuntary migration to, British-controlled Australia was also animated by larger geopolitical or strategic considerations. International trade rivalries, especially with France during the second half of the eighteenth century, contributed to the decision to occupy the south-east coast of Australia. The British navy, lacking naval stations along the coast of Africa and a port between India and the Pacific, was anxious to secure supply depots in the East in the event of future naval conflicts with the French, Dutch or Spanish.[35] Australian timber and flax (used in the manufacture of sails) became important commodities in the maintenance and projection of naval power. Convicts were used as a source of expendable labour in the building of military facilities, while political leadership was held by a series of governors who were also military men. Of all the governors, lieutenant governors and senior administrators who served in the colonies from their founding until 1855, only three were civilians.

In addition to their immediate duties associated with a penal colony, the military were also charged with displacing aboriginal peoples who resisted the process of English expansion and its accompanying appropriation of land. First contact with the indigenous population was defined by the fact that British explorers claimed lands by right of conquest; as hunter-gatherers with no fixed notion of territoriality, the aboriginal peoples were not recognized as legitimate sovereigns over the land which sustained them. It was a position reminiscent of earlier attitudes towards America's native peoples. Superior technology again played a significant role in settling the issue, but similar to the case of European settlement in the Americas, resistance was dramatically undermined by the presence of European diseases. Smallpox and influenza seem to have done the most damage to native peoples throughout eastern Australia.[36]

With the close of the transportation era, the government in London hoped to attract white settlers to the new colony by offering inducements of either free land or land at attractive rates, together with the possibility of convict labour to work the soil. A small number of Britons took advantage of these assistance schemes in the 1830s and 1840s. They were joined by the families of some convicts, also transported at government expense, but overall the attractions of migration to so distant a setting were few before mid-century. In 1828 the British colony of New South Wales was home to a white population of 36,598, 40 per cent of whom were convicts dispatched from the imperial centre after trial and conviction. Between 1832 and 1835 male convicts were joined by 2,000 women offenders, most of whom were from Dublin or Cork City in Ireland.[37] The ratio of free to convict remained steady through 1833, at which time the population stood at 60,794.

Transportation of convicts from Britain ceased in the 1840s, and with it the size of the free settler contingent expanded sharply. There were just over 400,000 migrants and their descendants in the Australian colonies on the eve of the gold rush at mid-century, a figure which constituted roughly 8 per cent of all those leaving the United Kingdom for overseas destinations between the years 1815 and 1850.[38] Wool provided the key export commodity prior to 1850, and most migrants engaged in pastoral enterprises or agriculture.

The discovery of gold in Victoria colony in the south-east understandably accelerated the migration process, as almost 500,000 newcomers arrived during the 1850s. A later gold 'strike' in Western Australia during the 1880s again fuelled migration levels. Half of these migrants received some form of relocation assistance from the British government, and this served to boost the number of whole families who travelled to the new colony. The city of Melbourne in Victoria colony had a population of 100,000 in 1854, while overall this one colony grew to 400,000 by 1857 and 540,000 in 1861.[39]

The Australian gold rush did not offer a solution to the problem of underemployment in the agricultural sector, but it did reduce the stigma of convict colony status associated with early settlement. By mid-century industrial Britain was no longer capable of feeding itself from domestic agriculture alone, and it was quickly understood that British migrants who travelled to Australia in hopes of striking it rich were likely to remain as potential agricultural labourers once the rush for mineral wealth had subsided. British policy makers envisioned new settlers in Australia as future consumers of Britain's manufactured products, and future Australian purchasing power would be provided through the export of foodstuffs and other raw materials to the metropolitan capital.

During the course of 1849 some 2,500 Australians had boarded ships destined for California and the gold rush fever which gripped that new territory of the United States.[40] It now appeared that labour resources that were essential to the development of the British colony were being siphoned off by the American Republic. The shortages had even led to the introduction of Chinese indentured servants before the start of the gold rush. They began arriving in 1848, with 2,500 Chinese in residence three years later and more than 25,000 in service by 1857.[41] The majority of Chinese were employed in the goldfields by 1855, but the hostility of white prospectors quickly led to the eviction of the indentured workers from mining operations. And in 1888, all of the Australian states followed the American precedent and adopted strict exclusionary rules respecting Chinese immigrants, fearful lest non-whites flood the labour market.

The end of the gold rush by the late 1850s meant a significant drop in the number of migrants arriving in Australia from the British Isles. The total non-aboriginal population in 1860 stood at just over 1 million. By 1900 it had risen to 3.7 million persons, while the native population declined from 180,000 in 1860 to 93,536 at the start of the twentieth century.[42] Most of the growth in the white community was due to natural increase; by 1901, 77 per cent of the colony's total population had been born in Australia. Of the remaining 23 per cent, 18 per cent were from Britain, with the small remainder having arrived from Germany or countries in South Asia.[43]

Transport under sail still took over four months, and the cost far exceeded that of passage to America. A total of 800,000 persons made the voyage to the colonies between 1860 and 1900, with many receiving some form of transport assistance from the destination colony. Assistance was often provided through revenues acquired in the sale of public lands, but not infrequently residents in the host colony would pay for transport costs associated with family and neighbours. Few non-Europeans arrived after 1860. Australia's strong colonial links with Britain and its Empire defined settlement policy in terms of white Anglo heritage. Migration restrictions during the later nineteenth and twentieth centuries were designed to preserve the national purity of the country, even at the expense of recruiting cheap labour for expanding industries. Today it is estimated that about half the population of Australia is of British stock, 30 per cent claim Irish roots, 15 per cent trace their ancestors to Scotland, while German, Italian, Greek and other Europeans constitute but a tiny fraction of the picture.[44]

When Australia was organized under a new government whereby the six colonies delegated specific powers and responsibilities to a central authority, the first significant policy matter to be treated by the new Commonwealth Parliament was immigration. In December 1901 a comprehensive Immigration Restriction Bill was passed, and its provisions set the precedent for the strict regimes against the free movement of peoples which would soon come to characterize a number of developed Western nations, including, most importantly, the United States. Adopted at the height of social Darwinist influence, when Australians 'had a clear concept of themselves as different from and superior to all non-European peoples', the legislation was popularly known as the 'White Australia' policy, and it served as part of a major effort to define the essential cultural characteristics of the newly established Commonwealth state.[45] Perceiving the rise of Asian powers such as Japan as a potential threat, and keen to maintain the Anglo-Saxon roots of the first colonial project, members of parliament viewed the legislation as an effective means of solidifying a sense of national and imperial identity at the moment of national consolidation.[46]

The White Australia policy also called for the repatriation of Pacific islanders who had arrived as indentured servants and laboured on the Queensland sugar plantations. By 1906 4,000 persons were expelled under this legislation and shipping companies involved in the transport of undesirable migrants were subject to heavy fines. The mechanism adopted to enforce the ban was a dictation test whereby prospective settlers had to answer questions administered in a European language of the examiner's choice. From 1904–9, 805 migrants took the test and 46 passed; after that date no one appears to have secured a positive mark.[47] For those who were permitted to remain in the country, a disturbing series of franchise, property and employment restrictions made their status extremely tenuous, in spite of the fact that Japan's rise to economic and military power undermined the racial assumptions respecting superior and inferior races.

Overall, the White Australia policy remained in force throughout the first half of the twentieth century, serving as an effective device in curbing the entry of Asian migrants, while encouraging the departure of others by withholding key civil rights. Australia's Chinese population, for example, declined from just under 33,000 in 1901 to less than 1,000 in 1921. By 1947, the success of the White Australia policy was overwhelming, for as 'the population of European descent doubled to over 7 million, the Melanesian population declined by more than 80 per cent, the Chinese by more than two-thirds, the Indian by over half, and the Japanese all but disappeared'.[48]

Between 1905 and 1929 over 700,000 British migrants relocated to Australia, and a majority received some form of government assistance in order to make their transport possible. Compared to only 140,000 non-British migrants for the first forty years of the twentieth century, the official government antipathy toward any but white Britons defined Australia as an exceptionally exclusivist portion of the larger British Empire. At the close of the Second World War an estimated 90 per cent of the inhabitants were of Anglo-Celtic stock, whereas the combined total for Asians and Aborigines had declined to just over 1 per cent.[49] Economic interests did not encourage revision of this restrictive regime, and while dissent and criticism were voiced, there was little hope that the dominant political culture would institute a re-evaluation of the policy, even in light of the racist ideology embraced by the German enemy during the Second World War. If anything, the Pacific war tended to solidify racist thinking among the white majority, as anti-Japanese propaganda highlighted the fanaticism and cruelty of the enemy.

It would take a number of years, together with shifting international perspectives on the issue of race and human equality, before a less prohibitive approach to immigration was adopted by Australia's political leaders. But when the shift did take place, beginning in the 1950s, the impact on Australian society was unprecedented. The period of greatest European migration occurred after the Second World War, when labour demands and defence considerations led to a broader acceptance of non-British Europeans under the assumption that new peoples could be assimilated into – and not accommodated by – the dominant culture. 'We must have a single culture' was the widely shared opinion of Bill Snedden, Minister for Immigration in the late 1960s, 'with everyone living in the same way, understanding each other, and sharing the same aspirations. We don't want pluralism.'[50] Census figures from 1947 revealed that over the previous fourteen years the country's overall population had grown by less than 1 per cent annually, and in some years departures from Australia exceeded arrivals.[51]

There was widespread acceptance of the argument that this large continent was underpopulated, and fresh memories of Japan's aggressive thrust to the south informed the thinking of defence experts on population questions. A government committee charged with studying the issue reported that future migrants from Britain alone would not be sufficient to meet postwar needs, especially in the building and industrial sectors. The government responded by opening the borders to non-British Europeans, including displaced persons. By 1963, a total of 2 million migrants had arrived in the country, with many winning assistance from the receiving country's national government. The majority continued to come from Britain, but Germans, Greeks, Turks, Portuguese, Yugoslavs, Dutch and Poles also joined the mix. Still slightly below settlement figures in the United States, Australia had become a more popular destination point than Canada or Latin America for white Europeans.[52]

But it was not until the mid-1960s that the Australian government lifted its long-standing discriminatory restrictions against non-European migrants. The pressing need for labour resources again served as the catalyst for the lifting of barriers against Asians who sought to relocate, and the government followed the lead of the United States and Canada in terminating ethnic criteria in admissions decisions. New eligibility categories were set, placing family reunion, professional skills and refugee status at the centre of the new regime. The government did not actively pursue Asian migrants as it had in the case of non-British Europeans, and there was no question of relocation assistance being offered to Asians, but still the impact of the new migration was dramatic.[53]

The Asian immigrant population in Australia climbed from 3 per cent of the total in the early 1960s to 40 per cent in the late 1980s, and as Australia's principal trade links gradually shifted from their traditional focus on Europe to emerging markets in eastern Asia, the pattern accelerated. During the twenty-year period beginning in 1970, Australia's exports destined for Asia grew from 49 to 67 per cent, while goods sent to Europe declined from 23 to 15 per cent of the total.[54] Asia is no longer viewed by Australians as a military or demographic threat, but as an economic opportunity for a land rich in resources but still underpopulated with respect to overall economic potential. In addition, recent decades have seen the emergence of Australia as a significant host nation for refugees, particularly those coming from war-torn Vietnam.

During the 1970s the government abandoned the goal of assimilation and turned instead to a multicultural, integrationist model for the future. In 1973 the Immigration Minister, Al Grassby, stated that 'the increasing diversity of Australian society has gradually eroded and finally rendered untenable any prospects that there might have been twenty years ago of fully assimilating newcomers to the "Australian way of life", to use a phrase common at that time.'[55] Migrants would now be encouraged to add to the richness of Australian life, not to adjust their cultural heritage to a prescribed formula. As early as 1965 the Labour Party removed its reference to a White Australia from its platform, and unions had abandoned their harsh anti-foreign rhetoric.

During the 1970s both major parties, Labour and Liberal, placed migrant issues high on their respective political agendas. Calls for improved housing, educational opportunities and professional development were all part of the minority rights agenda. And since most new migrants settled in urban areas, two states, New South Wales and Victoria, received the overwhelming majority of the new arrivals. In 1986, 2 million of the 3,247,000 people born outside Australia were resident in these two urban and industrial states.[56] By this date many of these migrants were Vietnamese, Filipinos and Chinese. As with Australia's Western counterparts, the issues of civil rights, ethnic identity and multiculturalism have engaged the attention of policy makers over the past twenty years, and overall the growing Asianization of the population has been progressing apace without substantial backlash.

LATIN AMERICA AFTER 1800

With the beginning of independence movements in Latin America during the first three decades of the nineteenth century, many liberal reformers in the newly established nations sought to encourage immigration – and thus address the problem of recurrent labour shortages – by lifting the centuries-old ban against non-Roman Catholic settlers. Overriding the fixed opposition of the Catholic Church, most of the new republics dropped their exclusionary religious qualifications and began to welcome migrants irrespective of their confessional points of view. The elites who governed these infant states expressed the hope that an influx of Old World settlers, preferably from northern Europe, would facilitate the emergence of a class of small farmers dedicated to the ideals of economic development and republican government.

These leaders operated under the assumption that European civilization was indeed the most progressive on earth, and that strong infusions of European human capital would quickly set the South American continent on the right developmental path. Unfortunately, such an outlook also reflected a more general contempt for the poorer citizenry, often of mixed race, who had inhabited the countryside for generations. In the event, the most optimistic plans were never realized, as the first half-century after independence witnessed only a modest growth in European migration to Latin America. It was certainly lower than that of the United States and, more surprisingly, lower even than the rate achieved in Latin America during the late colonial period. One recent scholar places the total migrant figure in the region of a modest 200,000 for the period 1816–50.[57]

For European emigrants before mid-century, there were a host of very practical reasons for *not* choosing South America as their destination. Cost of transport was pivotal, and passage to New York was both shorter and cheaper than it was to any of the major Latin American coastal cities. A comparatively liberal land policy in the United States offered the prospect of swift land ownership, the enormous social and economic advance from peasant to yeoman farmer, even for those at the bottom of the economic ladder. More stable political and judicial institutions in the United States (especially after 1865) together with a seasonal climate which was more familiar to Europeans, served as additional reasons for choosing North over South. It is no coincidence that the bulk of

Europeans who crossed the Atlantic for South America took up residence in countries featuring a temperate rather than tropical climate. Finally, the continued existence of chattel slavery in most of the key South American destination countries acted as a strong disincentive for potential agricultural migrants.[58]

In contrast with continued British migration to the United States after independence, few peninsular Spaniards arrived in the former colonies after crown authority had been repudiated. Creole-Iberian tensions had been relatively high prior to the colonial revolts, and with the expulsion of thousands of Spaniards by the Mexican government between 1827 and 1833, the climate of mutual recrimination and disdain only intensified. Spanish women and men continued to migrate to the two colonies which remained under imperial control – Cuba and Puerto Rico – but in every other settlement in Central and South America during the first half of the nineteenth century, non-Iberians were the principal additions to the population.

MID-CENTURY TRANSITIONS

Approximately 11 million of the 52 million individuals who travelled to the Americas between 1824 and 1924 selected the former colonies of Spain and Portugal as their new home. How do we explain this? The background and motivation of migrants to post-independence Latin America varied considerably. Some of the 7,000 British and Irish volunteers who fought in the army of Simon Bolivar, for example, remained on a permanent basis, while in Brazil roughly 1,000 French emigrants had settled by the early 1820s. The language and culture barrier in South America was not a significant impediment to relocation given that the largest percentage of migrants were Italian (38 per cent of the total). The seaport cities especially were popular sites for communities of non-Iberian merchants. Uruguay, for example, had a total population of some 74,000 people when it secured independence in 1828, but by 1842 the country was home to over 30,000 Europeans, many of them Italians. In the capital city of Montevideo alone, 60 per cent of the 1843 population of 31,000 were men and women of European origin. And by 1908,

17 per cent of the nation's population was foreign-born.[59] German and Swiss agricultural settlements in the south of Brazil, initially promoted by the respective governments in Europe, also attracted modest numbers. Organized by recruiters and landowners, over 5,000 German migrants had travelled to Brazil with the goal of founding agricultural communities before 1830. Similar settlements, consisting of French, German and Swiss nationals, were subsequently established in Argentina, Chile, Nicaragua, Peru and Venezuela.[60]

Other migrants, albeit fewer in number, chose a Latin American destination solely for the challenge and adventure involved in recreating their lives in a different environment. As in the United States, a handful of utopian communities were established, with leaders attempting to build the new society in a Latin American setting, but again we are speaking of very small numbers of people. Outside the 'big three' countries (Argentina, Brazil and Uruguay), which attracted most of those who crossed the Atlantic, migrants to Central American and Andean countries arrived in a better economic position than their peasant counterparts. European immigrants were among the more affluent coffee planters in Costa Rica, while in Peru they enjoyed key positions in the banking industry. Overall the economic variable must be recognized as the pre-eminent factor motivating all travellers from Europe. Whether well or ill-informed about the host country, Europe's peasant migrants hoped for new chances in a fresh environment, new opportunities for material improvement.

The major influx of Europeans into Latin America took place during the second half of the nineteenth century, and particularly after 1860. With Western Europe's overall population more than doubling from 187 to 400 million between 1800 and 1900, and particularly with the advent of cheap steamship transport by the 1870s, the relocation options available to common people broadened enormously. And thanks to the abbreviated crossing made possible by steam propulsion, mortality rates on the transatlantic passage declined dramatically.

The problem of securing ample and inexpensive labour, especially in the cash-crop-producing regions of South America, remained a constant issue for landowners, but a wider range of economic imperatives, all linked to the rapid development of industrial and consumer economies in Western Europe, best explains the remarkable upsurge in European migration to Latin America after mid-century. Exports from the former Spanish and Portuguese colonies grew more than ten times over the sixty-year period 1850–1910, and business and political leaders held that continued export growth depended on the availability of cheap immigrant labour. Industrial Europe developed a keen demand for the raw materials which were so essential to emergent consumer-based economies, and Latin America possessed many of these products in abundance. Base metals like copper and tin, nitrates for chemical fertilizers, rubber for the nascent bicycle and motor industries, meat products which from the 1880s could be transported long distance thanks to the advent of refrigerated ships, fruits destined for the United States: a wide array of products were now being exported to distant shores in bulk.

At the top of the export list, however, were grains and caffeine products, coffee in particular.[61] The economies of Brazil, Venezuela, Columbia, El Salvador, Guatemala, Haiti and Nicaragua became heavily dependent on the consumer demand of developed Western countries for this single export product. Given these factors, it is no surprise that most of those who arrived from Europe found themselves living and working in areas of export crop production – as producers of wheat in Argentina or on the coffee plantations of Brazil. A tenfold rise in Latin American exports during the second half of the nineteenth century, coupled with an overall population increase on the continent from 30 to 77 million during the period 1850–1912, might strongly suggest the existence of an adequate labour force, but in fact much land was still available for agricultural development, and the appearance of the first train lines in the 1870s made the transport of agricultural products to distant ports economically feasible for the first time.

Within this economic climate, traditional sources of plantation labour no longer sufficed. The importation of slaves had been made very difficult after the British navy began interdicting ships carrying unfree Africans in 1808, and by 1855 the Brazilian government ended the practice of importing bondsmen. Cuba reluctantly followed suit ten years later. Life expectancy for slaves working in subtropical environments had always been low, and reproduction levels never reached the point whereby the system could maintain itself in the long term without constant replenishment from the source of supply. One attempted solution to the worker shortage lay in the formation of an indenture system designed to lure impoverished Asians and South Asians into long labour contracts in return for passage, housing and wages. But even this project was by and large limited to some of the Caribbean islands and in British and Dutch Guyana. We will return to the phenomenon of Asian indenture in Chapter 4, but at this point we can say that it was but a partial and insufficient source of human muscle power for the cash-crop economies of Latin America.

The majority of mid- to late-nineteenth century migrants were by and large farmers who wished to continue working in that capacity. This rural, agricultural culture was in stark contrast to earlier Spanish colonial patterns of urban development and preferences for city life, but it was just the type of migrant most in demand given the economic priorities of many Latin American governments. The countries with the highest number of emigrants destined for the Americas in general and Latin America in particular were, not surprisingly, beset with economic difficulties during the second half of the century, including a depressed agricultural market, due in part to imports of grain from the Americas. Italy, Spain, Portugal and Russia were some of the least industrialized areas of Europe, while their respective agricultural output was unimpressive when compared with France and Germany.[62] The highest number of Europeans travelling to Latin America (38 per cent) during the second half of the century came from Italy, and most of these were agricultural labourers from the poorest segments of the population. Seeking to escape the consequences of economic downturn in the north and agricultural stagnation in the south, those Italians who began new lives in Latin America, while often illiterate, nonetheless believed that a more satisfying life in a rural, agricultural setting could be secured in the New World.

One factor that was crucial in the migrant's selection of a particular destination involved the work of shipping companies' hired agents. Often these agents would represent only the attractive features of the destination to a group of peasant farmers who had scant knowledge of the actual economic and political conditions in the host country in question. Landowners in Brazil and Argentina, for example, employed a number of recruitment agents in Europe during a period in the second half of the nineteenth century when the labour problem in the cash-crop agricultural sector was acute. In terms of demographic growth, their efforts had a significant impact. From 1900 to 1930 the population of Latin America increased by almost 70 per cent to 104 million, and many of these men, women and children were either migrants or the first generation of children of migrants from Europe.[63] Misrepresentation doubtless was widespread, and 'free' choice of settlement was often based on no more information that what was provided by a very interested party.

It is significant that over 90 per cent of all European immigrants to Latin America settled in just three countries: Argentina, Brazil and Uruguay. Between 1871 and 1915, 2.5 million Europeans settled permanently in Argentina alone, and four-fifths of these were either Italian or Spanish. This represented one-third of the country's entire population in 1914. By 1940, 30 per cent of the country's 14 million residents were foreign-born.[64] The capital city of Buenos Aires claimed to be a European city by virtue of the fact that at one point two-thirds of its adult inhabitants had been born in the Old World.[65] Almost as many migrated to Brazil during this period, again with the largest contingent coming from Italy.

Argentina, home to almost half of all European migrants to Latin America during the period 1851–1924, did not recruit settlers as long as the principal economic activity was the exportation of hides. But when labour-intensive wheat cultivation proved its profitability as an export commodity beginning in the late 1870s, the government successfully negotiated a lower fare structure with the major shippers, and in 1888 it even undertook to subsidize the transport costs of prospective migrants. The subsidy programme did not last more than a couple of years, but continued low transport costs, coupled with a favourable cost of living when compared with the United States, made it possible for millions of European migrants to find new homes in Argentina between 1880 and 1930.

Many of the Italian male migrants to Argentina were in fact seasonal workers, *golondrinas* (swallows) who would return home to Europe in May after the Argentine wheat crop had been harvested. Their work year was organized around the fact that the period of low agricultural activity in the Mediterranean coincided with the busiest time on the Argentine pampas.[66] These rugged farm workers would take cheap passage to the New World in the autumn and return home – in theory with some savings – just in time for a new round of agricultural activities in Italy or Spain.

Soon after the abolition of slavery in 1888, coffee producers in the state of Sao Paulo in Brazil also inaugurated a programme of subsidized passage for family units with at least one working-age male. This policy of subsidizing family rather than individual migration was designed to avoid the type of temporary labour so common in Argentina. During the final two decades of the nineteenth century, 1.6 million Europeans, mostly Italians, and virtually all of whom were attracted by the prospect of land ownership, landed in Brazil. With so many ex-slaves leaving their cash-crop positions after 1888, immigrant workers from Europe literally saved the coffee industry. In return for maintaining the coffee trees and working the harvest, immigrants were normally given free housing and land to cultivate their own food crops. Most labourers would sign on for at least a year in the coffee fields, and with their accumulated savings the migrant families would invariably attempt to purchase land. In the estimation of one recent scholar, the goal of upward mobility was in fact realized for many of these Europeans who settled in Brazil during the late nineteenth century.[67]

MODERNIZATION AND MIGRATION

The transoceanic passage of millions of Europeans to new homes in three distant continents during the century ending in 1914 represented a singular transition in global demographics. While the

Americas had earlier been appropriated from native peoples, the population impress of free whites had been nominal prior to the end of the Napoleonic wars in Europe. But with the exile of Bonaparte and the restoration of peace throughout Europe, a peace which would obtain for the next 100 years, European kingdoms east of the Elbe River moved into a vibrant era of industrialization and democratization. New unified nation states were formed in Italy and Germany, and far-flung empires were established by highly competitive European powers. As populations expanded dramatically in a period of increasing wealth, education, mobility and longevity, the possibility that life might be otherwise, that one's status was no longer set by one's birth, animated millions to seize the opportunity for international relocation.

The fact that Europe's highest out-migration took place during an era of great industrial and scientific development confirms the thesis that international migrants are not, by and large, isolated and impoverished rural peasants fleeing enormous economic hardship, but instead women and men who have been exposed to the first fruits of modernization, urbanization and the impact of global market economics. Marx's mid-century critique of capitalism and its social repercussions notwithstanding, it is undeniable that during the age of the Great Migration wages were on the rise, better public health measures were adopted, medical science began to tackle the age-old scourges of cholera, plague and typhoid, governments began providing workers with sickness, accident and unemployment insurance, and workplace conditions improved. The very fact that Europe's population increased from 188 million in 1800 to 463 million in 1914 – and this after deducting overseas migration figures of almost 60 million – suggests that ideas of progress were not just the wild imaginings of later historians.

The intensification of global market mechanisms over the course of the nineteenth and twentieth centuries has been a key factor in forwarding migration patterns. By 1914 there were over 30,000 commercial ships plying the oceans of the world, moving the wool of New Zealand, the rice of Burma, the rubber of Malaya and the cotton of India to a variety of global markets. The importation of cheap American wheat into a European market in the late nineteenth century, thanks largely to low costs associated with steamship transport, undercut European agriculture and facilitated the movement of peasant producers to the Americas. Between 1860 and 1914 world trade increased twelve times while world industrial output boomed.[68] European governments may not have actively encouraged migration during the nineteenth century, but neither did they continue to restrict or regulate the number and type of subjects who departed. During this century of unprecedented demographic growth, political leaders began to view settler colonies in terms of potential markets for the products of national industry. Expanded settlement, it was argued, would relieve population pressures at home while simultaneously contributing to social harmony in the sending country by insuring that the remaining industrial labourers would continue to find employment.

Receiving nations in Australasia and in America projected an insatiable need for labour prior to the First World War. The end of slavery and laws against indentured servitude in many receiving areas, coupled with lower transport costs, created an environment in which people of very limited means in Europe could become autonomous property owners or comfortable tradesmen in a fresh setting. The myriad hardships experienced by migrants who settled in maturing cities overseas were offset (for some) by the greater prospect of securing a better overall standard of living, if not for themselves, then at least for their immediate offspring. An intellectual and material economy of rising expectations became central to the migration psychology of free whites in these areas of the globe, fuelling an expansionist and competitive model of development. When paired with a level of political enfranchisement unmatched in the sending areas, the allure of these settler states became compulsive. The 'Europeanization' of the global community was becoming a fact of life just at the moment when these proud Western nations descended into the first of two suicidal military conflagrations.

FOUR

Empires and New Indentures

Europeans were by no means the only international migrants to play key roles in the transformation of the natural environment during the Industrial Revolution of the nineteenth and early twentieth centuries. In every major civilization, save perhaps the Muslim world, humans were on the move across land and water in significant numbers and under the auspices of expansive capitalist economic structures. For white Europeans, however, that movement was conducted largely as a matter of autonomous action, the decision of free agents who entered host countries without specific labour obligations. The task of securing meaningful work and adequate shelter upon arrival may have been daunting, but where to live and work, and how long to stay, were at least at the discretion of the migrant. Something of this autonomy and choice can be seen in the Russian claim to and occupation of Siberia, where sparsely populated stretches of the enormous Central Asian land mass were brought under the nominal control of tsarist authorities. A completely different model obtained in the case of non-Western migrants who ventured into lands under the control of Western peoples. For millions of travellers from South and East Asia, physical relocation to the Americas or to European colonial possessions was coupled with cultural disorientation, obligatory work contracts, and minimal chance for social and economic advancement. The dynamic and transformative power of industrial capitalism may have undermined the viability of slave labour, but it did not necessarily embrace personal freedom as the only practical and morally permissible alternative.

THE SIBERIAN ADDITION

The movement of millions of Western Europeans and Africans across the world's great oceans after 1500 was paralleled by another, lesser-known European migration, one which unfolded in an easterly direction across what were sometimes thought to be marginal, inaccessible, and inhospitable areas on the same land mass as Europe. The eastward march of Russian military adventurers, merchants, peasants, convicts and political prisoners across the Ural mountains, beginning in the 1580s and continuing into the mid-twentieth century, was crucially important both to the development of an absolutist and imperialist tsarist state during the early modern era, and to the physical transformation of one of the globe's key centres of mineral wealth.

Within the space of less than 150 years beginning in 1581, Russian exploration and claims to lands in the east extended some 6,000 miles from Moscow, first to the south-east in the direction of the Black and Caspian Seas, and then eastwards towards the Pacific. The subjugation and conquest of the land called Siberia (after the tiny Khanate of Sibir) was comparable in scope, strategic significance and overall economic impact to the Spanish and Portuguese incursions into the Americas. And the exploits of the first Cossack commander, Yermak Timofeevich, leading a handful of grasping warriors into the Siberian vastness, equals the ambition and self-confidence of the Spanish *conquistadores* from Columbus to Pizarro. The migration of Russians into this geographically diverse region marked the transition of the land-locked medieval Muscovy regime of the Stroganovs into the powerful Romanov Russian Empire of the modern era, making Russia both a European and an Asian power during the latter half of the nineteenth century.[1]

Whereas between the thirteenth and the fifteenth centuries Muscovy had served as a western frontier outpost of the ferocious 'Golden Horde', the associated khanates of the powerful Mongol Empire, in the seventeenth century roles were reversed as military power and imperial claims originated in the west and projected themselves east. As early as the third decade of the eighteenth century, Tsar Peter the Great was authorizing expeditions in the distant Bering Straits, activities which would eventually lead to the brief occupation of portions of yet another continent. And what had begun as the enterprise of merchants and raiders intent upon advancing the fur trade had become by the middle of the nineteenth century a state-directed colonization effort designed largely with the objective of mineral extraction and agricultural production.[2] From the early sixteenth century until 1763, all of Siberia was regarded as a single colonial unit under the control of a *prikaz* or bureau of trans-Ural affairs located first in Moscow and then in St Petersburg.[3] Some 20 per cent of Russia's population now lives in a area covering one-twelfth of the earth's land surface, which if independent today would constitute the world's largest nation. Although it remains one of the least densely populated areas on earth, with a total population of no more than 30–35 million people, Siberia and the Russian Far East (or collectively Northern Asia) remains a strategically and economically important holding for those who live west of the Ural Mountains in Russia proper.[4]

The relationship between the Russian core area and the enormous Siberian periphery has been firmly tied to colonialism for the past 400 years. Prior to the first Russian settlement, some 200 native tribes competed for land and influence across the large expanses of topographically varied territory. Previously occupied by invading Huns and Mongols, the entire population of Siberia at the close of the sixteenth century numbered no more than 250,000, and most of these were residents of the southernmost portion of the land mass.[5] This fact alone distinguishes the Russian conquest from the earlier Spanish actions in densely populated Central and South America. Living exclusively in a barter economy, the illiterate inhabitants of southern Siberia engaged in hunting and rudimentary forms of agriculture. Interregional trade was not uncommon, but these commercial exchanges never led to the emergence of strong territorial states. When the Russians arrived, penetration was normally along river routes, where forts were constructed and fur trading contacts with the native peoples first established. Rather than overwhelming the indigenous residents, these early settlements, whether sponsored by private trading companies or by the Siberian Department in Moscow, 'were, in fact, little islands in a vast ocean of forest, tundra and steppe, linked by fragile transport routes'.[6]

The early Cossack adventurers into Siberia were quickly followed by representatives of the tsarist bureaucracy. Military governors were assigned to overseas trade with the native peoples, while interaction with the two eastern powers capable of interfering with Russian operations, China and Japan, was minimal due to the isolationist stance of both empires during the course of the seventeenth century. Catherine the Great was eager to designate Siberia a part of the contiguous Russian Empire, and she discouraged references to the lands east of the Urals as colonies. But even when a unified governor-generalship was created for all of Siberia in the early nineteenth century, the practical challenges involved in administering such a gigantic area were insurmountable.[7]

Always the key motivating factor for explorers was resource acquisition, the hope of rapid and significant material gain. During the course of the seventeenth century, furs from Siberia constituted Russia's principal source of foreign trade.[8] Native peoples, quickly overwhelmed by the superior firepower of the Russians, paid tribute in the form of furs in return for maintaining a modicum of political autonomy. By the end of the eighteenth century, the indigenous tribes, now at approximately 280,000 persons, had become a minority in their own land. By 1720 there were nearly 700,000 native Russians living in Siberia, and these numbers would continue their modest growth over the next century, before a great burst of government-approved relocation took place after 1880.

As in the case of European expansion into the Americas, even when military conflict did not break out between migrants and natives, the inadvertent introduction of smallpox and measles had a serious impact on natural population increase among native peoples.[9] Occasionally in the seventeenth century, Russian Orthodox churchmen would make modest efforts to convert the largely shamanistic natives to Christianity, but since conversion would exempt indigenous peoples from paying tribute to the imperial authorities, such activities were discouraged. The Church at first forbade mixed marriages between Russians and indigenous Siberians, but later allowed these unions if both accepted Christianity.[10] Generally speaking, relations between the Russian and the tribute-paying natives were better than Amerindian contacts with Europeans. Clashes and senseless bloodshed were not absent from the Siberian experience, but the sense of racial superiority that informed relations in the Americas was largely muted in Russia's Eastern Empire.

During the course of the eighteenth century the Russian population in Siberia expanded to include over 1.5 million inhabitants, with the overwhelming majority of these migrants freely choosing their relocation destination. It is instructive to contrast this largely free migration with the approximately 2 million European (mainly English) inhabitants in what became the United States, where a majority travelled under some form of indenture. Siberia is today universally associated in the popular imagination with images of tsarist and Soviet (especially Stalinist) exiles, but these involuntary migrants and political undesirables together never formed more than a tiny minority of the overall population. As late as 1897, for example, only 5.2 per cent, or around 310,000 Russians in Siberia, were designated in the census as exiles.[11] Between 1861 and 1898 around half a million people were banished to Siberia for a wide variety of political offences, and most of these victims of the tsarist regime were males. Their contribution to brigandage and lawlessness was not insignificant in the social history of Central Asia, but freedom seekers clearly predominated in the migration process. Serfdom was never imposed on the inhabitants of Siberia, thus economic opportunities for resourceful pioneers seeking to better their lives contributed to the attractiveness of relocation.

It was during the nineteenth century that the Russian imperial state began to see Siberia, now double the size of the continental United States, as an important area for migration and potential agricultural development. And it was now that labour shortages in Siberia were filled by significant numbers of involuntary migrants in the form of criminals and political opponents of the tsarist state. Between the years 1835 and 1850, for example, 140,000 exiles, most in leg irons and on foot, traversed 2–3,000 kilometres to work in the royal gold and silver mines in western Siberia. Their numbers increased during the second half of the century, with 1.2 million unfree persons sent to work camps between 1867 and 1896.[12] A variety of factors came together during the final decades of the century to place the question of Siberia's future at the centre of Russian policy making. European and American imperialism in the Far East, Japanese expansion and industrial development, Siberia's potential vulnerability due to the lack of troops and the great distances involved in defending areas in the East from potential aggressors – all these served to focus the attention of imperial authorities in Moscow on the need to populate this enormous land. The goal, of course, was to create a unified, and Russified empire where ethnic nationalism and regional localism were subordinated to the needs of the imperial state.

Still, territories beyond the Urals did not attract large numbers of settlers prior to the advent of the trans-Siberian railroad in the 1890s. In 1800 there were still fewer than 1 million persons living in Siberia. And despite the abolition of serfdom in 1861, there was no great push eastwards by the newly emancipated peasantry. The population of Siberia (excluding the Far Eastern provinces) in 1858 stood at 2.7 million, and only 200,000 free agricultural labourers, together with half as many exiles, migrated to Greater Siberia during the decade of the 1880s. The completion of the rail link, advocated by strategic planners as essential to the prevention of centrifugal tendencies, transformed the migratory process. In a dramatic acceleration, roughly 4 million peasants relocated to Siberia between 1861 and 1914, pushing the total population towards 10.3 million by the start of the First World War, and while this out-migration did not solve the acute problem of overpopulation and land hunger in Russia, it did fulfil a Russian 'manifest destiny' in the East which had been impeded by the sheer distances involved prior to the advent of the rail system.[13]

In the decade after the 1905 Revolution, the government aggressively promoted migration to Siberia, offering subsidized fares and supporting the efforts of entire villages to send preliminary scouting parties, in an effort to alleviate pressure on land resources in Russia. Around 2 million men, women and children, most travelling as groups intent upon constructing entire villages after arrival, boarded the trains for Siberia in the period 1906–14 alone.[14] When the war began in 1914, almost 80 per cent of all inhabitants of Siberia were Russian, with the native peoples accounting for less than 10 per cent of the total population. In a burst of development, the newcomers laid railway lines, cleared forests for agriculture and established new villages, seeking in the process to begin life anew in a malleable, if harsh, environment.

Siberian extractive industries had from the start of the conquest provided the key motive for state involvement in migration. Focusing first on lumber and furs, subsequently on coal mining, and more recently on oil and gas production, Russian authorities have long viewed migration within the context of labour resources. At the close of the nineteenth century, 80 per cent of migrants from European Russia were relocating eastwards, not westwards to Europe and America. Overall agricultural yield increased 87 per cent during the final four decades of the century, a level of productivity which outstripped production levels common in European Russia. By the time of the Bolshevik Revolution in 1917, Siberian grain production eclipsed that of all other Russian colonial borderlands. Spring wheat was produced for the market thanks to efficient rail transport, while dairy products, especially butter, became important commercial products sold in a wider European market. By the eve of the First World War, there were over 4,000 creameries in Siberia, and their combined product accounted for 16 per cent of the world's exports of butter. Three-quarters of the total harvest in all areas of production was marketed outside the producing areas by 1914. As peasant incomes expanded in the years immediately prior to the war in Europe, the attractions of resettlement multiplied. Even the war, initially at any rate, proved to be an economic advantage for settlers east of the Urals, as agricultural cooperatives obtained lucrative contracts from the armed forces.[15]

Stalin's genocidal terror regime (1927–53) transformed Siberia into a massive labour camp where suspected opponents of the dictator met their end for the greater good of 'Socialism in one Country'. At the height of the regime's paranoid brutality, as many as 40 million persons were working in unspeakable conditions at hundreds of labour camps, what Solzhenitsyn labelled the 'Gulag archipelago'. Forced to toil as builders, loggers, miners, track-layers and tunnellers, millions died during the course of the Second World War while providing much of the industrial manpower and military *materiel* needed to rebuff the Nazi onslaught. Working prisoners to death was a deliberate objective of the regime, with Stalin eagerly employing the continent-wide land mass as a conveniently remote outdoor death chamber. In conjunction with the camp strategy, from 1928 the regime imposed collectivization schemes on native fishermen, reindeer herders and hunters, hoping to 'proletarianize' even nomadic peoples by subordinating them to the interests of the state. And when grain procurement west of the Urals fell below state mandates in 1927, Stalin led a bureaucratic raiding party into western Siberia in order to seize grain from industrious farmers who were now identified as kulaks. In 1929, Siberian peasants began to slaughter their own livestock rather than hand them over to an alien government. From 1930–1, when collectivization was fully under way, more than 300,000 Siberian farmers were exiled into the north; by 1937 resistance was broken and over 90 per cent of the Siberian peasantry who worked in agriculture were now toiling on mismanaged state collectives under capricious and brutal Party zealots.[16]

Once the dictator was dead, thousands who survived the terror returned to their homes west of the Urals, but Siberia lost none of its strategic importance as a resource pool for the Cold War Soviet State. Industrial development, power generation facilities, and after 1960, oil and natural gas exploration served to keep the region at the heart of the state's quest for hard currency earnings. Collectivization continued into the 1950s, while the central government pushed for greater urbanization and the abandonment of native herding, hunting and fishing lifestyles, and clan affiliations.[17] Unlike the many former union republics of the Soviet Union, which enjoy an indigenous nationality majority, Russians constitute an overwhelming majority of the inhabitants of colonized

Siberia. Thus while it remains today as a part of the Russian state, Siberia as frontier, as colony, as host for millions of impoverished migrants seeking release from the myriad oppressions of tsar and Party, remains at the core of its continent-wide identity, an identity not unmixed with a sense of remorse over the pace and scale of development. 'I see wasteland in place of forests,' writes the contemporary Siberian author Valentin Rasputin, 'which keeps spreading as the quotas grow; I see plowed fields withering and shrinking, and with what narcotic passion chemicals are injected into them; I see how hastily and badly new cities are erected, like heaps of flophouses, and how solidly they are encircled with apartment complexes and smokestacks.'[18] Migration and development have not been the sole monopoly of Europeans who have crossed the oceans. Subordinate to the industrial aims of Moscow throughout most of the twentieth century, the way of life of the native peoples is all but extinguished, bringing along with it another unfortunate parallel to the American experience.

NON-WESTERN INDENTURES

During the course of the middle to late nineteenth century, colonial governments in Canada, Australia, New Zealand, Brazil and South Africa all offered financial subsidies to prospective European immigrants in an effort to augment the numerical strength of white settler communities. During this period around 10 per cent of all migrants from Europe qualified for and received some form of support in their efforts to relocate. By way of contrast, nothing was offered to colonial peoples who wished to vacate overpopulated areas and take up residence in a portion of their respective empires where labour was in demand. Instead of encouragement, most non-European international migrants had to accept age-old indenture arrangements in order to secure assistance with their passage.[19] Especially in former slave-related rural and cash-crop farming occupations, work regimes which in some instances were akin to slavery became the established pattern of work and life into the early twentieth century. The new indentures were from a wide range of locales and their destinations were much more varied in comparison to the experience of their earlier European counterparts. Two of the three foremost non-European sending areas, India and China, were each under direct or indirect control of Western powers, while the third, Japan, was frantically seeking to achieve great power status alongside the already successful imperial states. But in all cases the indenture system when applied to non-whites involved not only the difficult adjustment to a harsh work regime, but in addition the challenge of adapting to an unfamiliar and often hostile majority culture. Unhappily, the migration of South and East Asian peoples in the service of Western states occurred just as pseudo-scientific theories of race and intellectual status were deforming the outlook of the West towards the rest of the world.

INDIA AND EMPIRE

Perhaps more than most places on earth, the massive Indian subcontinent has served as host to the widest variety of immigrants across the centuries, but the assimilative power of pervasive Hindu culture, over time, successfully absorbed most of these newcomers. From Aryan invaders beginning around 1500 BCE, to later Parthians, Sakas, Kushanas, and Huns, and more recently, and in much smaller numbers, Arabs, Persians, Turks and Britons, India has become a rich amalgam of varied migrant peoples.

Migration *from* India, on the other hand, has always been a rather modest phenomenon. During the reign of the great Mauryan Emperor Asoka in the late third century BCE, Buddhist missionaries ventured out to Ceylon, Burma and South-East Asia in a proselytizing enterprise which would eventually encompass both China and Japan, but the number of actual emigrants was negligible. In the path of these Buddhist holy men, traders and aspirant bankers would invariably follow, first to neighbouring Burma and then further south and east to Thailand, Malaya and Indonesia. Others, more ambitious still, ventured some 2,000 miles across the Indian Ocean to the east coast of Africa, there to inaugurate profitable trade links with coastal peoples, but these daring merchants cannot be compared with genuine migrant communities, for they had no intention of settling on a permanent basis in a new and unfamiliar land.

Although South Asia today is the second most populous region of the world (after China), less than one per cent of its one billion people live on other continents.[20] By the last decade of the twentieth century, some 9–10 million Indians were living in places remote from the world's largest democracy, and that efflux continues to grow at a modest rate, largely because many highly educated Indian professionals seek employment opportunities in more advanced industrialized nations. When compared with the fact that women and men of European ancestry (350 million) living outside Europe today account for about 40 per cent of India's total population, the unpretentious scale of Indian migration is placed into sharper relief. Excepting Singapore, Sri Lanka and western Malaysia, where Indians constitute around 10 per cent of the overall population, and in tiny Fiji, Mauritius and Guyana, where they are in a majority, migrants from South Asia's biggest country represent only a minuscule percentage of the total population in the nations and kingdoms where they have settled.[21]

One might explain the home-keeping penchants of the Indian population as one by-product of the insular outlook of the subcontinent's rulers, none of whom developed or supported a sea-faring tradition. The occasional long-distance merchant voyage aside, no major Indian dynasty embraced territorial or commercial ambitions beyond the shores of the massive subcontinent. Proposals for overseas colonization as a potential solution to social problems and/or overpopulation at home did not emerge in state policy discussions as they had in the royal courts of Western Europe. This essential political policy explanation for the paucity of migrants, however, is blunted by the fact that even during the period when India was under British imperial control – when there were no legal restrictions on the emigration of Indians to other parts of the Empire, when adequate transport resources were available, and when continuing widespread poverty at home might have provided an overwhelming incentive to leave – few chose to abandon their place of birth.

Perhaps the most plausible explanation for the small number of migrants from India over the centuries has to do with the sub-continent's unique social system. Despite a population which always placed enormous pressure on the land, the Hindu caste system emphasized the importance of communal cooperation and support at the local level. Before the mid-nineteenth century, caste restrictions seem to have made overseas travel, especially for upper-caste Indians, very difficult indeed. Exposure to and interaction with people from many backgrounds beyond the 'black sea' made the life of the devout Hindu migrant problematic at best.

Doubtless the most familiar example is that of Mohandas Gandhi himself; the future leader of India's independence movement was excommunicated by his caste after he decided to travel to England for his education in the 1870s. Hindus who returned home after extensive travel or work abroad sometimes underwent long rituals of purification before reintegrating into their caste. Sustained contact with strangers who knew nothing of this social and religious system was fraught with spiritual danger. Those Indians who rejected caste mandates, on the other hand, such as the thousands of Sikh emigrants who settled in late nineteenth-century East Africa, or others who settled in Canada in the early twentieth century, made an easier adjustment to their new environments. Uninhibited by majority norms respecting group exclusivity, the Sikhs readily adapted to changing economic environments and took up a variety of occupations as the need arose.

During the first three centuries covered by our survey, then, intercontinental migration of Indians was numerically insignificant. When the Portuguese explorer Vasco da Gama first arrived off the western coast of India in May 1498, the Hindu ruler of the bustling port of Calicut treated him in much the same manner as he had dealt with Arab and Chinese traders for decades: in exchange for gold, ivory, silks and jewels, Indians at Calicut provided the supplicant foreigners with pepper, cloves, cinnamon and ginger. No one imagined at the time that da Gama's two ships would be followed by thousands of Dutch, Portuguese, French and finally British vessels over the course of the next three centuries, but in light of the 3,000 per cent profit realized by that first bold voyage, the subsequent European interest in India is not surprising.

But it was always trade in goods, not venues for permanent settlement or (as in the case of West Africa) demand for unfree labour, which animated Europe's contacts with South Asia. The terrible transatlantic slave trade, binding West Africa first to the sugar islands of the Caribbean, and later to the plantation economies of South America and parts of North America, never affected or absorbed the subjects of the Muslim Mughal emperors. And just as few inhabitants left India for transoceanic destinations before the nineteenth century, so too only a handful of Europeans settled in India during the entire period of British imperial control. Unlike the epidemiological disaster visited upon the Americas by European diseases such as smallpox and measles, a disaster which facilitated the rapid settlement of Europeans and African slaves in the Americas, no comparable demographic calamity ensued in the wake of European contact with India. Thus, there would never be a Western population 'takeover' of India similar to that which occurred in the Americas or Australasia.

The Portuguese came to dominate trade along the west coast of India during the sixteenth century, thanks in large measure to superior military technology – in particular the mounted cannon on their ships. Lightly armed Arab dhows were no match for the on-board firepower available to the Portuguese. In 1502, for example, da Gama reduced a large part of the port of Calicut to rubble in retaliation for Muslim attacks against Portuguese traders who had taken up residence there. But with a total population of less than 1 million subjects in a Europe of escalating religious and national rivalries, the Portuguese crown never attempted to create permanent settler colonies in India.[22] Satisfied with the commercial potential of trade in spices, the crown's viceroy in the East, Alfonso d'Albuquerque, established the west coast island port of Goa as a base of operations, and this tiny stronghold would remain in European hands for the next four centuries. As imports of Indian spices increased from 250,000 pounds per year in 1501 to 2.3 million in 1505, undercutting the overland shipment of spices to

Europe which was controlled by the Ottoman Turks and their Venetian collaborators, the need for territorial control and Portuguese settlement in order to secure trading privileges was clearly absent.

Those few Westerners who did come to reside in South Asia were by and large either the employees of one of the great European trading companies, or imperial administrators charged with overseeing colonial interests. A handful of Portuguese Jesuits had taken up residence in Goa by the late sixteenth century, but their proselytizing efforts were largely ineffectual. At the start of the eighteenth century, most of the military and civilian residents in India were British. The Island Kingdom's efforts to establish permanent links with South Asia had not begun until more than a century after the Portuguese first arrived. In 1608, one year following the establishment of Jamestown colony in Virginia, a ship owned by the newly chartered East India Company dropped anchor off Surat, at the time the Mughal Empire's principal port in the north-west. Captain William Hawkins failed in his efforts to secure a trade treaty with the Emperor Jahingir during this initial visit, but one decade later Sir Thomas Roe was able to win permission for the East India Company to establish a 'factory' at Surat. Roe cautioned his countrymen against seeking to wrest any territory from the powerful Mughals, emphasizing the importance of good diplomatic relations if lucrative trade opportunities were to develop.

In this way the English managed to encroach upon Portuguese trade in the region, and by 1687 a new base of operations was established at the port of Bombay.[23] Together with east coast stations at Madras in the south and later at Calcutta in the north-east, the East India Company enjoyed monopoly trading privileges and reaped enormous profits for its investors. And with the generous royal charter granted by King Charles II during the 1660s, the Company also enjoyed the right to coin its own money and to wield full legal jurisdiction over all English subjects living in company ports. Now a virtual state within a state, Company power was limited solely by the fact that at the time of this legislation only about one hundred English employees lived in the subcontinent.

These numbers would rise over the succeeding 250 years, but only in a minute fashion. The 1861 British census in India recorded a sparse 110,000 civilian and military personnel in residence, and this total expanded to 166,000 by the last decade of the century. Virtually all of these migrants hoped one day to return home to Britain, but in fact the combination of long tours of duty coupled with susceptibility to diseases like malaria meant that many career servants of the Empire never departed Indian shores. Beginning in the late eighteenth century, and especially after the establishment of direct British crown rule in 1858, there were strong 'pull' factors for commissioned officers and civil servants to complete a tour of duty in India.

The majority of these individuals were from middle-class backgrounds, men who aspired to genteel status and who viewed a posting in India as one means of securing improved salary and social standing. Rarely did one find officers or civil servants drawn from the highest aristocracy assigned to India. Those who were in residence – military and civilian alike – normally isolated themselves from the indigenous population and enjoyed an overall standard of living which they could never hope to secure at home. Mixed marriage was discouraged by both Indian and British communities, although at least one governor of the East India Company, Lord William Bentinck, viewed the possibility of racial intermixing with some favour.[24] This was in the 1830s, and not surprisingly Bentinck's counsel was studiously ignored by his contemporaries. Fifty years later, at the height of British imperial power and in an intellectual climate infused with racism, such sentiments were unimaginable. The 1901 census listed only 87,000 people of 'Eurasian' background living in the crown's richest colony, and most of these were illegitimate. At the height of British migration overseas, when an estimated 20 million Britons were boarding steamships for new destinations and new lives, British India would remain distinguished by the paucity of Europeans within her midst. Not for nothing did Gandhi later insist that the most efficacious means to end colonialism lay in the simple refusal of the overwhelming majority to cooperate with their numerically insignificant captors.

The real start of intercontinental Indian migration is closely associated with wider global developments in the treatment of agricultural labour in tropical climates. In particular, the abolition of slavery in the British Empire in 1834 provided the watershed occasion for the renewal of a European-sponsored indenture system, only now the pool of indentures was to be found outside Europe proper. Prior to 1800 almost 30 per cent of the 2–3 million Europeans who had migrated overseas had done so as indentured labourers. Now the bonded labourers would be recruited almost exclusively from colonial venues around the world. The French had earlier enslaved thousands of Indians for colonial plantations on the islands of Mauritius and Reunion, but with the end of black bondage in the British, French, Danish and Dutch colonies, planters sought to replace their unfree labour pool with semi-free indentured workers from recently acquired colonial possessions.[25] Capital accumulation in a colonial setting would thus continue to be predicated on the existence of a cheap supply of labour.

The British-inspired indenture system began in 1830 and was only abolished by act of parliament in 1916; during the almost full century of its existence approximately 1.5 million Indians became part of London's expanding global empire as semi-free workers. At the start of the period, reform-minded politicians were eager to rebut the accusation put forward by critics that landed and commercial interests were seeking through indenture to replace chattel slavery with a new form of exploitation. Evidence of government sensitivity to the charges was clear; in 1839, for example, ministers temporarily halted contract migration to the island colony of Mauritius after reports of brutal treatment of indentures were made public, and mechanisms were quickly established in India in order to prevent the recruitment of unwilling or unsuspecting workers. The British Secretary for the Colonies, Lord John Russell, wrote in February 1840 that 'I should be unwilling to adopt any measure to favour the transfer of labourers from British India . . . which may lead to a dreadful loss of life on the one hand, or on the other, to a new system of slavery.'[26] Given that the vast majority of Indian indentured workers were from lower castes, the reservations of officials both in London and Delhi were legitimate.

Procedures for recruitment and transport were developed very quickly. Indentured migrants would receive return passage (giving them the option of returning home at the end of their contract), together with maintenance, wages, housing, clothing and medical care while living in the new setting. In return the indentured worker would contract to work for five years. Each colonial government was permitted to appoint agents in India for the recruitment of workers, while the Government of India was charged with supervising the agents' activities at the various ports around the country. All potential recruits were interviewed first at the local level, and again after rail transport to Calcutta or Madras, where most potential recruits assembled and waited (sometimes for weeks and even months) for appropriate passage overseas. Almost 15 per cent of those who were interviewed at local level and then transported to Calcutta dropped out of the recruiting process prior to embarkation. Many found more attractive opportunities in the cities; others simply changed their minds. In addition to this screening process, the government in London insisted that both women and men, including married couples, be allowed to migrate, and this provision insured that between 30 and 40 per cent of indentured workers were female. Forty per cent of the women who migrated overseas were married, and one very important result of this recruiting model was the development and expansion of Indian communities in a number of island colonies.

Despite these and other efforts to identify and dismiss corrupt recruiters, however, the official regulatory system was in constant tension with emergent *laissez-faire* arguments about the right of free individuals to enter into labour contract without hindrance from the crown. And with India's overall population reaching almost 300 million by the year 1900, proponents of indenture argued that the impact of migration on the economy of India would be insignificant.

Migrant destinations were truly global during the course of the nineteenth century: East and South Africa, Ceylon, Fiji, Trinidad,

Jamaica, British Guyana and Mauritius – all embraced significant numbers of impoverished Indians, hoping to improve their economic status through indenture. For prospective migrants, 'push' factors were significant. In addition to the pressure of population growth (in India, from 185 to 300 million between 1800 and 1900), British penetration into the Indian economy contributed greatly to the decision to migrate overseas. The commercialization of agriculture, increasing landlord demands, the shift from rent in kind to cash, and the introduction of discriminatory taxes on Indian manufactured goods all provided incentives for poor labourers to seek employment overseas.[27]

Indeed the Indian 'coolie' phenomenon must be situated within the longer context of British colonial policy on the economic front. In 1814, approximately 1.2 million pieces of Indian manufactured cotton products had entered the British home market. Thirty years later only 63,000 pieces made their way into British shops. It was during these years, as British industrial manufacturing was in its adolescence, that Parliament imposed import duties, as high as 80 per cent, on Indian-manufactured textiles. These restrictive tariffs completely undermined the commercial viability of Indian manufacture for export, while the flood of cheap British products devastated the Indian crafts and textile sectors. Britain's industrial cities absorbed raw cotton from India and sold the finished textiles in the subcontinent using economies of scale that could not be replicated in India. And as Western medical advances, public health measures and famine relief projects contributed to a rapid rise in India's population from 255 million in 1872 to 305 million in 1921, a widening crisis of underemployment developed.[28] Where Europe's growing population was able to exercise the options of factory employment at home or migration to the colonies, Indian villagers had no ready alternative to endemic poverty under increasingly unfavourable demographic conditions.

In a vast subcontinent, the principal areas of recruitment were centred in north-east India, where between 1838 and 1917 some half a million Indian subjects of the crown left their places of birth for the long passage to the sugar islands. Many of these intercontinental migrants were internal labour migrants before signing their indenture, and almost all agreed to contracts which normally called for five years of service with provision for housing, rations and return passage if the emigrant decided to go back to India at the end of the agreed term. Only about one-quarter of those who survived the experience, however, elected to return to India. While most individuals initially hoped to save their wages and return home at the end of their contract, not infrequently these plans were abandoned after the migrant was established in his or her new home.

Once situated in their overseas environment, labourers were expected to work six days per week, nine hours each day, and rates of pay varied between islands and plantations. Not surprisingly, conditions were very harsh on the plantations, with Indian migrants living in dilapidated former slave quarters and discipline enforced through the use of whips and stocks.[29] On the island of Mauritius, between 1834 and 1910 over half a million indentured migrants arrived to work on British-controlled sugar plantations. By 1871 the Indian population on the island stood at 216,000 or 70 per cent of the total population. Mauritian planters dominated the economy, which by 1900 was dedicated almost exclusively to sugar production for export. Planters paid one-quarter of the cost of transport for the ten-week journey.

Conditions were very harsh on the island, with labourers living in barracks and managers (*sirdars*) wielding arbitrary authority over the lives of the workers. Mortality rates were high, especially for children born into such conditions, and the lot of women workers was particularly cruel. By 1910, one-third of those who had accepted indenture in Mauritius had returned home to India after the completion of their term.[30]

In each of the colonies, additional government agents were hired to oversee labour conditions, but often those responsible for oversight looked upon indenture as a humane means whereby impoverished Indians might improve their living conditions.[31] From mid-century to the 1880s, West Indian sugar producers enjoyed a period of signal prosperity, and while living and working conditions for indentured workers did not improve, colonial authorities justified the status quo using the argument that plantation life in the Caribbean was preferable to village conditions throughout most of India. And despite the hardships and abuses, many of those who remained in the colonial setting achieved some economic advancement. For the majority who remained after the completion of their indenture term, for example, crown lands were offered in place of the promised return passage to India. Eventually some of these men became independent farmers and some rose to the level of substantial sugar producers themselves.[32] In most colonial venues, the average income of Indian migrants actually exceeded that of the numerically dominant population. This was true in Kenya, Uganda and Tanzania, as well as in Fiji and Malaysia, and the same may be said more recently for Indians in Great Britain and the United States.[33]

In addition to plantation islands around the globe, British colonies in eastern and Southern Africa were also important destinations for Indian indentured labourers during the mid- to late nineteenth century, despite the availability of a more than adequate native labour pool in these African colonies. Trade between East Africa and India had been conducted for centuries before the advent of British colonial rule; Indian ocean-going ships known as *khotia* were, like the more familiar Arab dhow, extremely durable and versatile. Indian traders were especially visible on the island of Zanzibar, where the Indian rupee stood as the principal currency.[34]

But European penetration into Africa changed the nature of the relationship between Indians and Africans in a substantial manner. After establishing bases of power, often brutally, over the peoples of East Africa, Europeans employed Indians in a number of capacities. When the Portuguese wrested Mombasa from the Arabs and built the imposing Fort Jesus during the sixteenth century, for example, they employed Indian masons to complete the stone work.[35] Key to the more lasting penetration of Indian migrants into East Africa was the late nineteenth-century British plan to build a railway from the coast (the Kenyan port of Mombasa) to Lake Victoria in present-day Uganda. About 39,000 Indians, many from the West Indian state of Gujarat, worked on the construction of the railroad, and while most who survived the experience chose to return home at the end of their service, some stayed on as employees of the railway or as small business people.[36] They were joined by other, more affluent Indians who paid their own passage to East Africa in order to take advantage of the trading and business opportunities opened up by the construction of rail lines. Known as 'passenger Indians', many of these people remained in East Africa after construction was finished, assuming a wide range of business roles, particularly at the retail level, in their adopted homes.[37] In German-controlled Tanzania, and in the British colonies of Uganda and Kenya, Indian businessmen were important figures in almost every town.

Unfortunately, but perhaps not unexpectedly, Indian economic success deeply disturbed white settlers who saw no need to extend equal rights to those from other parts of the Empire. When Natal was awarded self-government by the British in 1893, the 50,000 white settlers immediately set out to end Indian immigration and to discriminate against those 50,000 Indian residents who had built livelihoods for themselves among half a million Africans. Trading licences were restricted, and special taxes were imposed on Indians who were residents in the colony. While the British government protested, little was done to defend the Indian colonists; 'It is selfish', lamented Sir John Woodburn, a British official in India, 'it isn't magnificent and it isn't magnanimous but it is human nature.'[38]

The same abandonment of the hope that inhabitants of the Empire would share uniform rights and privileges was played out when the Boers were awarded power in South Africa in 1910. Here over 100,000 Indian labourers, again mostly indentured, had taken up residence by 1900. Once again the colonial administration made the lives of those Indians who stayed on after the completion of their contract very difficult. Excluded from all but the lowest levels of civil administration, facing bothersome restrictions on the purchase of land, discriminatory legislation designed to exclude them from certain trades, and the refusal to grant naturalization status to migrants, the Indian community was in a precarious situation.

Despite growing discrimination and immigration regimes imposed by white colonial settlers, the economic power of the South Asian community in Africa continued to grow during the first half of the twentieth century, with enterprising Indians building up their economic influence out of all proportion to their actual numbers. In Kenya, for example, Indians represented less than 2 per cent of the overall population in 1962 (roughly 177,000 out of a population of almost 8 million), but their numbers were concentrated in the capital of Nairobi, where they made up almost one-third of the city's population and controlled main street businesses.[39] Sadly, with the coming of African independence in the 1960s, the popular resentment once focused on Indians by European colonial settlers was now turned against successful South Asians by black nationalist leaders; newly independent governments sought first to marginalize and subsequently to remove the Indian businessman from his property.

Intermarriage between South Asians and Africans had never been anything other than exceptional, and during the first half of the twentieth century relations between the two peoples remained formal and somewhat distant. The brutal actions of dictators like Uganda's Idi Amin in the early 1970s, following the confiscation of thousands of Indian shops by the Kenyan government in the 1960s, were built upon decades of black African resentment of the economic influence of South Asians. Some 50,000 Asians (half the total residents) were summarily expelled by the xenophobic Amin in August 1972, while in neighbouring Kenya an Indian population of over 175,000 in 1962 had dwindled to 25,000 by 1972. The economies of both countries, but particularly Uganda's, suffered serious reversals in the wake of the many discriminatory actions against Indian residents, a sad testimony to the importance of the Indian contribution to East African economic development.[40]

Half a world away and at roughly the same time, the Burmese government of General Ne Win was busy pursuing an equally callous policy of removal. Indian migrants had played a very significant role in the Burmese economy during the century of British rule, and by 1931 there were just over 1 million living in the country, many in key occupations like rail transport and banking. But half a million were forced to flee the country after the Japanese invaded in 1941, and in the postwar period an Emergency Immigration Act placed sharp restrictions on returnees. Still, there were almost 800,000 Indians resident by 1950. In 1962, General Ne Win seized power and inaugurated a socialist reform programme which included the nationalization of most sectors of the economy. Indian residents were ordered out of the country, and by 1964 the Government in Delhi classified more than 300,000 recent arrivals as refugees.[41] Confiscation of personal property was the final humiliation imposed on these refugees as they left Burma. Like their Ugandan counterparts, India's migrants had been repudiated by their xenophobic hosts, labelled as exploiters and colonialists, irrespective of their many contributions to adopted homelands. Even in Fiji and Guyana, where they constituted a majority of the population, Indians have been denied political power.

In the post-Second World War period, two groups of Indians have migrated overseas. Young (mostly male) students have left for education and training, while Indians of higher caste and significant educational background began to leave their homeland for greater personal opportunities. Great Britain, Canada and the United States have been the chosen destinations for over 3 million Indian students and professionals. The oil-rich Gulf States have also absorbed almost one and a half million migrants from the subcontinent – almost the same size as the total Indian presence in Europe. Businessmen, physicians, technicians, managers, diamond traders, money-lenders, and more recently engineers and computer specialists, have migrated to more industrially advanced nations where their services are highly rewarded. In 1981 more than 250,000 Indians counted themselves among the professional classes around the world, and the number has doubtless increased over the past two decades. In Britain, for example, where open immigration was allowed from Commonwealth countries until restrictions were imposed after 1962, 11 per cent of Indian men were in professional jobs by 1989, compared with 7 per cent for whites.[42] The impact of this 'brain drain' on India's economy, especially in light of the continuing widespread poverty at home, is an issue that is intensely debated today.

LEAVING THE MIDDLE KINGDOM

The earliest migration from China can be associated with a great age of maritime trade inaugurated under the southern Song dynasty in the early twelfth century. Contacts with South-East Asia and with islands in the South China Sea afforded a very small number of native Chinese the opportunity to experience different lands and cultures, and to work as sojourners in a foreign culture. While never committed to the building of a maritime empire, the Song imperial government outfitted a strong navy, fostered harbour development projects, and encouraged a variety of overseas commercial links. Chinese naval and merchant vessels were much larger in size and capacity than their contemporary European counterparts, and under the Mongols (1279–1368) armed flotillas were sent out to challenge trade rivals like the Japanese and the Javanese. During the early decades of the Ming dynasty, and especially between 1405 and 1433, enormous fleets were dispatched under the leadership of the Muslim naval commander Zheng He to explore new lands boardering the Indian Ocean, the Persian Gulf, and along the east coast of Africa.

Somewhat surprisingly, this dramatic outward thrust, involving hundreds of enormous vessels and thousands of seamen, came to an abrupt end in the 1430s. As the capital of the Empire was shifted north from Nanjing to Beijing, and as military resources were redirected to land-based armies designed to rebuff the still-threatening Mongol presence in the north, Chinese officials turned inward and abandoned interest in the barbarian outside world. Overseas trading enterprises were banned by the government, and those Chinese who dared venture beyond the seas were declared outlaws.[43] Within a century of this retrenchment and neglect of naval defences, Portuguese explorers would begin to solicit commercial contacts with the Middle Kingdom, even establishing a trading outpost on the Pearl River Delta south of Canton (later Macao).

This incursion, together with the escalation of Japanese piracy along the coast, led the imperial government to rethink its isolationist posture. Beginning in 1567 Chinese merchants were again allowed by the government to engage in limited overseas trade. Large quantities of silver, extracted from mines in Central and South America, made their way round the globe and into Chinese hands as Europe's appetite for finished products and luxury goods seemed insatiable. By the 1570s the Spanish conquerers of Mexico had founded a colony at Manila in the Philippines, and soon a Chinese merchant community established itself in an effort to promote greater commercial exchange with the mainland. Market forces were beginning to play an increasingly significant role in China's economy. By the end of the century more than twenty Chinese junks per year were landing in the Philippine islands, their holds crammed with silks and cotton fabrics, gunpowder and luxury articles crafted in brass, copper and wood.[44] The south-east coast of China became the origination point for most of this robust overseas trade with Europe, and it was from here that the first emigrants from the Chinese mainland began their exodus.

When the Ming dynasty was overthrown by the upstart Manchu invaders in 1644, a long era of imperial vacillation commenced over international trade and the ancilliary migration which it facilitated. Thousands of Ming loyalists from the south-east fled to the Philippines and Taiwan in the wake of Manchu advances. Once it consolidated power throughout the country, the new dynasty outlawed foreign travel, largely out of fear that prospective migrants were animated by a desire to establish bases of opposition to the regime from overseas colonies. In 1717 the Qing Emperor's government specifically prohibited the emigration of Chinese overseas and requested the assistance of foreign governments in returning emigrés to China for punishment. And the consequences were severe. A regulation issued in 1799 announced that 'All officers of government, soldiers, and private citizens, who clandestinely proceed to sea to trade, or who remove to foreign islands for the purpose of inhabiting and cultivating the same, shall be punished according to the law against communicating with rebels and enemies, and consequently suffer death by being beheaded.'[45] Not until 1893 was this draconian ban on emigration officially lifted.

Prior to 1500, then, Asian out-migration in a global context was fairly insignificant, limited to seafarers and adventurous merchants, and to those who were willing to ignore the imperial prohibition. During the period 1500–1800 the pace of illegal migration quickened, but the vast majority of men who relocated overseas prior to the nineteenth century settled in nearby South-East Asia and in colonies controlled by the Dutch, British, French and Spanish. Here Chinese merchants established a number of trading contacts with their Western counterparts, while poorer labourers accepted positions in agriculture and the service trades. Carpenters, cobblers, masons, weavers and unskilled labourers all played a numerically small but economically significant role in the nascent European colonies of South-East Asia. A handful of Chinese even made their way to Spain's American empire prior to 1800 via the Manila connection, working mostly in the domestic urban sector as housekeepers and servants. In 1635 a group of Spanish barbers submitted a petition to the viceroy in Mexico City demanding the removal of Chinese barbers from the city's centre. The complaint centred on the long hours worked by the Chinese, evidently in violation of accustomed business practices.[46]

The entrenched imperial opposition to overseas migration can be explained in some measure by reference to traditional Mandarin attitudes toward merchants and artisans. In the hierarchy of orders in traditional China, the Confucian scholar-bureaucrat looked askance at the dealings of the trader and producer. Never truly supported by the government, the business-oriented Chinese were regularly marginalized and always suspect. And this prejudice continued even in the face of stunning demographic changes which threatened to erode the government's ability to maintain economic self-sufficiency. The Qing government faced an enormous problem of overpopulation, and lacked the technology and organization capable of increasing agricultural yield. In 1600 China's population of over 100 million already exceeded that of Europe as a whole, and the figure exploded to an amazing 430 million by the middle of the nineteenth century. While new lands had been opened up to peasant farmers in the intervening period, such expansion could not keep pace with the number of people dependent on the soil for their survival. Family plots shrunk generation after generation, and younger children found little prospect of securing a living in the traditional village setting.

Invariably, displaced peasants headed for the cities and, despite continuing official restrictions, for overseas destinations. The population of Shanghai, for instance, grew from 107,000 in 1880 to 1,250,000 in 1911, one year before the collapse of the empire.[47] Nearly a million and a half Chinese, mostly male, migrated to Thailand from 1882 to 1917, while another million took up work as miners and rubber workers in Malaysia. When Taiwan was ceded to Japan in 1895, some 300,000 Chinese migrants were obliged to return to mainland China. In total, by 1900 some 7 million Chinese were living outside the mainland. As one recent scholar has observed, 'At the end of the day, one cannot long escape the simple logic of demography: the press of numbers, no less than merchant venturing, made migrants of the many Chinese who subsisted on farming.'[48]

In addition to internal demographic strains, beginning in the nineteenth century, a new and fundamentally different stage in Chinese migration began as the major European powers sought out larger labour resources in an effort to replace recently liberated African slaves and make their respective empires pay. Following an age-old pattern, poor countries would provide the surplus labour needed by their wealthy superiors. Although the Qing continued to view their empire as the only state that really mattered in the global community at the start of the nineteenth century, in reality a host of internal weaknesses placed the Middle Kingdom at a serious disadvantage as Western powers demanded greater access to Chinese markets.[49] Two wars against Britain (1840–2, 1856–60) over trade practices ended in defeat for the Celestial Empire, while a serious internal rebellion from 1850–64 almost toppled the regime. As many as 20 million Chinese died during the horrific Taiping civil conflict (ironically, the rebels were led by a convert to fundamentalist Christianity), while millions more were displaced from their homes during the fighting.[50] Conditions within the country continued to deteriorate after the Taipings were dispatched. British empire-building in South Asia had already assumed a direct territorial form by the mid-nineteenth century, and now China emerged as a key target of market-oriented imperialists who successfully recruited the British government into the role of military enforcer.

Slowly but inexorably, the Manchu rulers were losing their grip on the centuries-old Mandate of Heaven; no longer was the ruling household capable of maintaining civil, economic and social equilibrium. With the British defeat of the Chinese in the second Opium War of 1856–60, the imperial government was obliged to sign a convention whereby the emperor permitted his subjects to work in any of the British colonies, or in other foreign parts. These migrants would embark from the so-called 'treaty ports' along the south-east coast. France, Spain and the United States also quickly won the same concessions from the Qing. Against the backdrop of the end of slavery in the Western world, together with the annexation of lands in South-East Asia and the need for labour in a rapidly industrializing international economy, China, with its unrivalled population and troubled imperial polity, became a key source in the global resettlement of labourers. Estimates of contract labourers, 'coolies' who left the mainland for points overseas during the nineteenth century, range from a low of 3 million to a high of 6 or 7 million.[51] As in so many cases around the globe, significant Chinese migration was led by the the destitute, the illiterate and the unskilled. And their debt would increase at the moment they booked passage as hired labour.

Between 1850 and 1875, one and a quarter million Chinese were recruited into overseas contract labour by foreign agents and shipping companies. One-fifth of these were destined for the mines of Cuba and Malaya, and the plantations of Latin America. During the final quarter of the nineteenth century, an additional million 'coolies' were recruited and shipped to locations in South-East Asia and South Africa.[52] Half a million Chinese were living and working near Singapore by the early 1870s, while an equal number were settled in the Dutch East Indies. Suffering a mortality rate of between 50 and 60 per cent on transoceanic voyages, thanks largely to unspeakable conditions on board, these unfortunate victims of callous labour brokers became the first native Chinese to contribute to the emerging Western-dominated world economy. One hundred thousand lived in Peru by 1875, working on railway construction and cotton plantations. Thousands more worked on sugar plantations in Cuba, experiencing conditions virtually indistinguishable from those of the slaves whom they replaced.[53]

The imperial Qing government was virtually powerless to protect its subjects from the exploitation visited upon them by foreign recruiters and their agents. An investigating commission was sent to Cuba and Peru during 1873–4 and the findings demonstrated the myriad abuses faced by coolies. Press-gang kidnappings, terrible conditions aboard ship, unremitting labour in the host countries – all pointed to the inability of the imperial authorities to protect their own nationals. Although the government was able to establish consulates in the areas of highest Chinese settlement by the close of the century, and while this was helpful in terms of maintaining links with successful Chinese overseas, effective mechanisms for ensuring the health and well-being of migrants were entirely absent.

The overwhelming majority of ethnic Han Chinese who emigrated overseas before the First World War were natives of two provinces along the south-east coast, Guangdong and Fujian. Few Mandarin-speaking inhabitants of the north, and virtually no residents of western provinces, relocated overseas. Proximity to major sea routes is one explanation for the focused exodus. Japan's southern islands, the Philippines and Taiwan are all near Guandong and Fujian. The latter province is about the size of England, mostly mountainous, and after 1500 it offered inhabitants less arable land than any other province in China. As it was visited by multiple famines in the seventeenth and eighteenth centuries, it is no surprise that a high proportion of the country's migrants would hail from this part of the south-east. And the numbers of emigrants continued to rise, despite the restrictive immigration policies of Western nations, until the 1930s. The collapse of the dynastic system in 1912 ushered in nearly three decades of warlordism and its attendant civil unrest. Not surprisingly, many Chinese sought refuge overseas. At the start of the Second World War, almost 9 million Chinese, the bulk of whom hailed from Guandong and Fujian, were living outside the borders of China, the majority in South-East Asia.[54]

In terms of total population, however, the demographic impact of overseas emigration on China itself has remained minimal. What was important throughout the course of the twentieth century was the value of remittances sent home by successful Chinese abroad. In addition to assisting individual families, remittances helped to encourage the growth of commercial enterprises in places like Canton and Singapore. Perhaps more than any other migrant community, the Chinese tended to view their emigration as but a temporary affair. Of the 1.5 million who resettled in Thailand between 1882 and 1917, for example, almost two-thirds eventually returned home. 'For commitment to one's native place, one's ancestral home, few people could beat the Chinese.'[55] Not unlike the Irish, the Chinese were profoundly reluctant to leave their ancestral home, irrespective of how difficult life might be in the land of their birth. Many left soon after marriage, hoping to save their overseas earnings in order to return home someday, buy land and improve their family's standing.

But very much unlike the Irish, overseas Chinese did not pursue political careers or engage in sustained political activity as a national group. Migrants to South-East Asia and to the Americas tended to be better informed about Western economic development, and the prejudices which they encountered overseas helped to fuel their strong sense of nationalism, their desire to return home and assist in the process of Chinese modernization. Successful migrants returned to their native soil with a strong commitment to economic development, to a free press and to Western-style education, but all in the service of national revival. Many of Sun Yat-sen's most important financial supporters in the early twentieth century, for example, were successful overseas Chinese. Since this time the overseas Chinese have been viewed as distinct assets to the state, a remarkable reversal of centuries-old prejudice against those who had abandoned the homeland.[56]

By the close of the twentieth century, the descendants of the first humble unskilled workers who had migrated overseas had, in not a few cases, emerged as the economic elites in their host countries. The Chinese experience in America is a case in point. Today, the largest Chinese community outside mainland China is located in the United States of America. It is, however a very novel formation. As recently as the middle of the 1840s, there were no more than a handful of Chinese in the continental United States. The first significant wave of settlement took place in the wake of the 1848–9 gold rush. The overwhelming majority were unskilled males, products of an ancient culture where it was not uncommon for single men from rural areas to resettle on a temporary basis while saving towards the purchase of land.

Although San Francisco was referred to as *Jinshan* or 'mountain of gold', early hopes of instant riches were quickly disappointed. Of the more than 300,000 Chinese who entered the United States between 1850 and 1882, only one-third remained on a permanent basis. Most who settled permanently eventually found themselves employed as laundrymen and casual labourers, while, later in the 1860s, thousands would find work in transcontinental railway construction. Some of those who had wives and families back in China were destined never to return, their dreams of prosperity dashed in the stark climate of post-gold rush California. Remittances were made to support families, and there was always the prospect that men might at least retire back in China, but as they fanned out across the continent in search of work, the prospects for repatriation dimmed. Just as the descendants of Europeans moved west during the nineteenth century, so the Chinese labourer moved east. By the last quarter of the century there were Chinese agricultural workers as far south as Mississippi and Alabama, and nascent working-class communities in north-eastern urban centres like Boston and New York.[57]

The hostility faced by earlier migrants was a phenomenon not limited to the United States. Wherever they had settled – South-East Asia, Latin America, the United States – the Chinese had been exposed to deep resentment and disdain. As in the case of the Jews of eastern Europe and the Indians of Fiji and East Africa, the spectacle of impoverished migrants rising in a few generations to economic affluence, mainly in middlemen careers related to small business, kindled the resentment of host populations around the globe. In the United States, hostility toward the Chinese was born of many variables: envy; fear that dedicated Chinese workers would undercut the bargaining power of organized labour unions; a perception of the Chinese as mere sojourners who had no intention of staying in their American host setting; and disdain for unfamiliar language and social customs.

The economic depression of the 1870s exacerbated these feelings, magnifying anti-Chinese sentiment at the national political level as early as the 1880s. In 1882 legislation was passed which suspended the immigration of Chinese skilled and unskilled labour for a period of ten years, while simultaneously prohibiting those Chinese who were already resident from securing citizenship. President Grover Cleveland declared in 1888 that the Chinese in America were 'ignorant of our constitution and laws, impossible of assimilation with our people, and dangerous to our peace and welfare'. Cleveland's Republican Party opponent in that year, Benjamin Harrison, expressed similar racist sentiments. Increasingly after this date, harassment, violence and the threat of deportation became the constant worry of Chinese workers from Hawaii to New York. All of this deplorable conduct toward migrant communities occurred even as the presence of American Christian missionaries in China increased. By the 1920s over 11,000 Catholic and Protestant workers were in the country, struggling to bring the Christian message from a nation which had displayed little understanding of or sympathy for Chinese culture abroad.[58]

During the late 1930s, as Japanese aggression against China intensified, and especially after the United States allied itself with China during the Second World War, anti-Chinese sentiment began to abate. Many Chinese served in the United States' armed forces and merchant marine during the conflict, and the general labour shortage facilitated the entry of more Chinese into jobs which had previously been closed to them. In 1943 the Chinese Exclusion Act of 1882 was repealed in an effort to counter Nazi propaganda, and the Chinese in America regained the right of naturalization. The modest number (8,000 from 1945–50) of new arrivals to the US after that date contained a majority of women; many of them were reunited with their husbands after many years of separation.

Hostility between the Chinese Communist Government and the United States after 1949 guaranteed that few Chinese would spend time in America. The old imperial pattern of introversion and proscription was embraced again by the government of Mao Zedong during the Great Leap Forward (1958–9) and again during the Cultural Revolution of 1966–76. Legal emigration from China was halted, although thousands continued to seek freedom from the Marxist regime by fleeing overseas. After the death of Mao in 1976 and the rise to power of Deng Xiaoping, limited market reforms, including the lifting of restrictions on travel, spurred a new round of migration. And in 1992, in the wake of the Tiananmen massacre, the United States Congress passed legislation to allow students to apply for permanent resident status. Over 50,000 took advantage of the opportunity.[59]

After the Second World War the isolation of the Chinese-American urban population into Chinatowns slowly ended, as better-educated and highly skilled Chinese joined their white counterparts in the move to suburban neighbourhoods. Small businesses, especially groceries and restaurants, proliferated, and the skilled professions were at last opened to all. The Immigration Act of 1965 ended decades of discrimination against Chinese migrants. Applicants from all nations were now assured equal treatment, with each nation assigned an annual quota of 20,000.

In recent decades Chinese overseas migration has been dominated by skilled labourers, entrepreneurs and students who bring with them to their host countries (and almost always to a large urban setting) a great deal of intellectual and financial capital. Unlike so many of those who preceded them in the nineteenth and early twentieth centuries, these were migrants by choice who sought greater opportunities in which to employ their professional skills. Students from China (including here Taiwan and Hong Kong) composed almost a quarter of the total of foreign students at universities in the United States during the 1990s.

By the end of the century the median income of native-born Chinese Americans exceeded that of their non-Asian counterparts by almost 60 per cent.[60] And these post-Second World War migrants hailed from a wide variety of locales in China. For the first century of Chinese migration, most who settled in America were from the Pearl River Delta, and especially the region around Canton. Now the profile was much more diverse, and while Chinese made up only 0.7 per cent of the entire US population in the mid-1990s, they were by far the largest Asian group resident in America.

JAPANESE INDENTURE

Comparatively speaking, Japanese migration overseas has been a very modest affair over the course of the last five centuries. Many of us are familiar with the fact that during the rule of the Tokugawa shogunate (1638–1868), foreigners, with the one exception of Dutch traders, were expelled from the country. A long season of isolationism took hold as the executive authority of the monarch was subordinated to the will of the leading military family. Less familiar is the correlative policy of the government to forbid emigration from Japan. Subjects who left the country, or those who dared to return after having done so, did so on pain of death. Prior to this time, small communities of Japanese could be found in the Spanish-controlled Philippines, South-East Asia, and in Korea, but the Tokugawa ban on resettlement guaranteed that no Japanese would become part of Europe's quest for labour resources during the West's age of global expansion. The handful of Japanese sailors who served as crew members on Spanish galleons after first contact was established in Manila in 1592 never became the leading wedge of a process which might have a fundamental impact on the domestic scene or in host countries.[61]

All of this changed with the Meiji Restoration in 1868. The reform government was eager to adopt Western models of political and economic advancement, and it was within this late nineteenth-

century context of admiration for and envy of the West that the first
migrants headed out across the Pacific for the hoped-for
opportunities of advanced industrial civilization. Over 3,000 foreign
advisors, mostly engineers and other technology-related specialists,
assisted the Japanese government in its efforts to modernize the
economy. And some 11,000 Japanese students were sent overseas for
specialized training at European and American universities. Few
remained abroad; keen nationalists, these students returned home
with technical skills and a sense of confidence that Japan could
catch up with its mentors in very rapid fashion.[62]

Emigration from Japan, often under the aegis of indenture, was
first permitted by the new modernizing monarchy in 1885, although
the total number of migrants remained small when contrasted with
the European experience. The Americas had already been occupied
by Europeans by the time that Japanese migration began, and labour
opportunities there were therefore limited. In that first year a meagre
945 persons headed out across the Pacific for Hawaii. But the pace
accelerated thereafter. Roughly 1 million Japanese left their homes
on a permanent basis for opportunities around the Pacific during the
45-year period 1885–1930. More than half of these had settled in
the United States by the start of the twentieth century, and when
racist immigration restrictions were established in that country,
migration patterns shifted toward the west coast of South America,
especially Peru, and to Brazil.

Before the outbreak of the Second World War, some 235,000
Japanese were living in Latin America, with the vast majority of the
total (almost 190,000) resident in Brazil. Migration from Japan to
European offshoot countries in the Americas and Australia began to
decrease once other host nations adopted the American model of
exclusionary immigration policies based on migrants' origins. This
reversal was compounded by the the growth of a Japanese Empire in
Asia beginning in the 1920s, an Empire that Japan's military leaders
would come to describe as a 'co-prosperity sphere' but which in fact
was nothing less than a traditional imperial institution following the
time-honoured Western precedent. During the 1930s the bulk of
Japanese migrants, more than one million, were relocating to

occupied lands in Korea, Manchuria and Formosa. In 1940 some 1.7 million Japanese were living and working abroad, and all but 500,000 were situated in conquered Asian territories.[63]

The first cohort of Japanese migrants, those who settled in European offshoot countries in the Americas, were almost exclusively agricultural labourers, while the subsequent migrants to points across Japan's Asian Empire were largely bureaucrats, merchants, military personnel and urban workers. The latter groups were obliged to return home to Japan after the end of the Second World War, a humiliating reverse exodus of over 6 million subjects of the emperor.[64] For the earlier generation of humble emigrants who sought not imperial glory but modest economic advancement, on the other hand, their removal from Japan was permanent, and their offspring would move rapidly into positions of economic and political influence in their nations of birth. The relative success of the Japanese in most areas they settled is exceptional in light of the harsh discrimination they faced during the early years of the twentieth century, and the economic setbacks they endured in so many countries during the course of the Second World War.

These first migrants were destined for a land that, while gradually coming under the shadow of the United States, was still, until 1898 an independent monarchy: the Kingdom of Hawaii. Beginning in 1868, and continuing with some regularity until the 1920s, migrants were recruited by private agencies representing plantation interests on the Hawaiian islands. A system of indenture was established and very harsh discipline was maintained on the sugar plantations. Terms of indenture involved three years of labour, while transport costs were borne by the employers. Most of the 28,000 Japanese who entered Hawaii between 1868 and 1884 were young males, and most of these landed as sojourners, hoping one day to return to Japan once they had accumulated some savings. The United States government ended all indentured labour contracts in 1900, but most settlers continued to work in agriculture-related enterprises. Native-born Japanese Americans tended to experience better race relations on the islands in comparison to their reception on the US mainland. Still, language barriers and the tendency of the migrants to avoid integration with dominant populations posed a range of problems for the first generation of settlers. Sons and daughters would be more successful in their efforts to advance both economically and socially.[65]

A small number of Japanese worked as indentured servants in Mexican coal mines and on railway construction projects during the first decade of the twentieth century, but the preference for agricultural work led more voyagers to Peru and especially to Brazil. Roughly 33,000 Japanese, many of them arriving as indentured labourers, settled in Peru between 1898 and 1940. More than 100,000 Chinese had already arrived as agricultural labourers beginning in mid-century, and the popular disdain which was exhibited against these first Asians was later visited upon the newcomers. But at the outset of the process, Latin American leaders thought that the Japanese would bring with them some of the energy which was transforming the economy of Japan at the end of the nineteenth century.[66] As in the case of Hawaii, conditions on the Peruvian sugar plantations were very harsh indeed, and the central government took few steps to insure the well-being of the immigrants. Second- and third-generation Japanese Peruvians were able to overcome much discrimination to establish themselves in urban centres as owners of small commercial firms, but the fact that the government, which was not at war with Japan until 1945, sent almost 2,000 Japanese to internship camps in the United States during the Second World War, indicates the level of majority hostility toward the migrants.[67]

Emigration to Brazil began in 1908, with most Japanese taking up positions in the coffee plantations of Sao Paulo. Transportation subsidies were offered by the Sao Paulo government until 1925, when the home government took over this responsibility. Despite much discrimination, migrants to Brazil were able to become independent proprietors of land fairly quickly after completion of their indenture. Throughout the most fertile regions of the country, the income of Japanese settlers rapidly rose to the average for the country.

In the aftermath of the First World War, the government of Japan made a concerted effort to coordinate and centralize the whole process of migration. The impetus for this can be traced to concern over population pressures. The volume of food imports was increasing after 1920, while the economy was no longer expanding. A number of colonization and transport companies were merged into a single Overseas Development Company, and local recruiting efforts were placed under close official control. With high postwar unemployment, the state encouraged overseas settlement. Beginning in 1923 emigrant transport was subsidized up to 60 per cent, and after 1930 all of the costs related to transport were assumed by the state.

Many of Japan's more aggressive colonial theorists of the early twentieth century viewed the establishment of empire as an essential outlet for emigration, a place where the nation's excess population might create new and thriving agricultural settlements and produce surpluses which would be utilized in support of the homeland. These hopes were never realized, of course, especially since so many of the migrants were more interested in quick profit from land speculation or preferment in colonial government than they were in agricultural production. Not surprisingly, their presence was deeply resented by Koreans and Taiwanese who watched as their lands were expropriated and their autonomy curtailed. Government schemes to encourage agricultural labourers to resettle outside Japan were in the main a failure, despite inducements involving everything from free passage to low-cost start-up loans.[68] Thus, the goal of demographic redistribution was never achieved, and the Japanese remained a tiny, and, like the British in India, physically isolated minority in each of their colonies. For those who did travel to Manchuria, Korea, or Taiwan, opportunities to rise to positions of political power were few; military occupation and its priorities always pre-empted the emergence of a civilian colonial elite.[69]

Japan is today one of the world's great industrial and technological powers, and it has reached its pre-eminent economic position very rapidly. From defeat and widespread devastation in 1945 to financial and manufacturing superpower fifty years later, the island nation is unique in having achieved its global pre-eminence without reliance upon the immigration of new peoples. Retaining a very high degree of cultural homogeneity, modern Japan remains one of the few democratic and developed nations where in-migration and diversity are not part of the social landscape. Comparisons with another island, and one-time imperial nation, Britain, highlight the unique features of Japanese culture. Just as many Britons see themselves as distinct from their continental neighbours, so too many Japanese would argue that their civilization is distinctive in relation to its Asian counterparts. Like the British, the majority of Japan's population of around 126 million lives in large urban centres. But whereas Britain has become an increasingly heterogeneous state since the end of the Second World War, Japan retains its largely exclusivist cultural identity. While hesitant to reflect critically upon its bellicose imperial past, democratically elected Japanese leaders do not feel obliged to enter the lists of receiving nations within the developed world, and widespread political support for *sakokku* (keeping the country closed) reflects continued popular endorsement of the notion that Japan is somehow unique among the nations of the world, and that this uniqueness is anchored in ethnic and cultural homogeneity. In the words of one recent observer: 'The notion of Japanese society as a big kinship group is a widely accepted myth and social cohesion and order are seen as consequences of it.'[70] Given the continuing centrality of this myth in popular consciousness, the anomaly which is Japanese immigration policy will not be altered in the near future.

This is not to say that migrants have not played a significant role in the nation's recent history, but the role has more often than not been a tragic one. During the years when Japan occupied Korea (1910–45), a large number of low-wage Korean peasants arrived in Japan to engage in unskilled activities such as coal mining and labour-intensive manufacturing. In the decade after 1921 alone, 400,000 Koreans migrated to Japan, and by the beginning of 1940 there were over one million, mostly concentrated in urban centres. Stereotyped in the 1930s as being indolent and volatile, the Korean migrant community 'was perceived as being largely composed of ignorant, filthy and morally deficient paupers who were prone to criminal behaviour'.[71] Still, during the course of the Second World War, the Japanese imperial government encouraged both forced and voluntary migration of Koreans into war-related industries. More than one-third of the victims of the Hiroshima bombing, some 30,000 persons, were Koreans working in Japan. During the last decade of the twentieth century, there were just under 700,000 resident aliens from Korea in Japan, and just under 140,000 from China. While the majority of the Koreans are second, third and fourth generation residents who speak Japanese as their first language, only about 200,000 have become Japanese nationals. The majority are not afforded political rights and are denied access to employment opportunities in the public sector.[72] These two groups represent exceptions to an otherwise restrictive policy.

Instead of meeting labour shortages with foreign workers, Japanese industry began to concentrate on manufacturing overseas. Still, shortages of unskilled workers during the 1980s led to an influx of workers on short-term contracts. Reaching 1.6 million, or 1.1 per cent of the population, the largest contingents arrived in Japan from nearby Korea. Combined with an estimated quarter of a million undocumented 'overstayers' who remained in the country after the expiration of their visa permits, these migrants ensured that Japan gradually joined the global trend towards labour migration. But in 1990 the government passed additional immigration control laws, and in the aftermath some 25,000 illegal workers were expelled. The majority of the approximately 700,000 foreign residents today represent professional and skilled labour, students, researchers and intra-company transferees. Illegal immigrants, numbering around 200,000, continue to work in construction trades, factories and restaurants. Supporters of the ethnic exclusivism thesis have successfully recruited a number of Latin Americans of Japanese descent to work in Japanese plants. In 1996, for example, there were over 200,000 Brazilians in the country, with most employed in the automobile industry.[73]

LABOUR AND MIGRATION

The persistence of contractual labour schemes as a central component of capitalist, market-oriented agriculture and industry around the world speaks to the exceptional nature of free international migration over the past 500 years. With the decline of slavery in lands controlled by Western colonists, the global sweep of recruitment for indentured service drew a variety of different cultures into the orbit of Western economic enterprise. Not until the beginning of the twentieth century did free migrants come to dominate the movement of peoples across international boundaries.

In particular, the incorporation of South and East Asians into the orbit of Western-controlled settler states inaugurated a period of worldwide movement which continues to this day. Never again would international migration be the prerogative of white Europeans seeking economic advancement and political freedoms; rather the movement of people across oceans and continents now became an integral part of making civilizations less distinctive, less isolated from dominant political and military powers. Even as Western states began to impose exclusionary, and unprecedented, immigration regimes in the early twentieth century, the process of bringing diverse cultures and traditions together under conditions of difficult labour helped to redefine nationalism itself. The Europeanization of the globe, begun in the sixteenth century, certainly accelerated during the course of the nineteenth and early twentieth centuries, but a correlative process of internationalizing European settler zones both enriched and reshaped existing cultural formations. The result would be a world where political allegiances often transcended ethnicity, religious identity and racial category. But the transcendence was not complete; the twentieth century was to engage in some of the worst examples of hatred for and cruelty towards 'the other'.

PART THREE

The Era of Global Migration, 1945–2000

During the second half of the twentieth century, a dramatic increase in both the number of international migrants and the variety of global sending areas raised new questions about the right and ability of autonomous sovereign states to regulate their borders. The rapid economic recovery of advanced Western nations after the war led to acute labour shortages (especially in unskilled and semi-skilled sectors) both in Europe and in the United States. Temporary residency schemes were adopted in a number of Western European countries, while in the United States undocumented migrants from Latin American countries found employers who were more than willing to engage the services of 'illegals' in a range of low-wage agricultural, service and industrial enterprises.

The welcome was extended only so long as the economic good times continued, however, placing recent migrants in the unenviable situation of serving at the behest of larger global economic forces. During the 1970s, as Western economies slowed in the wake of the OPEC oil shocks, international labour migrants became the victims of focused political attacks, resurgent racism, and amorphous xenophobia. Despite these impediments, the very uneven development trends between industrialized states in the northern hemisphere and newly independent developing nations in the south created additional incentives for poor people to seek relocation opportunities in more affluent areas.

In the aftermath of the Second World War, the United Nations adopted a Universal Declaration of Human Rights which appeared to open the way for the unhindered relocation of persons who feared persecution in their home country. The Declaration was non-binding, however, and in a Cold War political environment, nations on both sides of the ideological divide, together with non-aligned countries, continued to maintain strict immigration regimes. Direct suffering or apprehension at the prospect of persecution had become a legitimate reason for crossing international borders, but there remained no guarantee that the asylum seeker would be accepted by other states.

The refugee issue became especially problematic during these decades, with regional conflicts, inter-ethnic disputes and natural disasters, occasioned in part by economic failures in developing states, all contributing to the flight of millions within continents and across oceans. The advent of inexpensive jet air transport during the 1960s greatly facilitated the movement of people across international frontiers, and presented potential host countries with new security challenges at a wide range of entry points. Refugee acceptance policies often became enmeshed in Cold War politics. The United Nations established the Office of the High Commissioner for Refugees in 1950 in order to assist individuals who had fled oppression, but the Soviet Union and its Eastern Bloc subordinates refused to cooperate with UN efforts in this area. On the other side of the ideological divide, the United States, which became the largest recipient of international migrants in the postwar era, distinctly privileged refugee applications from countries under the domination of communist governments, while residents of authoritarian and sometimes brutal regimes were denied entry due to the fact that the political and military leaders of the country supported the United States in the Cold War.

At the close of the twentieth century, the prospect for ever-expanding international migration seemed to hinge on two large but closely related variables. How would the pace of globalization on the economic front affect the efforts of poor nations to modernize at a rate which would ameliorate the outflow of job seekers? In a demographic environment where population growth consistently outstripped employment prospects, and where low levels of education and lack of infrastructure hampered economic development schemes and access to investment capital, the ongoing dilemma of poor nations appeared to be little affected by the end of the bi-polar Cold War world. Related to economic underdevelopment was the troubling expansion of undemocratic forms of government where rulers played upon the ethnic and religious divisions inherent in their polities in an effort to deflect popular indignation over growing poverty levels away from failed political structures and towards minority populations.

The viability of the pluralistic nation state was very much in question in a number of areas around the globe at the start of the twenty-first century. The paradoxes were numerous: financial and trade integration on a worldwide scale, but widening gaps between rich and poor states; the assertion of international human rights and the prerogative of autonomous sovereign states to recognize and protect those rights; the rhetoric of multiculturalism, which in one respect is inherently open to the movement and integration of peoples, and the increasing frequency of inter-ethnic and religious strife in Africa, in South Asia, in south-east Europe. The contradictions ensured that the process of relocation remained at the centre of the human experience, but, increasingly, movement across borders took the form of brutal 'push' factors.

FIVE

Global Transitions since 1945

Despite the fact that two world wars and a global economic depression during the period 1914–45 severely cut short the movement of peoples across international borders, the twentieth century established new benchmarks in both the scale and variety of human migration. There were approximately 1.6 billion people in the world when the century began, and just over 6 billion when it ended, a demographic change 'without historical parallel'.[1] In 1900 most people lived in rural villages and depended exclusively on surrounding fields for much of what they consumed. Only in Britain did more than half the population live in urban settings where food production was not the main occupation of the inhabitants. During the next century, and in particular after 1945, rapid urbanization, combined with ever larger concentrations of people in towns and cities, became normative on every continent.

Much of the population growth was a direct result of breakthroughs in agronomic science, the so-called 'green revolution', and, more importantly, of extensive international efforts to control and eradicate disease. Over the past fifty years vaccinations, water treatment, antibiotics and other public health measures have had an enormous impact on curbing diseases like tuberculosis, measles, dysentery, malaria and smallpox. The efforts of the World Health Organization – in cooperation with national governments – to reduce death rates, accounted for larger numbers of people living into their reproductive years. Preventive medicine rather than simple fecundity transformed the population profile of the earth in a very brief interval. This overall growth, when combined with Cold War foreign policy struggles, and, more recently, with rapid internationalization on the economic front, served to accelerate the migratory phenomenon. When added to the unprecedented numbers of war refugees and victims of racial and ethnic hatreds, the world at the close of the twentieth century was one marked by massive displacement and relocation.

If it is possible to identify one overarching theme in the last fifty years of international migration, it is that points of departure are more diverse and that former sending countries, especially in the developed West, have become substantial destination areas for very large numbers of poor and unskilled migrants. The attractions of Western urban culture were increasingly accessible (at least vicariously) through the spread of twentieth-century technologies like the cinema, radio, television, and, most recently, the Internet. Inhabitants of self-sufficient rural villages around the world were introduced to Hollywood-manufactured images of affluence and leisure in Western cities. Poor rural labourers the world over increasingly contrasted their own isolated existence with the potential of the cosmopolitan centre. Rarely did the deleterious side – the anonymity of urban life, the slums, the low-wage jobs – feature prominently in the broadcast media images of life in developed urban spaces, especially those in Western democracies. In the estimate of one recent observer, 'The central fact of the twentieth century is that the modern Western world has swept the rest of the world into its economic, technological and, less straightforwardly, cultural orbit; the societies affected by this process have resisted, acquiesced, joined in with enthusiasm, and often all three in varying combinations.'[2]

In the first decade of the twentieth century, more than 8 million Europeans left for America, but that number plummeted to less than 0.8 million during the years 1981–90.[3] Between 1951 and 1960 and 1980 and 1990, on the other hand, the number of immigrants from emerging states rose from 12 to 88 per cent of the total. According to a recent estimate, 'the percentage of migrants admitted to Australia, Canada and the United States which came from developing countries increased from 7.8, 12.3, and 41.1 per cent respectively in the early 1960s to 53.7, 70.8, and 87.9 per cent by the late 1980s'.[4] The same trend, although not as dramatic, can be observed in the major European countries. Once the great sending area for settler societies in the Americas and Australasia, Europe shifted from a net emigration zone to a pivotal receiving area, as a combination of lower fertility rates since the Second World War and expanding economies created new opportunities for foreign labourers in EU countries.

Central to this larger theme, of course, is the unshakeable constant of the nation state. The appropriate setting for legitimate governance remains in our day, as it has at least since the seventeenth century, firmly at the level of the territorial state, whatever the particular political configuration each state maintains. Despite the emergence of the global economy, inexpensive long-distance transport networks, instant electronic communications and access to information, a half century of United Nations' efforts to implement the principle of collective political, legal, and even military action, and the close of the costly and dangerous Cold War conflict between communism and capitalism, the world at the start of the twenty-first century remains one where the sovereign nation state remains the context within which people of different cultures define their core identities. The implications for migration under this long-standing organizational paradigm cannot be overstated. The 'other', the outsider, the newcomer, the un-assimilated remained in place: so long as state sovereignty was defined largely in terms of promoting the interests of a particular people, the problem of migration remained a deeply divisive political issue.

During the final quarter of the twentieth century, debates about the wisdom of accepting new migrants from non-Western cultures into advanced industrial democracies centred on three key issues. Would the introduction of large numbers of unskilled workers undercut the economic status of current workers, especially those involved in the semi-skilled and unskilled sectors? Would the new immigrants overtax existing social services; would they be able to provide for themselves and their families without substantive assistance from the welfare state? And finally, would these new peoples ever fully assimilate into the dominant culture, or would there emerge instead a type of cultural hybridity or multicultural exclusivity dedicated to stressing differences?

Earlier European migrants to the Americas, it was argued by some, succeeded fairly quickly in learning the majority language, embracing the principal values of material culture, and aspiring to full participation in the existing political process. With greater diversity in terms of points of origin, religious background and political experience, critics wondered whether more recent migrants could be expected to follow the same path towards social and cultural integration. Defenders of restrictions pointed to the need for maintaining a modicum of cultural unity, especially in democratic states where social cohesion must invariably be the product of a shared consensus. Open borders in an age of relatively inexpensive transport could result in a massive incursion of people seeking access to higher standards of living. The result would be to destabilize the existing political community, irreparably straining the existing social service infrastructure.

Quite often the popular media compounded negative stereotypes of new migrants and asylum seekers, highlighting their illegal status and their alleged penchant for claiming state benefits originally designed for citizen taxpayers. In point of fact, however, many of the aspersions cast against Asian, African and Latin American migrants beginning in the 1970s merely echoed similar estimates of Irish, Italian and especially eastern European settlers during the pre-First World War era. The argument that Roman Catholic, Jewish and Eastern Orthodox migrants would never appreciate, much less understand, the democratic process was a commonplace at the turn of the twentieth century.

Recent Western proponents of diverse immigration, on the other hand, have kept alive an argument first put forward by nineteenth-century political economists who insisted that the free movement of peoples was every bit as essential to economic progress as the free movement of goods and capital. Over the past fifty years this thesis has maintained that migrants bring new drive and ambition to the host country, setting solid examples of commitment to hard work and human betterment. In addition, unskilled migrants are always needed for less attractive jobs in a modern, increasingly service and technology-centred economy.[5] After the Second World War, the core

154

developed nations in Western Europe and America experienced a fertility rate at or just below replacement level. As a pattern of negative growth developed in conjunction with higher quality of life expectations among already affluent populations, demand intensified for additional labour to carry out the so-called 3-D tasks: dangerous, dirty and demanding. And these were almost always poorly paid, tedious and insecure jobs where high levels of education were not required.[6]

For the first time in the human experience, then, migrants from Africa, Asia, the Middle East and Latin America entered countries where there was little land available for settlement; instead, many of these newcomers took up jobs in industry and service, sending remittances home, and working with the full intention of eventually returning to their native land. Seeking citizenship status was no longer a priority for many of these migrants to developed countries. In Germany during the 1980s, only 6 per cent of foreign residents intended to apply for citizenship, while only 2 per cent of Mexicans in the United States had taken up citizenship after ten years or more of residency.[7] Many others never did return, however, and in the case of Europe these 'guest workers' from North Africa and the Middle East successfully petitioned for the entry of family members, swiftly transforming Western Europe into a multicultural society. The dilemma facing policy makers and politicians in the developed world almost always involved balancing popular concern over assimilation of new populations (normally from Asian or Latin American points of origin) and the growing need for labour in the low-wage sector businesses.

The West was not alone in facing challenges presented by new migrants from non-traditional sending areas. The break-up of the Soviet Union in 1991 led to major dislocations for Russians across the old Empire. In oil-producing states throughout the Middle East, OPEC price spikes in the early 1970s led to massive capital improvement and infrastructure projects, all of which propelled Muslim leaders to imitate the earlier European model of recruiting temporary foreign labour, without, however, following Europe's move toward cultural pluralism and the extension of civil rights.

And by the 1980s and 1990s, rapidly industrializing countries in Asia, including Taiwan, South Korea, Singapore, Malaysia and Thailand, all played host to significant numbers of international labourers due to their respective needs for unskilled and low-skilled workers. Migration systems over the past half-century undoubtedly became extremely varied and linked more closely with broader developments in an emerging global economy. The numbers of migrants worldwide, voluntary or refugee, had never been higher than at the start of the twenty-first century, yet sovereign states the world over continued to struggle strenuously to channel, restrict and control the numbers and determine the backgrounds of those admitted to residency. In a world where the movement of information, goods and people was less costly than at any previous period in the human experience, and where internationalization has been widely embraced on the economic front, the opposite trend was unfolding in the field of human migration. The tightening of immigration regimes, and the privileging of individuals with specific professional skills raised serious and troubling questions about fairness and commitment to human rights.

EUROPE AS HOST

Contemporary estimates suggest that as many as 15 million foreign nationals, many from outside the European Union, currently reside in lands that were once the leading sending regions of the globe. The roots of this demographic shift can be found in the three decades following the end of the Second World War, when two types of international migration changed the face of the leading industrial powers in Europe. The first consisted of so-called 'guest workers' from Europe's southern and eastern margins, men and some women who were attracted to Britain, West Germany, Belgium, France, Switzerland, the Netherlands and Luxembourg in order to meet significant labour shortages. In the postwar era, enormous rebuilding projects in war-torn countries created significant labour shortages, and migration opportunities increased dramatically for both skilled and unskilled labour from the periphery of Europe. In the developed world unemployment averaged a mere 2.6 per cent between 1950 and 1973, down from 7.5 per cent during the period 1920–38; thus there was little resistance on the part of native workers to enhanced international labour migration.[8] Most of the new jobs were in booming construction trades, factories and service occupations.

By 1973, foreigners made up 10–12 per cent of the labour force in France and West Germany.[9] The latter was the unquestioned leader here, with the federal government inviting workers from Turkey, Italy, Greece, Portugal, Yugoslavia, Tunisia and Morocco to assist with the industrial re-building of this war-torn land. The promotional migration only began in earnest after the erection of the Berlin Wall in 1961; before this date labour shortages were met in the main by fellow citizens fleeing the communist regime in East Germany. From 95,000 temporary wage earners in 1956, the number of foreign workers in West Germany escalated to 2.6 million in the peak year of 1973. In France, temporary, often seasonal, labourers from Spain and Portugal numbered 150,000 annually. By 1970 over 2 million foreign-born workers, together with around 700,000 of their dependents, were resident in the Fourth Republic. Even in tiny Switzerland, which was spared the widespread wartime destruction, one-third of the labour force consisted of foreign nationals during the early 1970s.

Sending countries such as the Republic of Turkey viewed the migration of their unskilled citizens as contributing to the reduction of serious unemployment levels at home. And funds sent back to family members in Turkey after 1960 played a key role in the overall economic well-being of the Republic. In the case of some 800,000 Turkish workers in Western Europe in the early 1970s, for instance, remittances represented nearly 70 per cent of Turkey's foreign currency earnings or approximately 5 per cent of gross national product.[10] At the same time it was hoped that the guest workers would be schooled in trades that would be of value to the domestic economy once the overseas labour contracts had expired. The dominant attraction for the temporary labourer was high wages, at least in comparison to what was currently on offer in their country of origin. From the point of view of the democratic European receiving states, on the other hand, the 'guest worker' programmes of the 1950s and 60s were designed exclusively to provide a reasonable solution to a temporary and anomalous post-Second World War labour scarcity. There was to be no permanent residency offered, no access to the benefits of the welfare state apparatus, no official accommodation for cultural and linguistic differences.

None of the host countries felt obliged to offer 'guest workers' opportunities for permanent citizenship rights; often even basic civil rights were restricted and dependents were not encouraged to join the invitee. After 1968 all workers within the European Economic Community were permitted free movement within the union, but even this drawing down of international borders within the Community did not slow the pace of the 'guest worker' phenomenon. Indeed, it was not until the general economic slowdown associated with the first OPEC oil embargo in 1973 that the recruitment of foreign workers into EU countries ceased.[11] Facing escalating energy prices and higher levels of unemployment, Western European political leaders responded by stopping most guest worker initiatives.

In West Germany, for example, over 1 million citizens were unemployed in 1975, and as 2 million foreign workers were still in the country, the government was compelled by political realities to abandon all further worker recruitment.[12] But while new worker migration was halted, liberal family reunification policies in most European receiving countries meant that the actual number of new migrants continued to grow during the 1970s. In West Germany the number of foreign-born men began to decrease after 1973, but the number of women actually continued to grow, a testimony to the strength of the movement for family reunification. In 1982 there were over one and a half million Turks resident in the Federal Republic, and more than two-thirds of these were dependents.[13] Overall by the early 1990s, there were approximately 8 million non-European Community residents living and working in EC countries. The temporary worker phenomenon of the immediate postwar period, actively promoted and organized by host governments, had clearly resulted in the creation of a more ethnically diverse society.

Clearly, most of the state-run programmes to engage foreign migrants as temporary workers failed to unfold as its sponsors had hoped. By withholding from guest workers the opportunity for citizenship while dictating their length of stay, housing options and type of work available, host nations sought to engage workers and not potential citizens. However the relatively open political culture in the receiving countries, together with the emergence of non-governmental organizations dedicated to advancing the civil rights claims of these workers, served to facilitate the process of transforming temporary sojourners into permanent residents. National legislation passed during the 1960s, when civil rights and anti-discrimination laws were priorities in all Western democracies, offered specific advantages to family members of migrant workers who sought reunification in the destination country.

The other key source of migration to Western Europe after 1945 involved persons coming from the colonies and previous colonies of the major powers. More than half a million former subjects of the British Empire from the Caribbean and from South Asia were resident in the United Kingdom by 1961, as free movement of peoples within the newly created Commonwealth of Nations became a key feature of the post-colonial era. Most of the ex-colonials enjoyed citizenship rights, or at the very least the opportunity to secure such rights, while guest workers from the periphery of Europe were largely unsuccessful in this respect. By 1981 there were over 1.5 million UK residents who had moved from Commonwealth countries around the world, and 60 per cent of these were born in Asian or African countries. A similar pattern emerged in France, as that former colonial power in North Africa became home to Algerians, Moroccans and Tunisians; by 1970 the total from all three countries was almost 850,000. And by the early 1960s, even the Netherlands adopted the pattern, accepting 300,000 men and women from the former Dutch East Indies.[14]

Since Britain was dismantling the largest of the colonial empires after the Second World War, the impact of new migration here was exceptional. The ethnic, racial and cultural composition of the British Isles, and of England in particular, changed in a dramatic

159

fashion in the fifteen years after the defeat of Nazism. Former colonial peoples, now members of a community of independent nations comprising a new Commonwealth, streamed into England in pursuit of greater economic opportunity. Excluding Irish migrants, 3.2 million newcomers arrived from sending destinations as geographically distant as Jamaica and Barbados in the West Indies to India and Pakistan in South Asia. With the exception of approximately 200,000 war refugees (mostly Poles) who were permitted to remain in the country after the Soviet takeover of eastern Europe, most of the postwar arrivals were welcome respondents to an acute British labour shortage. A strong economy with an annual average growth rate of 2.6 per cent between 1945 and 1962 provided the backdrop to the influx of Commonwealth residents to the heart of the old empire. In a now familiar pattern, chain migration emerged very quickly, with male residents sending remittances home in order to pay for the relocation of additional family members. Most settled in England's major industrial cities, where factory work and small service-oriented business careers became the norm for the new minorities.

Predictably, the first restrictions placed on Commonwealth residents occurred in the midst of a economic downturn with the passage of the Commonwealth Immigrants Act of 1962. Sharp controls on wage-earner immigration were imposed, but in an important exception, family dependents of those who had previously settled on a permanent basis were able to relocate to Britain for another decade. This 1962 legislation made all future entries from Commonwealth sending countries subject to specific skills requirements. Just over 30,000 such entry vouchers were issued in 1963, but the total fell to 2,290 in 1970.[15] Family reunification was allowed to continue after 1972, although subsequent legislation further reduced the number of non-whites who were allowed to settle in the country.

During the Margaret Thatcher era of the 1980s, Britain became one of the most restrictionist of the European nations. Still, the scale of the earlier migration had recast the racial and cultural character of the island. From food to music, language and dress, urban England had become remarkably multicultural. And with the

160

passage of the 1965 Race Relations Act, discrimination in public places, together with incitement to racial hatred in speech and print, was made a criminal offence. In 1968 the Act was extended to include housing and employment. Of course much de facto discrimination continued, especially for the non-white communities, but national and local government bodies had taken important steps designed to curb the worst inequalities.[16]

Economic advancement had been the central reason for the postwar migrations into Europe, both from the point of view of the host countries and with respect to the migrant populations, and it is fair to say that Europe's economic revival after the experience of global war owed not a little to the labour resources provided by guest workers and former colonial peoples. Despite this major contribution, both groups tended to suffer from discrimination, held the lowest-paid unskilled jobs, and often were reduced to living in segregated urban districts. A host of cultural differences sometimes exacerbated social tensions between white Europeans and residents from Europe's periphery and from colonial settings in Africa, Asia and the Caribbean, while treatment at work, inadequate schools and housing, and insufficient social services all combined to reinforce the social and economic marginalization of new peoples. And as the European Community began affording citizens of each member state equal treatment with respect to migration and labour opportunities, the non-European resident faced additional challenges in the search for meaningful employment.

ISLAM, OIL AND GUEST WORKERS

Postwar developments in the six wealthiest oil producing Gulf States (Saudi Arabia, Kuwait, Bahrain, Qatar, Oman and the United Arab Emirates) were very different, although here too the guest worker phenomenon became the chosen solution when labour demands became acute. Much of the region was still under indirect Western control in 1945, but Europe's retreat from global empire facilitated the move toward regional autonomy in the Muslim Middle East. When petroleum prices skyrocketed in the early 1970s, these states, while eager to modernize and industrialize, did not have the requisite number of skilled workers to complete the work at an acceptable pace. In particular, Saudi Arabia, Kuwait and the United Arab Emirates all undertook massive infrastructure development projects in the 1970s and 1980s, and the need for manual labour vastly outstripped the ability of the subject, largely rural population to provide.[17] With a total of only 18 million inhabitants, or 7 per cent of the entire population of the Middle East, the demand for manual employees in this region remained very high throughout the period 1970–90.

Overall educational levels were low in the Gulf States, the role of women in the workforce was minimal, and a transport infrastructure was largely absent. The migration experience in these areas was thus predicated upon the rapid creation of an industrial base and capital projects, a situation unique in comparison to that experienced by migrants in highly industrialized and urbanized countries in the West. South and East Asians, together with large numbers of Africans, entered Muslim countries as temporary workers whose remittances home contributed significantly to a number of domestic economies.

But unlike the Western host nations, the oil-producing states were not pluralist democracies but hereditary monarchies where legislative and executive power lay firmly with the respective ruling families. These kingdoms were thus better equipped to treat their migrant workers merely as economic units and not as rights-bearing human beings. None of the Gulf States, for example, recognized the right to asylum, and no one was permitted to enter these countries without a specific, pre-approved job contract. In addition, ownership of land by foreigners was not allowed and the right of appeal against government decisions respecting the status of non-residents was absent. There were no advocacy groups working on behalf of foreign workers in these states as there were in the democratic West, and residency permits were available for only one or two years. Access to housing and health care operated under the terms of the original work contract, while expulsion without cause became the prerogative of the interior ministry in each kingdom.

The overwhelming majority of foreign-born workers resident in Gulf States were employed in the lower end of material production or service trades, while professional posts and the upper levels of private enterprise remained the monopoly of native elites. Male workers often resided in barracks, and families were not allowed to relocate alongside their male wage earners. And wage discrimination between native and foreign workers in the same field was commonplace, a practice again marked by the absence of any legal recourse against alleged discrimination. More than any other receiving area in the modern world, Arab oil countries enjoyed unrivalled success at maximizing the economic potential of foreign labour while denying the temporary residents basic social and political rights.[18]

During the early 1970s, initial migrant labour flows into the newly affluent kingdoms came from neighbouring Muslim states. Egypt led the way as a sending country, while Jordan, Yemen and Sudan provided additional human resources. In the 1980s the number of sending countries multiplied, and workers from South and East Asia became important contributors to the expanding oil economies. Indians comprised the largest group of migrants to the region, with just under 1 million resident in 1990. On the eve of the Gulf War, foreign workers constituted a majority of the labour force in all of the oil states, reaching nearly 80 per cent of the overall workforce in Kuwait, Qatar, and Saudi Arabia.[19] In that year there were over 7 million foreigners in these sparsely populated countries, 50 per cent of whom were from Indonesia, Korea, the Philippines and Thailand, but none of these recent arrivals could hope for a permanent place of residency within these societies. With their varied religious, cultural and linguistic backgrounds, they were easily distinguished from the subjects of the respective monarchs in the region. This made it much easier for Arab authorities to prevent temporary migrants from assimilating into the predominant culture, a challenge which was more difficult during the early years of migration in the 1970s when most foreign workers were from neighbouring countries.

The Gulf States' migration zone is thus unique, with undemocratic state authorities successfully (thus far) preventing the massive numbers of foreign migrant labourers from having a significant impact on the Muslim social order or the exclusive political regime. Rigorous entry requirements, segmented labour opportunities, wage discrimination, no provision for family reunification or land ownership, and few efforts to integrate fellow Muslims into the host country's social and political culture have enabled the Arab oil states to create a singular migration system, one very much antithetical to the model in the rest of the developed world, where migrant participation in the political and cultural life of the host nation has eventually become an important addition to their initial labour function.

The penchant for oil-producing states to commodify labour was not solely the preserve of Middle East kingdoms. During the oil boom of the 1970s, unskilled and undocumented foreigners from a number of West African states had made their way to Nigeria in order to secure employment. Again, as in the Arab world, public and private spending on internal Nigerian development projects created a strong demand for contract labour. But when world oil prices slumped in the early 1980s, the Nigerian government, fearful of the potential for social disorder as unemployment rose, ordered an estimated 2 million illegal migrants to leave the country. Most of those affected were Ghanaians. This 1983 removal was followed by the expulsion of an additional quarter of a million persons in 1985. In a global context, as many as 5 million people, many of them foreign workers, were uprooted from their host nations in the wake of the Gulf crisis and war of 1990–1.[20]

If one measure of a country's intellectual and economic dynamism is its ability to fully incorporate new cultural and experiential perspectives into its national life, if embracing diversity is truly a long-term asset to the well-being of the state and its citizenry, then the current Gulf State migration model will, in the long run, contribute little to the advancement of this region of the globe. Cultural and political exclusivity may yield short-term economic benefits as long as finite oil resources continue to privilege the native elite who now constitute a minority of the overall labour force in this region. But the recent practice of maximizing the economic potential of migrants while shutting out the broader cultural and intellectual assets of migrant populations may, in the end, foster the very sort of cultural stagnation which doomed an earlier Muslim polity in the Ottoman Empire.

ASIA AND NICS

The newest zone of significant international migration has involved a select number of small Asian Pacific countries, especially newly industrializing states in South Korea, Taiwan, Malaysia, Hong Kong and Singapore. Together with Australia, whose government abandoned a long-standing 'whites only' immigration policy in the mid-1960s, these Asian hosts have followed the Western economic model of industrial capitalism and low-wage labour recruitment with, until the late 1990s, remarkable success.

Beginning in the early 1980s, Singapore, Hong Kong, South Korea and Taiwan all undertook to recruit additional unskilled workers for the booming construction sector. Many came from Indonesia and the Philippines, countries that stood as the two chief sending areas during the last two decades of the twentieth century. In the early 1990s, some 20 per cent of Singapore's labour force consisted of migrants from neighbouring Thailand and the Philippines, the vast majority of whom were engaged on projects related to housing and transportation. Over 400,000 citizens of the former Dutch-controlled Indonesia were resident in Malaysia and Singapore by the end of the twentieth century, and some even relocated to Australia. Filipinos could be found in a very wide range of countries where labour shortages emerged on account of rapid economic and industrial development. A quarter of a million were working in Newly Industrialized Countries (NICs) in the early 1990s, while the overwhelming majority of Filipino migrants (almost 1 million) could be found in the United States, with another half million in Gulf States.

By 1970, only 3 per cent of settlers in Australia were from Asia, but this number had increased to 37 per cent in 1995. New entrance requirements which privileged migrants with specific skills enabled professionals from around the Pacific rim to enter this western outpost. By 1990, only about half the foreign-born persons in Australia were born in Europe, an important decrease compared with earlier decades. A similar pattern emerged in the other European settler region of New Zealand, as significant migration flows from neighbouring Pacific region states helped to diversify the population.

The one modern industrialized nation which has avoided this emerging cultural diversity is Japan, where labour unions and the government have effectively triumphed over the business community's desire for less restrictive immigration policies. By and large Japan elected to solve its postwar labour shortage in the manufacturing sector by relocating production facilities outside Japan proper. Overseas, Japanese-owned facilities are commonplace within the larger global marketplace, while a high degree of ethnic homogeneity has been preserved on the Japanese islands.

Still, even with Japan's preference for establishing manufacturing plants overseas, labour shortages continued to beset domestic producers into the 1990s. In the last decade of the century, openings in the construction industry were substantial. There were 1.3 million legal migrants in Japan in 1993, but a number of temporary 'trainee' programmes allowed foreign workers to remain for up to three years. In addition, there are another 250,000 visa overstayers. Businesses moved quickly to narrow the gap between available jobs and applicants. In the early 1990s, the Tokyo Chamber of Commerce called for an expansion of the legal quota for foreign workers over the current 600,000 number, but politicians resisted these entreaties.[21]

Overall, it can be said that migration patterns in the Asia-Pacific region appear to be following the model witnessed earlier in the industrializing West. NICs serve as magnets for workers in countries where the early stages of development have upset traditional modes of production and employment, and where high rates of fertility exacerbate the already difficult prospects for meaningful employment at home. Some of the receiving areas, Japan in particular, have imposed severe immigration restrictions, but elsewhere the flow of migrant labour across international boundaries seems destined to expand over the next decades. As governments in sending countries struggle to deal with rising populations and limited job opportunities, their advocacy of emigration, and in some cases their penchant for estimating remittances as part of their national planning targets, indicates that the international migration phenomenon is perhaps just at its beginning stages in this area of the world.

LATIN AMERICA'S DILEMMA

In the case of Latin America, much of the international migration which took place after 1945 occurred within the American continent, but economic difficulties and endemic political instability also secured for the region a dubious distinction as the first European settler region to become a significant emigration area. In the southern portion of the continent, comprising the nation states of Brazil, Argentina, Chile, Uruguay and Paraguay, the majority population is of European origin. Further north and west (including Central America) the population is largely native Indian and *mestizo*, while the islands of the Caribbean are today populated by a majority population that is of African origin.

Three of the South American countries, Uruguay, Argentina and Brazil, began the process of industrialization in the late nineteenth century and, as we have seen, became important destination countries for very large numbers of European migrants, and in particular migrants from Italy, Spain and Portugal. In almost two centuries beginning in 1800, roughly 14 million Europeans settled in South America, with almost three-quarters of the total relocating to Brazil and Argentina. Immigrant communities came to dominate the populations of industrial cities like Buenos Aires, Sao Paulo and Montevideo before the Second World War, while after the war arrivals from Europe clustered in Venezuela, where development made possible by petroleum revenues spurred industrial growth. Overall, European migration declined in the postwar period, however, as economic conditions at home allowed for greater opportunities without relocation.

International migration within the South American continent increased sharply during the final half of the twentieth century. Of course cross-border movement had been a hallmark of seasonal agricultural labour since the establishment of independent republics in the early decades of the nineteenth century. People who were accustomed to moving in search of harvest-related work now found themselves traversing international boundaries in the wake of Spanish and Portuguese decolonization. A good deal of this seasonal movement continued after the Second World War, especially in border regions where people of similar cultural heritage were formally separated due to the fact of state building.

Beginning in the 1970s, however, a new form of rural to urban migration boosted the volume of international migration in countries like Venezuela and Argentina. Almost half a million foreign workers from other South American countries moved to Venezuela in search of work related to the oil industry. And in Argentina during the same decade, while the European-born population declined by some 500,000 due to deaths and return migration, almost 200,000 Latin Americans from other nations became residents. Indeed, Argentina alone remained an in-migration country in the postwar period. The 1980s witnessed the rise of military government and defeat in a conflict with Britain over the Falkland/Malvinas islands, but these conditions did not seriously curtail relocation flows. During the course of the 1980s 402,000 arrived, mostly from neighbouring states like Uruguay, Paraguay and Bolivia, and the bulk of the new arrivals settled in urban centres like Buenos Aires.

None the less, by the 1980s Latin America and the Caribbean basin as a whole had become a net exporter of persons, and most of these migrants were destined for work in North America. The burgeoning populations, declining economies and indebtedness of the sending countries, together with regional military clashes and Cold War ideological conflict, all contributed to the outflow phenomenon. In Mexico alone, a population of 20 million in 1940 had grown to almost 70 million by the early 1980s.[22] But while the adoption of the North American Free Trade Agreement in 1994 called for the free flow of goods and services across Mexican, American and Canadian borders, this economic opening, ostensibly designed to facilitate the advancement of all three economies, did not include the unfettered transfer of human capital.

At the very time that the federal government was adopting greater restrictions and regulations respecting the movement of peoples across international borders, the United States continued to recruit Mexican labourers for low-wage temporary employment in agriculture and manufacturing. In fact the Immigration and Naturalization Service (INS) actually assisted US agricultural employers in a modern-day contract labour scheme by permitting temporary service by undocumented Mexican nationals. Estimates placed the annual number of undocumented aliens at 300,000 per year during the 1980s.[23] Many of these workers elected to stay in the US at the end of their term of employment, thus expanding the problem of undocumented aliens. But during the 1990s the INS budget was boosted in an effort to better secure the US–Mexico border and to restrict undocumented residency, as resistance to permanent status for Latin Americans living and working in the United States remained strong.

The advent of military government in much of the southern cone (Argentina, Chile and Uruguay) during the 1970s also led to a modest outflow of skilled professionals. Roughly 80,000 migrants from these countries entered the United States during the 1980s, unfortunately compounding the economic development woes faced by the sending nations. Since the early 1960s, military struggles in Cuba, Guatemala, El Salvador and Nicaragua, often with strong Cold War surrogate components, resulted in the outflow of millions of Central Americans, most of whom sought refuge in the United States.[24]

IDENTITIES IN THE NORTH AMERICAN REPUBLICS

The United States has long prided itself on its special character as a 'nation of immigrants' dedicated to the principle that new arrivals contribute to the strength and vitality of the republican enterprise.

169

For most of its comparatively brief history as an independent nation, citizens of the American republic have welcomed migrants, but occasionally there have been periods of strong xenophobia. Restricting immigration was never a political issue before the 1900s, and has been only periodically since that time. As we read in Chapter 4, women and men from north-western Europe dominated the flow to the United States until the close of the nineteenth century; after that time settlers from southern and eastern Europe made their presence felt, especially in large urban areas along the Atlantic coast. Between 1880 and 1920 men and women from Italy, Austria-Hungary, the Balkan states and Russia constituted 40 per cent of newcomers to the United States. The only serious restrictions on this celebrated migrant flow involved an 1875 law which excluded criminals, prostitutes and Asian contract labour, and an 1882 law that forbade the introduction of Chinese workers. Enforcement provisions were weak, however, since federal authorities did not have the resources or manpower to supervise all ports of entry. Immigration control was essentially a state enforcement matter.

In the wake of the influx of new migrants from southern and eastern Europe, dominated by non-English speakers and representing Catholic and Russian Orthodox Christianity, Congress enacted a new set of prohibitory laws. The first serious restrictions on the flow of migrants to the United States began within the context of heightened nativist concerns over assimilation and social order. Congress had established a federal Bureau of Immigration in 1891 in order to bring some order and regularity to the enforcement of existing statutes, while additional legislation in the early twentieth century further limited the type of migrant who could enter the country. Fairly sweeping categories – anarchists, the illiterate, the mentally ill, unaccompanied children, persons with physical handicaps – all could be denied entry at the discretion of port authorities.[25] The literacy requirement, enacted in 1917, effectively stemmed the flow of migrants from outside north-western Europe. That same year Congress officially barred all Asians from entering the country. Finally, in the Quota Acts of 1921 and 1924, the federal government imposed strict controls over all prospective entrants, but the 1924 legislation based each quota on the number of each country's nationals living in the United States in 1890. By using the 1890 census as a benchmark, the law drastically reduced migrant flow from outside north-western Europe.[26]

By the second decade of the twentieth century, then, migration had become a major national policy issue within the United States. Previously limited to the job of processing and documenting new arrivals to the nation of immigrants, federal authorities now took up the assignment of enforcing legislative mandates which for the first time in the nation's history determined what type of person could join the American republic, and how many might be admitted in any given year. Since this time, the focus of debate over migration has centred on the national legislature. Since the process was no longer in the hands of employers, state or local officials, the role of the United States as a land of new beginnings for all who could secure transport was now at an end. Self-interest as defined by the representatives of a democratic electorate had effectively redefined one of the essential foci of the republican experiment.

The highly restrictive legislation of the 1920s was only amended some forty years later with the passage of the 1965 Immigration and Nationality Act. Passed within the context of the American civil rights movement and revulsion over the racist overtones of the rules established during the 1920s, this law put an end to nationality quotas and replaced this criterion with a new set of guidelines designed to privilege family members of citizens and permanent residents, together with skilled professionals who could best contribute to the material development of the nation.

Throughout the 1980s, almost 70 per cent of all foreign residents in the United States entered as relatives of permanent residents or citizens, while 18 per cent came as refugees and only 9 per cent as workers.[27] Each sending nation was now limited to 20,000 immigrants annually, with a cap of 290,000 total for each year. These numbers were flexible, however, as Congress exempted both refugees and immediate relatives (spouses, children) from the cap. In 1996 the overall cap was raised to 675,000. The result was a dramatic acceleration in the number of new settlers to the United

States. From 1965 until 1996, 20.1 million migrants came to this one country. In the five-year period ending in 1996 alone, over 6 million new migrants arrived, rivalling in volume the peak decade of migration without restrictions (1900–10) when close to 9 million (mostly Europeans) were admitted.[28]

The majority of new migrants were born in Asia and Latin America, not Europe. Whereas over two-thirds of all legal immigrants to the United States during the 1950s were from Europe, by the 1990s this figure had been reduced to 17 per cent, while Latin American sending countries accounted for half the total by the end of the century. Another 30 per cent arrived from Asian nations. When coupled with a considerable influx of undocumented workers, largely from Central America, the total number of foreign-born residents at the close of the twentieth century compared with the busiest years of open immigration policies of one century earlier.[29] It is undeniable that the United States 'now accepts more immigrants than all other countries combined'. And the status of the United States as the world's premier receiving nation has given rise to a contentious political debate over the wisdom and purpose of the current national policy. It is currently projected that by the middle of the twenty-first century, non-Latino whites will represent less than half the total population of the United States, while the next largest group (about 26 per cent) will be Hispanic.[30]

Attitudes towards this issue rarely corresponded to political affiliation. Conservative republican business interests often supported generous immigration policies, citing its benefits to the manufacturing and agricultural sectors of the United States economy. Constant infusions of new unskilled migrants, these advocates claimed, would lower overall labour costs and spur the entrepreneurial spirit of the newcomer. Other conservatives decried immigration with the argument that unskilled residents inordinately overburdened the tax-supported social welfare system, while still other conservative voices lamented the increasing ethnic diversity of the country and the potential for social conflict. Liberal Democrats were also to be found in the anti-migrant camp, pointing to the adverse effects that cheap labour had on the bargaining power of

American workers. On the other hand, many liberals celebrated the cultural variety and richness brought to the American landscape by new arrivals. Restrictions violated the democratic principles upon which the nation was founded, it was argued, while any policy which retreated from the original ideal of open access to all was, in the end, ethically untenable. The matter of human rights was difficult to avoid.

ACCESS AND HUMAN RIGHTS

Prior to the First World War, the migration decisions of most individuals were subject to very little intervention or intrusion on the part of political authorities. China was a major exception to this generalization, of course, as were the Spanish, Portuguese and French empires in America after 1500. Still, in comparison to the various migration control regimes established during the course of the twentieth century, the paucity of sovereign state controls in earlier ages is exceptional. During the course of the Great Migration after 1850, this *laissez-faire* posture was firmly endorsed by classical political economists who insisted that the free movement of peoples was as essential to economic progress as the unhindered movement of goods and capital.

The establishment of national immigration regimes after the First World War, as well as the reconfiguration of these regimes during the 1960s in an effort to end racist preferences, merely substituted one form of discrimination for another. For while race and national origins were no longer to be privileged in terms of entry into developed nations, educational background and skill level, normal concomitants of wealth and access to the professions, smoothed the relocation process for the affluent and hardened barriers against the movement of poor people. By the 1960s international migrants were as likely to be highly qualified and specialized professionals or employees of multinational firms as they were to be unskilled manual workers.

As we have seen, after 1945 the developed European settler nations (Canada, Australia, the United States) afforded immigration preferences to regions which were linked to the receiving nation by a specific historical relationship. But during the 1960s and 1970s, as reforms in the host countries put an end to discrimination based on race, ethnicity and point of origin, a new measure of acceptability was introduced, one which centred on the overall ability of the migrant to contribute to the economic well-being of the receiving country. Successful entrepreneurs, scientists, technicians and other skilled persons, irrespective of their point of origin, were able to secure new and expanding opportunities in the most advanced industrialized nations. Increasingly, those who controlled sufficient capital or possessed professional skills made possible through expensive educations could relocate without serious impediment, while those lacking educational and financial resources were condemned to suffer under sometimes oppressive governments.[31]

Laws defining minimum professional qualifications for prospective migrants certainly advantaged the receiving country's short-term scientific and economic status, but such policies also unfairly privileged economic elites while undermining the sending country's ability to pursue a Western-inspired modernizing agenda. The movement of commodities and capital is almost always accompanied by the movement of people. But the growing inequality between the wealthiest Western nations and the rest of the world after 1945 severely aggravated the out-migration patterns of highly educated citizens, a phenomenon sometimes referred to as 'brain drain', and compounded the development problems of sending states. The negative impact on the many developing countries was enormous, especially in terms of a state's ability to improve health services, technical advancement and managerial expertise. Clearly the economic interests of the host country too often served as the chief criteria under which national immigration policy took shape, leaving the more troubling issue of social equity on the margins of public debate.

Another troublesome determinant of migration flows between 1945 and 1990 involved foreign policy conflicts in an emerging bi-polar world. It is clear that since the end of the Second World War international migration patterns have been functions of both economic variables and larger geopolitical tensions. International relations and the dynamics of the Cold War have contributed extensively to the movement of peoples across borders, but in many cases the formulation of immigration control policies took little account of these political factors. As noted earlier, the principal receiving countries tended to accept the bulk of their migrants from nations where the host state had once exercised direct colonial authority or even indirect neo-colonial economic and political influence. In these cases migration was less the result of individual choice and more the unwelcome fallout of ideological – and sometimes military – conflict. When the Soviets crushed the Hungarian Revolution in November 1956, for example, almost 200,000 refugees flooded across the border into Western Europe, with most settling in neighbouring Austria. The large flow of migrants from Vietnam, El Salvador and the Philippines to the United States after 1970 similarly coincided with the massive military and defence-related foreign aid secured by these nations.[32] Almost 1 million Vietnamese exiles eventually settled in the United States, with Canada, Australia and Western European nations accepting a much smaller total.

These involuntary migrants were faced with adjusting to political, cultural and religious traditions quite distinct from those embraced by the majority population of the homeland. By the end of the century 60 per cent of all foreign-born residents in the United Kingdom were from Asian and African countries where Britain once wielded direct colonial suzerainty, while almost all Algerians living in Europe were residents of France. The idea that destination countries are decided by individual migrants on the basis of a rational calculation of economic betterment, while perhaps a plausible explanation for much nineteenth-century migration from Europe, was no longer tenable. Receiving countries are not passive victims of migration processes; the past or current relationship of the receiving country to the migrant's place of origin is often extensive and complex, and frequently it was and continues to be a relationship between unequals. Admission to states was often a function of the ideological relationship between the sending area and the dominant power.

The Global Community

The unexpected demise of communist regimes across eastern Europe and in Russia during the late 1980s raised fears that a great westward shift of population would occur as the disparities between economic conditions in the former Soviet bloc and the West became apparent. The collapse of the Soviet Union and its East European satellite states posed a special human rights dilemma for the Western democracies, all of whom had roundly condemned the Soviets for their refusal to allow emigration during the Cold War. Once those restrictions were lifted, however, the prospect of receiving large numbers of economic migrants (there were approximately 1.2 million men and women who crossed into Western Europe in 1989 alone) created a significant problem for Western political leaders.[33]

Surprisingly, most of the migration flow in the new states of the former Soviet Union did not conform to this projection. Instead, the greatest level of movement took place among the successor states themselves. In 1991, millions of Soviet citizens found themselves instant foreigners in a host of newly formed republics. Twenty-five million Russians, 7 million Ukrainians and 2 million Belorussians were resident in lands once unified under communist control but now reconfigured along linguistic, ethnic and historical lines. In the wake of the collapse of the Soviet Union in the late 1991, millions of people crossed these newly established borders, with 2.7 million Russians, unwelcome in previously occupied states, returning home. The repatriation process was at best painful during the 1990s, with Russians in particular experiencing the disdain of the indigenous populations of regions where Soviet communist officialdom once lived amid privilege and plenty.[34]

In addition, 2 million ethnic Germans returned from former Soviet satellite states to a reunited Germany, and an alarmed German government pumped money into former Soviet states in an effort to slow the reverse migration. Unhappily, while the end of the Soviet Union eased military and ideological tensions between the world's superpowers, a resurgence of ethnic, religious and nationalist tensions has marked not a few of the reconstituted nation states of eastern and south-eastern Europe. As a result, new patterns of migration have presented the global community with unprecedented challenges, and these have often been felt most acutely in more affluent receiving nations.

Even post-apartheid South Africa has wrestled, in large measure unsuccessfully, with the problem of unwanted labour migrants. The white minority government had vigorously expelled undocumented residents during its long ascendancy; in 1993 alone some 53,000 migrant workers were required to leave the country. But in the first year of democratic majority rule, Nelson Mandela's government expelled almost 160,000 undocumented migrants, most of whom were from neighbouring Mozambique.[35] The primacy of the nation state ideal remains secure even in areas of the world where the detrimental influence of Western colonialism had its greatest impact.

International migration, it seems, will continue to grow as the north–south divide widens, and as economies the world over become more integrated. As long as the economic disparity between developed countries and their aspirant counterparts continues to widen, the prospect of removal to more affluent nations will remain a constant in the human experience. The contemporary signposts are not propitious. Income distribution in many developing nations continues along an increasingly inequitable path, while population growth and environmental degradation point to greater political challenges for governments which in many instances have not been responsive to the emerging global human rights regime.[36]

For good or ill, a dominant monocultural ideal formed at the heart of the economies of emerging nations after the Second World War. Development, consumption, material measures of individual self-worth – these sometimes troubling characteristics of contemporary life around the world presented serious challenges for humans and their environment by the year 2000. Issues of sustainability, never considered thoroughly during the height of the industrial age, now emerged as important policy questions. And the larger challenge of ends to be pursued, of human flourishing, of whether continual development and growth are ethically and psychologically satisfying human goals in their own right, became intimately connected to the migration phenomenon.

At the end of the twentieth century the average income of three-fifths of the world's population, largely men and women living in India, China and sub-Saharan Africa, was only about one-twentieth that of people living in the richest countries. Perhaps not surprisingly, only a small number of poor countries have managed to catch up with the developed West over the past half century.[37] Poor people will always seek to improve their lot, and the educated elite within developing nations will aspire to participate in the wider range of opportunities offered by economically advanced Western democracies. Only when significant improvement on the economic and political fronts takes place, as witnessed in the Republic of Ireland during the 1990s, will current migration trends abate and in some cases (again using the Irish example) reverse themselves. But whether current definitions of economic success can be sustained at a global level over the long term is very much a matter of intensive debate.

One of the ironies of migration at the end of the twentieth century was that while economic globalization worked to denationalize economies, while controls on the flow of capital, technology and information were removed, every nation state continued to insist on its sovereign right to manage and restrict the entry of new peoples. States seem willing to relinquish sovereignty on key economic fronts, but were distinctly less than enthusiastic about including the free movement of persons as a component part of global economic transactions.[38] The end of the bi-polar world and of costly proxy wars in the name of competing political ideologies has done little to ameliorate the essential inequalities which remain at the heart of immigration policies. While international migration has reached new levels, points of destination, at least welcoming ones, manage to contract. Reception policies in modern states continue to reflect national self-interest rather than global equity.

SIX

Refugees in the Modern World

There have always been refugees, people driven from their place of birth and residence by famine, war and persecution. Over the centuries both individuals and large groups have experienced involuntary removal at the hands of their own political elites or by hostile invaders. From the Jewish exile in ancient Babylon, to the flight or *hijrah* of the Prophet Muhammed from Mecca to Medina, to the removal of Amerindians to the western United States by white Europeans and their descendants, the experience of loss, of cultural uprootedness, and other myriad hardships associated with resettlement mark every culture and stand as a centuries-old testimony to humankind's tendency towards inhumanity.

But even while the phenomenon continues as a depressing constant of the human experience, three factors distinguished the situation of twentieth-century refugees the world over. The first involved the sheer scale of the experience. There were more forcibly displaced persons during the last 100 years than at any earlier period in recorded history. Europeans led the way in homelessness during the era of the First and Second World Wars, as intra-European refugee migration became a fixture of social reality across the continent. Political upheaval and racist ideology combined to force massive human dislodgement. Over 7 million people crossed international borders in Europe during the First World War, while perhaps 25 million were compelled to relocate, mainly in an east–west direction, between 1939 and 1945.[1] Estimates of as many as 15 million persons fled for their lives upon the creation of independent India and Pakistan in 1947, while 2 million left China for Hong Kong and Taiwan after the success of Mao's communist revolution in 1949.[2] Five years after the end of the Second World

War there were almost 8 million refugees living in West Germany, 3 million of whom were Germans intent upon abandoning their homes in the Communist East German state.

Since the mid-twentieth century, Africa and Asia have secured unfortunate notoriety as major refugee areas. In 1990 the estimate of migrants worldwide was 80 million, or approximately 1.7 per cent of the world's population, and some 20 million of these were refugees or asylum seekers. Requests for asylum rose dramatically after the defeat of fascism in 1945. Political, religious and ethnic tensions, sometimes made worse in the broader context of Cold War rivalries, propelled the involuntary movement of peoples, mostly in the direction of developed Western democracies. Of the estimated 20 million refugees in the world today, 30 per cent reside in wealthy developed nations.[3]

A second variable is rooted in the emergence of restrictive admissions criteria, especially in the wealthiest nations of the Western world. Sovereign nation states whose leaders were committed to improving the quality of material existence for their own citizens, fiercely defended their right to exclude migrants, and this included displaced refugees. As early as 1932 an international Convention at the Hague affirmed the exclusive prerogative of the state to grant citizenship, and while a 1952 Convention on Refugees confirmed egress from a country as a universal human right, no mention was made of the right of ingress to a potential receiving country. The right of asylum remained firmly under the discretion of individual states, a reality that has presented particular difficulties for refugees the world over. Hannah Arendt, herself a refugee from the racist policies of 1930s Nazi Germany, observed in the 1960s that throughout history 'forced migrations of individuals or whole groups of people for political and economic reasons look like everyday occurrences. What is unprecedented is not the loss of a home but the impossibility of finding a new one.'[4]

The final development, closely related to the second, concerned the new prominence given to refugee issues within the international community, and in particular within the United Nations. The myriad horrors of the Second World War guaranteed that human rights issues would be a subject of central concern to the international community after 1945. This was especially true in democratic states where rights language was, and is, an important part of civil discourse. International cooperation in this area of human experience was in its infancy when the United Nations was established. According to UN Conventions adopted in the 1950s and 1960s, a refugee is an individual who 'owing to a well-grounded fear of being persecuted for reasons of race, religion, nationality, membership of a particular social group or political opinion, is outside the country of his nationality and is unable or, owing to such fear, is unwilling to avail himself of the protection of that country'.[5]

Whenever involuntary migrant issues emerged, human rights became part of the equation, often pitting the idealistic rhetoric of democratic states against the nationalist commitment to border security. The effort to maintain cohesive civil societies where common values could find expression within the framework of liberal, democratic political institutions was complicated by the increasingly diverse nature of migrant populations. Affirming the inherent right of individuals to migrate when faced with acute economic deprivation or with political, religious or ethnic persecution (or the fear of it) at home would be meaningless so long as refugees remained at the mercy of restrictive and anarchic entrance criteria. How to enhance the quality of life for those who have exercised an internationally recognized right to flee oppression quickly emerged as one of the most intractable problems facing sovereign nation states at the start of the postwar era.

Human rights as first articulated in the West during the late eighteenth century claimed to transcend national borders and oblige all nations to conform to a single universal standard. Rights language has informed the founding documents of a number of states in the West over the past two centuries, but only after the Second World War were formal conventions agreed within the United Nations concerning the specifics of global rights. The 1948 Universal Declaration of Human Rights is not a legally binding international treaty but it has been interpreted as a worldwide benchmark on permissible international practice. Subsequent UN

Conventions on Genocide (1948), Racial Discrimination (1965) and the Political Rights of Women (1981) have further clarified the emerging human rights regime. Despite these transnational agreements, however, the locus of authority respecting international migration remains with the sovereign state, and the prospects for international cooperation seem, at the start of the twenty-first century, less than propitious.

AN EARLIER WELCOME

Until the late nineteenth century, governments and peoples rarely troubled themselves over what amounted to communities of foreign exiles living within their midst. And while there were often groups of fugitives and dispossessed within the borders of Europe's many kingdoms, rarely did this situation complicate relations between royal heads of state. Religious minorities, for instance, were often harried by the crown after the start of the Protestant Reformation in the sixteenth century, but more often than not such groups were accommodated by other monarchs as assets to their own kingdoms. Thousands of Irish Catholic rebels fled to France after the failure of the 1688 rising against English rule and subsequently served on the continent in the armies of Louis XIV. Similarly, Protestant Huguenots fleeing the persecution of Louis's regime in the late seventeenth century, were invited by King Frederick William of Prussia to settle in his patrimony. Still other Huguenots could be found living – and prospering without distraction from authorities – in London and Dublin. In Russia, both Peter the Great and Catherine the Great, keen to westernize their Empire, regularly welcomed enterprising exiles into their cities.[6]

Before the advent of the twentieth-century welfare state, the influx of refugees did not pose an acute political problem in terms of the allocation of fiscal resources. Indeed the suffering experienced by exiles in a foreign land was not markedly different in kind from the daily hardships faced by the majority population in the host kingdom or country. The special trials endured by refugees were akin to the material life conditions of all peoples who struggled with

182

nature in subsistence economies. Not until the nineteenth century was the word 'refugee' (from the French *refugie*) even associated with involuntary exiles in the broadest sense, and even then the designation was normally limited to individual, high-profile political exiles.

Throughout much of the first half of the nineteenth century in Europe, most refugees were specifically political exiles, fugitives fresh from the front lines of one failed revolution after another. And remarkably, political radicals were easily absorbed by host countries, with governments paying little heed to their presence or to their frenetic organizing efforts. Whether it was Polish emigrés fleeing to France after the failed 1831 revolution against their absolutist Russian overlords, or Germans, Italians, Austrians and Frenchmen decamping to London or Geneva after the collapse of the European liberal revolutions of 1848, political refugees quickly found succour in a variety of neighbouring states. The troublesome Karl Marx, for example, lived quietly in London with his family after 1849, and the same disinterested reception awaited other high-profile revolutionaries like Giuseppe Mazzini of Italy and Louis Kossuth of Hungary. During the course of the century not a single refugee was refused entry into Britain; indeed, refugees could simply disembark without having to register with the police or any other state authority. Remarkably, in France the government even provided modest support stipends for notable refugees. An 1832 law 'Concerning Foreign Refugees Residing in France' defined the newcomers as persons residing without their own government's protection.[7]

The rather generous reception awaiting those who had worked avidly to overthrow a neighbouring government can be attributed in part to the social standing of the exiles. Most were educated and affluent (or at least formerly affluent) persons of either aristocratic or bourgeois background. Rarely were these foreign agitators thought to pose a serious threat to the receiving country. Numerically insignificant, with few contacts in their new environs, it was hardly likely that exiles would stir up trouble in their temporary abode. Nor were refugees particularly interested in trying the patience of their hosts. Most were too concerned with re-establishing their revolutionary credentials back home, always planning, always hoping for decisive vindication. And for destination countries like Britain and France, the refugees seemed to embody the very core principles of liberal government now embraced by the political establishments in Paris and London. Exiles from lands controlled by the autocratic Turks and Russians, or by the absolutist Bishop of Rome in the case of central Italy, deserved at least a modicum of support from liberal states. After all, harbouring refugees rarely triggered diplomatic problems for the receiving kingdom. Requests for expulsion were occasionally honoured, but the surprising inability of central governments to identify and track down foreign residents was well known. Police had precious few resources on the detection front, and the public, at least, was rarely keen to assist in the apprehension of noted exiles who had overstayed their welcome.[8]

This exceptionally benign disposition toward political refugees began to give way in Europe during the last three decades of the nineteenth century, as the forces of militant nationalism, imperialism and state building transformed the political and ideological landscape. At the start of the Franco-Prussian War in 1870, 80,000 German residents were summarily expelled from France, and when a victorious Germany claimed the French-speaking province of Alsace-Lorraine as part of the spoils of war in 1871, 130,000 French vacated their homes rather than subject themselves to Bismarck's rule. And this was only the beginning of what quickly became a pattern of physical disruption. In the Balkans, where Ottoman authority was challenged repeatedly by nationalist insurgents, Christian and Muslim refugees criss-crossed newly established borders as a host of regional conflicts erupted prior to the outbreak of the First World War. Further north, in the wake of the assassination of Tsar Alexander II in 1881, thousands of Russian radicals were chased out of the Empire, and many of these political refugees were hardened conspirators who posed an acute problem for host governments which were committed to maintaining diplomatic relations with the reactionary regime of Alexander III.

GLOBAL WAR, DISPLACEMENT AND DENIAL

The catastrophe of the First World War, leaving in its wake some 10 million dead and another 20 million wounded and permanently disabled, generated a refugee crisis of extraordinary proportions within Europe and across the lands of the Middle East. The technology of total war, when combined with virulent nationalism, intruded its way into civilian life as never before, destroying the productive capacity of the enemy in a manner which drew no distinction between soldier and non-combatant. By the end of the conflict there were almost 9.5 million refugees in Europe, most of whom were concentrated in the East, and few of whom entertained any reasonable prospect of returning to the land of their birth unassisted. Whether they were former prisoners of war, conscripted labourers, exiles from Bolshevik Russia, Germans expelled from various parts of the continent, Poles scattered by the ravages of highly mobile armies, Armenians fleeing their Ottoman Turkish masters, or Balkan peasants forcibly removed by the majority ethnic and religious populations of their newly independent states, international mechanisms for dealing with the fate of involuntary migrants were tragically deficient.

The Armenian refugee catastrophe during the First World War stands out as the product of one of the most brutal state-sponsored and directed policies of the entire 1914–18 global conflagration. A Christian minority of about 2 million living in the Ottoman Turkish Empire, the Armenians had been able to maintain their cultural identity throughout more than 500 years of Muslim rule in Anatolia. With the advent of the traditionalist Sultan Abdul Hamid II in 1876, however, the condition of the Armenian community deteriorated precipitously. The Turkish Empire was in rapid decline by this date, with secessionist movements in the Balkans compounding a constant Russian threat to Ottoman power in the Black Sea region. Calls within the Armenian leadership for an independent state triggered a campaign of fierce persecution and, in the end, massacre.

Repeated attacks led to thousands of Armenians fleeing across international borders into Russia and Persia during the First World

War. Anticipating some of the features of the later Jewish Holocaust of the Second World War, the ramshackle Turkish state, now an ally of Germany, utilized new bureaucratic methods and ideological fervour to engage in the mass extermination of an entire religious community. It is now estimated that close to 1 million people, or about half the total Armenian population, was killed or died of starvation during 1915–16 alone. In late 1915 the Turkish Minister of the Interior, Talaat Bey, announced tersely that 'The Armenian question no longer exists.' Those fortunate enough to escape the violence made their way to the Caucasus in southern Russia or to Syria in the south-east.[9]

With the dismantling of the Ottoman Empire at the end of the war in 1918, an independent Armenian republic was established in the Transcaucasus, but within two years separate assaults by the new Soviet government to the north and by Kemal Ataturk's Republic of Turkey to the west succeeded in carving up the fledgling nation. Tens of thousands of refugees perished in the region during the fighting, many of them, particularly the young, victims of starvation and disease.[10] The victorious Allied forces, facing greater challenges in the rebuilding of war-torn Western Europe, simply abandoned the Armenians while Ataturk's government steadfastly denied that its Ottoman predecessor had ever engaged in an act of genocide. The abhorrent disclaimer continues to this day.

POST-WAR INTERNATIONAL AGREEMENTS

Multilateral treaties concluded at the end of the First World War were informed by the buoyant Wilsonian principle that people must be permitted to choose their national affiliation and move into newly established states without hindrance from government authorities. The spirit of the Versailles peace settlement intimated that individuals, not states, should define national allegiance. As the peacemakers at Versailles attempted to redraw the map of Europe along national and ethno-linguistic lines, the hope was that persons displaced by the war would now enjoy the opportunity to determine their political loyalty free from the coercive structures of the state in which they currently found themselves residing. And minorities who elected to remain within the borders of newly defined states were to be afforded equal civil and religious rights.

As we have seen, in 1921 the newly formed League of Nations created a special High Commission for Refugees. Under the leadership of Norwegian scientist and explorer Fridtjof Nansen, the Commission received no funding from the League but instead was expected to rely on philanthropic resources in order to carry out what was thought to be a temporary assignment. One of its primary tasks during the 1920s involved facilitating the movement of 'undocumented' refugees across Europe. Individual 'Nansen' passports and similar identification first became widespread requirements only after the start of the First World War. During the conflict international travel was sharply limited, of course, and in the immediate postwar era, border crossings occurred only at the sufferance of an expanding regime of state bureaucracies.[11]

Although Polish, Turkish, Russian and Balkan refugees continued to rely on the assistance of the Commission throughout the 1920s, Nansen and his associates were confident that the refugee problem would be resolved through growing international cooperation. The rise of xenophobic fascism during the 1930s, however, together with the failure of the United States to join the League of Nations, seriously undermined the efforts of the Commission. And the temporary ascendancy of the brutal fascist world-view in the late 1930s and early 1940s would constitute a dark preamble to one of the worst refugee crises in the human experience.

THE JEWISH TRAVAIL

The Nazis had no intention of furthering the refugee phenomenon as part of their drive to create a racially 'pure' state in the centre of Europe. Their design was to rid the world of the myriad errors of liberalism, democracy, individualism, internationalism, and conscience, and since all of these pernicious and debilitating innovations were attributed to the machinations of the Jews, the 'final solution' was elevated to the status of a holy mission. Under the Nazis, the efficiencies of modern science and technology were employed in the service of mass murder on a scale never before witnessed by civilized societies. Killing centres were established in Germany and within occupied lands, and Jews were rounded up with ruthless efficiency. Over 6 million would lose their lives before the horror was brought to a close by invading Soviet and Allied forces in May 1945. And for those who had eluded the death camps, removal and exile – the fate of so many Jews over the centuries – would conclude with the formation of a separate national home, a new nation state in a world of divisive nationalisms.

The idea of restoring the historic state of Israel was always framed within the context of bitter memories. The ancient Jewish diaspora is without much question the best known of the involuntary migrations within the Western context. With the leaders of Israel scattered by the conquering Assyrians in the eighth century BCE, the community of the faithful began a centuries-long experience of removal and relocation, a people who claimed affiliation with a specific place but who lived without a kingdom. The treatment of the Jews in the Roman Empire, despite the destruction of the Temple by Roman authorities in the first century CE, was relatively benign. The majority of the Jewish population lived outside the lands which the Romans renamed Syria Palestine, working as farmers, traders, artisans and businessmen in Alexandria, Rome and a host of other urban centres. They were left unhindered to pursue their faith as long as they paid homage to the rulers and gods of the Empire, but the collapse of Roman authority in the West and the emergence of the Catholic Church as the pre-eminent power in medieval Europe led to a sharp deterioration in the position of Jews as a minority population.

The intolerance of the medieval Church towards non-believers contrasted with the practice of most Muslim leaders in North Africa and the Middle East, lands where the majority of Jews lived in the centuries after the fall of Rome. Confident, prosperous, militarily strong, and sophisticated in both the sciences and philosophy, the Islamic lands were more comfortable with the presence of religious minorities in their midst, extracting special taxes and forbidding Jews to act in self-defence when attacked, but otherwise permitting them to live without hindrance. The same attitude toward 'the other' characterized the Germanic pagans who swept into lands formerly held by Rome, and where Jews had established themselves under Roman protection.[12] Unhappily, all of this changed with the consolidation of papal power in the eighth century.

Jewish traders and middlemen had helped to re-establish Europe's links with the much more prosperous eastern Mediterranean during the early Middle Ages, but an urban and commercial lifestyle made their communities easy targets for intolerant neighbours, especially when that intolerance was advocated by leaders of the Church in Rome. Christian monarchs maintained an ambiguous relationship with European Jews. Often dependent upon Jewish moneylenders, royal households normally felt obliged to protect this minority population from anti-Semitic mobs, but on occasion some leaders would seek to remedy their own debt status by expelling their creditors while using Jews as convenient scapegoats for their own mismanagement of the realm.

Such was the lot of England's Jewish community in 1290. During the era of the Crusades, Christian armies would often attack European Jews en route to their work against the Muslim infidel in the Holy Lands. Later, during the terrible plague of the fourteenth century, Jews were accused of designing and forwarding the spread of disease, and Church authorities did little to disabuse the general population of such malicious allegations. Disdain for and hostility toward Jews intensified across Europe, with one result being that non-Christians were forbidden to own land, serve in the military, enter guilds or participate in politics. Jews were marginalized into occupations which were considered to be immoral by Christian authorities and into neighbourhoods separate from the rest of the city population. The combination of religious hostility and economic exclusivity fostered the popular conception of the Jew as alien, as outsider, as disloyal in light of his commercial connections with co-religionists in other lands.

Two significant Jewish migrations took place at the start of our survey, one the result of deliberate state policy in Christian Spain and the other involving the movement of German Ashkenazic Jews eastward into Slavic Poland-Lithuania. Jews had resided and prospered in Spain since the time of the Roman Empire. When the Visigoth kings converted to Christianity, the economic and political position of the Jewish community deteriorated. It was thus with some sense of relief that Jews witnessed the successful invasion of Muslim armies into Spain during the early eighth century. Characterized by a cultural, artistic and intellectual renewal, especially between the tenth and thirteenth centuries, Muslim Spain afforded Jews the opportunity to extend their commercial contacts with the entire Mediterranean world while simultaneously inaugurating a remarkable intellectual flowering whereby texts from ancient Greece, the Middle East, and as far away as India were translated out of Arabic by Jewish scholars and into Latin for the benefit of later generations of poorly educated Europeans.[13]

In northern Spain, however, where small Christian kingdoms survived, a protracted *reconquista* against the Muslim settlements was inaugurated and continued until 1492, when at last the peninsula was united under the joint monarchy of Ferdinand of Aragon and Isabella of Castile. In that fateful year, Jews were ordered out of the kingdom as part of a larger effort to cleanse the realm of all who were not born into the Catholic fold. Even Jews who had converted to Roman Catholicism, the so-called *conversos*, were expelled. Those who refused to leave were denounced and some were burnt at the stake.[14] It was a self-inflicted policy blunder of enormous proportions, stripping the kingdom of its most enterprising population and providing Spain's Protestant enemies in England and Holland with the talents of hundreds of thousands of involuntary exiles. The Spanish or Sephardic Jews who scattered around Europe and the Mediterranean basin had been obliged by Spanish authorities to surrender their property and possessions at the moment of their exile, but they took with them their intellectual capital and soon became leaders in a host of new urban communities elsewhere.

Some of the Sephardic migrants settled in the Muslim Ottoman Empire, where they constituted 11 per cent of the population in Istanbul by the end of the fifteenth century. Initially, their Muslim overlords were tolerant of the recent migrants, affording them commercial opportunities and the right to engage in professions like medicine. But as Ottoman military power waned during the course of the seventeenth century, attitudes toward the Empire's minority non-Muslim populations also took a negative turn. The treatment of Jews within all the Islamic lands hardened as military and material conditions deteriorated, and as the majority of Jews lived under Muslim-dominated states until the nineteenth century, the status of those Jews who had remained in Christian Europe, or who had migrated to Europe, began to appear less offensive. Still separate from the majority Christian population in terms of residence, language, dress and demeanour, Jews nevertheless participated in the rapid economic and cultural development of a number of Western European kingdoms.

The French Revolution contributed to the process of secularization and civil equality irrespective of religion. In 1791 Jews were recognized as equal before the law, and Napoleon Bonaparte's regime extended this principle across Western Europe during the early nineteenth century. The French Constitution of 1793 offered asylum to foreigners who had been expelled from their country of birth 'for the cause of liberty'. By the mid-1800s political exclusion and cultural animosity were abating in some quarters, and Jewish assimilation into the emerging secular culture of the industrializing West proceeded apace. But considerable popular opinion still held a negative view of Jewish contributions to the nation state. And the nature of this popular disdain for the Jews changed during the course of the nineteenth century. Based largely upon religious belief and practice during the Middle Ages and Renaissance, hostility now began to take the form of contempt for ancestry, for 'racial' affiliation with Semites, irrespective of beliefs. Jewish converts to Christianity like the *conversos* in Spain, while once welcomed into the majority culture, were now excluded on the basis of lineage, or blood, irrespective of belief.[15]

REFUGEES FROM RUSSIA

When the Kingdom of Poland was erased from the political map of Europe in the late eighteenth century, Russia's portion of the carve-up included almost 800,000 Ashkenazic Jews, most of whom were the descendants of earlier migrants who had fled east in the wake of German intolerance. The addition of so many Jews to the Russian Empire was an unwelcome development, especially in light of the fact that Catherine the Great had issued a decree in 1727 banning Jews from the country. Russian officials now restricted Jews to their current locations in occupied Poland and to portions of southern Russia, areas collectively referred to as the pale of settlement. A programme of Russification was undertaken whereby Jews were conscripted into the military for thirty years, while the traditional long beards and long coats worn by males were forbidden. Four million Jews lived in Russian-controlled lands during the final quarter of the century, and most of these were concentrated in north-west and south-east sections of the unwieldy Empire: Belorussia, Lithuania, the Ukraine and Poland.[16]

Anti-Semitism remained a strong force among the bulk of Russian Orthodox population, and in the aftermath of the assassination of Alexander II in 1881, new waves of mob violence against Jews emerged, often with the complicity of local and national authorities. Strident nationalism had no place for those outside the ambit of Russian Orthodoxy: an escalating series of regulations designed to drive Jews away from the skilled professions and from the right to own land all contributed to the exodus. While never officially forced to leave their homeland by Russian authorities, the lives of Russian Jews were made extraordinarily difficult and their treatment capricious by the agents of the absolutist tsars. The indiscriminate assaults continued until the end of the Romanov autocracy in 1917. These pogroms led directly to one of the largest Jewish migrations in history. The bulk of the exiles, over 1.5 million, left for the United States between 1881 and 1914, at a time when migrants from eastern Europe to the US numbered almost 2 million.[17]

Anti-Jewish conduct was a distressing hallmark of other late-nineteenth century states, and as emigrants huddled in the major cities of Western Europe, the growing scale of the refugee phenomenon began to make its mark on popular consciousness.

The German imperial government showed no enthusiasm for the impoverished newcomers, encouraging their transport via German ports and aboard German-owned steamships to continue on to America. Even Britain, long the champion of open entry, passed the 1905 Alien Act which required refugees to demonstrate that their status was the product of persecution on religious or political grounds. Fortunately for the initial receiving countries in Western Europe, the problem of large numbers of poor migrants from the east did not oblige them to re-think national policy in a fundamental manner. So long as America remained open to all who could afford passage, the refugee issue was not a permanent dilemma requiring state action.

For the entire period 1880–1995, over 8 million Jews relocated from a variety of Christian and Muslim-dominated countries to the United States, to Western Europe, and to Palestine. Of this total, 2.4 million migrated between 1880 and the end of the First World War, 1.6 million between 1918 and 1948, and the remainder since the start of the Cold War.[18] Sixty-three per cent of all migrants in this final period, *c.* 1948–95, turned to the new state of Israel as their destination country, and the single largest sending area during this period was, not surprisingly, eastern Europe. Thirty-three per cent of all migrants to Israel left their birthplaces as a direct result of the Holocaust experience.

THE EMERGENCE OF ZIONISM

The Jewish communities of medieval Europe, North Africa and Babylon were not, by and large, united in their attachment to a lost homeland situated in Judea. This changed dramatically towards the end of the nineteenth century, however, as groups of Jews from eastern and central Europe began to settle in Ottoman-controlled Palestine. By the start of the First World War there were some 85,000 Jews in Palestine, or about 12 per cent of the total population.[19] Increasingly, Jewish identity was being associated no longer with shared customs and religious traditions, but pre-eminently with a specific territory, a development closely related to

193

the rise of nationalism across Western Europe at this time. In the view of the Zionist movement's leadership, Jewish efforts at assimilation in Europe and elsewhere had been repeatedly rebuffed, even in countries like republican France where the ideals of liberty, equality and fraternity were ostensibly part of the predominant political culture.

The leader of the Zionist movement in late nineteenth century Europe, Theodor Herzl, was a middle-class Viennese journalist. After reporting on the infamous Dreyfus Affair of 1894, where a Jewish army officer was wrongly accused of spying for Germany, Herzl came to the conclusion that European Jews needed to establish their own territorial homeland and refuge. While Western liberal states had afforded Jews both opportunities and protection, Zionists argued that the popular perception of them was both unpredictable and inherently distrustful. They also argued that formal citizenship rights in the countries of Western Europe did not compensate for the unease felt by many regarding their permanent status.

The leaders of the Zionist movement secured an important commitment in November 1917, when the British Foreign Secretary, Lord Balfour, issued a declaration calling for the establishment of Palestine as a national home for the Jews. But after having made pledges to both Arab nationalists and European Zionists during the war, the British took possession of Palestine for themselves and subsequently received mandate power from the League of Nations over the contested lands. Neither Arabs nor Jews were satisfied with this situation, and while the British did not discourage European Jews from migrating to the area after the war, living conditions were quite difficult and levels of return migration to Europe were very high. There was little expectation on the part of British authorities that large numbers of Jews would migrate to such difficult environs. In 1932 only 9,500 had relocated to Palestine, but with the emergence of state-sponsored anti-semitism in Germany during the 1930s, the numbers continued to grow until by 1940 there were half a million Jews settled on the land.

Communal farms called *kibbutzim* emerged between the two World Wars, while agricultural productivity made steady advances.

Modern factories were built and Tel Aviv began to emerge as a thriving economic centre. Although Jews were still a minority, Arab nationalists viewed overall British policy as a direct threat to their land. Supporters and financiers of the Zionist enterprise argued throughout the 1920s and 1930s that Jewish presence represented a progressive and democratic influence in the region, but frustrated Palestinians interpreted developments within the context of a wider system of Western colonialism and imperialism, one characterized by the imposition of unwanted Europeans on indigenous peoples in distant lands.[20] Solicitous of Arab support on the eve of the Second World War, Britain declared that further Jewish migration would be restricted, and that within ten years an independent Palestine with equal rights and protections for both populations would be established. The Second World War pre-empted this and all other plans, and in the wake of the Holocaust a new sense of urgency surrounded the status of Europe's remaining Jews.

The Holocaust eliminated the main centres of Jewish life in eastern and central Europe and permanently reconfigured the focus of Jewish settlement during the second half of the twentieth century. Over 3 million Jews lived in Poland before the Second World War, but by the late twentieth century that number had plummeted to around 10,000. The mass murder which took place in Poland during the war was followed by renewed outbreaks of anti-semitism after 1945 in the wake of the Soviet decision to appoint Jews to many important political posts both in Poland and elsewhere. Most of those who left their homelands after 1950 relocated to Israel, and this was generally true of migrant Jews from other Soviet-dominated Eastern Bloc countries.

DISPUTED HOMELAND

The founding of the independent State of Israel in 1948 stands as a powerful modern example of one diaspora that has been successful in its efforts to secure a territorial homeland, but at the very high price of displacing others. In one respect the founding of the Jewish state can be seen as an ingathering of those who had for centuries been part of an involuntary victim diaspora, providing an essential refuge for the remnants of European Jewry while also absorbing Jewish populations who were living a precarious existence within the borders of Arab countries. From a different point of view, Jewish settlement in Palestine involved the unilateral and unwelcome colonization of lands already occupied by Muslim inhabitants.

After the defeat of Hitler, many Arabs interpreted talk of an independent Jewish state as little more than old-style European imperialism, now reinforced by the military and financial might of the United States. Riots and terrorist attacks marked the final period of British rule in Palestine (1945–8), with both Jews and Muslims engaging in acts of indiscriminate violence against one another. Declaring an independent state immediately after the British withdrawal in May 1948, Israeli forces swiftly and surprisingly defeated an Arab coalition whose aim was to destroy the fledgling state. In the wake of that capitulation, some 1 million Muslims were expelled from Palestine by Israeli authorities, creating an enormous refugee problem in the region and fuelling a legacy of hatred and distrust between neighbours.

With strong support from the United States, Israel was able to consolidate its hold on the contested land, but the continual displacement of Palestinians in the wake of subsequent regional conflicts served to harden animosities between the Israelis and the 'stateless' Palestinians. In 1950, a special UN Agency, the United Nations Relief and Works Agency for Palestinian Refugees in the Near East, was created, and it continued to offer relief services to the Palestinian communities at the end of the century. In 1999 the agency had registered 3.5 million Palestinians as refugees in the West Bank, Gaza, Jordan, Lebanon and Syria.

The majority of the founders of the new State of Israel, while favouring the notion that citizenship should be descent-based, were secular Jews from eastern Europe and Russian lands who viewed migration to Palestine as an opportunity for freedom and economic opportunity. In this outlook they were much like the vast majority of pre-war Jewish migrants who had opted for the United States as the appropriate place for achieving these largely secular goals. Still, the fact that citizenship rights were immediately extended to immigrant Jews under Israel's 'Law of Return', while Palestinians who had been residents long before the founding of the new state only grudgingly received these same rights, contributed enormously to the ongoing international debate about the proper place of this diaspora homeland in the international community.[21]

And for most Jews living in the West (and more than half the world's Jews outside Israel live in the USA, the UK and France), the Zionist invitation to join with co-religionists in a territorial homeland was not compelling enough to abandon their adopted countries. The goal of assimilation into the political, educational and professional culture of the secular West was exceptional, especially for Jews living in the United States, even in light of much discrimination. For many of these women and men, Jewish identity did not include a particular national and territorial allegiance, but instead centred on the idea of religious and cultural difference within one polity. Given the treatment of Jews within majority Christian cultures over the centuries, such a stand was a bold affirmation of the principle that diasporic communities, and cultural identity, could flourish within diverse cultures; that identity could be 'deterritorialized'.[22]

Even with the establishment of a national homeland in the mid-twentieth century, then, the majority of the world's 10 million Jews continue to live in diasporic communities. And today the overwhelming majority of Jews live in just five countries: Israel, Britain, France, Russia and the United States. The minority status of Jews (excepting the Jews in Israel) has long been a feature of their cultural identity. There are more Jews living in the US than in Israel, for example, but the almost 6 million American Jews represent just 2 per cent of the total population. Not only are the Jews unique by virtue of the fact that the diasporic community is larger than the population of the historic homeland, but the principal receiving area has shifted repeatedly over time. At different periods the largest concentration of involuntary migrants could be found in Muslim lands, at another time in Christian eastern Europe, and most recently in North America.[23]

The overall global population profile of Jews since the 1970s has been flat, with near zero population growth worldwide but significant population growth within Israel due to the migration process. In fact, over the last fifty years Israel has emerged as one of the most prominent countries of destination for international migrants.[24] In 1990, over 30 per cent of the nation's population was foreign-born. Only in the United States and in Western Europe did the size of the Jewish population remain stable; thus if a general pattern can be identified, it would reflect a movement away from less developed areas of settlement (North Africa, the Arab Middle East, eastern Europe, the Soviet Union and Asia) and towards more economically developed and politically democratic areas. During the seven year period 1989–96, more than 1 million Jews migrated from the Soviet Union. Three-quarters of this total, or about 690,000 migrants, settled in Israel, with the United States receiving the second largest number (around 270,000).[25] Israel's sweeping 1950 'Law of Return' allowing for unrestricted immigration, full citizenship rights and even material assistance for Jews regardless of their national origins, clearly had a decisive impact on the demographic profile of the Middle East.

One distinguishing factor of migration to Israel over the last fifty years has been its family or household unit character. The relocation of entire families, sometimes including three generations, represented a deep commitment on the part of the migrant to permanent relocation. The usual pattern of unattached males seeking employment opportunities in a foreign country, with the ultimate goal of return migration, has not been operative in the Israeli experience. Another special feature involved the varied sending backgrounds – cultural, linguistic, social – of the migrant populations. While it is a myth to view migration to the new state after 1948 as one in which Jews from around the world packed up and relocated on ideological grounds (in fact those who came to Israel were overwhelmingly Holocaust survivors and those who were prevented from entering Palestine during the Second World War by British authorities), still the refugees brought with them varied experiences from eastern and central Europe.

With the influx of so many Jews from the former Soviet Union after 1990, the question of reception in the host country emerged as an important issue. Unlike any other modern nation state, Israel faced an ongoing challenge with respect to reception and assimilation. As a nation of migrants where citizenship is open to all Jews irrespective of national origins, social and ethnic divisions between Jews of American or Western European origin (Ashkenazim) and those who hail from Asia and Africa (mostly Sephardim) are substantial, with the former group enjoying primacy in both the economic and political life of the nation. The number of Soviet Jews who arrived in Israel in the single year 1990 was 200,000, equalling the total for the entire period since independence in 1948.[26] Many Arab leaders feared that the large influx of Jews from the former Soviet Union would serve to reinforce the exclusive Jewish character of Israel, exacerbating an already considerable separation between the two communities and preventing the possibility of fashioning an Israeli identity which transcended the religious divide, a state for all citizens instead of one dedicated primarily to the advancement of Jewish interests. Arabs also feared that additional Jewish settlements would be established in the occupied territories while Jewish migrants would replace Arab workers in the construction and service trades. These considerable differences frustrated all efforts to secure a political settlement in the region by the close of the century, leaving extremists on both sides with inordinate power to shape public policy.

POSTWAR DILEMMAS

Refugee migration across international borders became more frequent in the world's developing countries with the close of the Second World War and the start of the Cold War. Internal civil conflict precipitated by clashing Cold War ideologies, together with heightened ethnic divisions, contributed to the displacement of millions of people in Africa, Central America, the Middle East and in South-East Asia. When joined with unanticipated natural disasters and the technical inability of developing countries to address these crises in a timely fashion, the involuntary flight across borders, usually to neighbouring countries with similarly inadequate resources, fuelled a debilitating cycle of political and economic failure in poorly developed regions of the globe.[27] Since the 1950s, over 95 per cent of refugee movements have originated in the developing world. And neighbouring states, particularly in Africa, were often reluctant to accept political and economic refugees, since the target country often faced similar economic problems and feared an escalation of ethnic conflict should new, ethnically diverse populations begin to take up residence in countries already struggling with a host of economic and political difficulties.[28]

Certain general trends can be readily identified in refugee migration since the end of the Second World War. Clearly the Cold War rivalry between the Western powers and the Soviet Union involved a number of developing states in proxy wars and civil conflicts. Korea, Vietnam, Angola, Somalia, Cuba, Nicaragua – in these states and in others like them, superpower rivalry contributed to militarization, internal conflict and the destabilization of society, with the usual outflow of refugees seeking protection from the devastating impact of civil war. As refugee numbers escalated from 5 million in the early 1970s to over 20 million at the start of the twenty-first century, wealthy nations, often directly or indirectly responsible for much of the suffering endured by asylum seekers, sought to draw a distinction between 'political' and 'economic' refugees, denying the latter entry into rich countries. But since civil conflict normally led to impovershment for many, the line between political and economic precipitants to migration was often blurred. Prior to the collapse of the Soviet Union, eastern Europeans who managed to make their way to the West were categorized as political refugees; during the 1990s their status changed to the less-welcome one of economic migrant. The same re-classification occurred with respect to Vietnamese fleeing their homeland before and after 1975.

The grey area between political and economic refugees has been highlighted by recent adumbrations of the original 1951 United Nations' Convention Relating to the Status of Refugees. That document, agreed to by 134 nations at the close of the twentieth century, limited the definition of refugee to a fairly narrow band of human rights abuses. A much broader interpretation was offered by the Organization of African Unity (OAU) in 1969, when the definition of refugee was extended to individuals who fled their country because of external aggression, occupation, foreign domination, or events disturbing public order in a significant manner. This more inclusive definition clearly better reflected the post-colonial realities in many sub-Saharan states. And in 1984, representatives from a number of South American states issued the Cartagena Declaration, ascribing refugee status to anyone fleeing generalized violence and/or international conflict.[29]

DIVIDED SOUTH AND SOUTH-EAST ASIA

The end of the Second World War ushered in the age of colonial independence movements around the globe. Europe's political hold over peoples and land in Africa, the Middle East and South Asia was successfully challenged by indigenous elites who demanded the implementation of the ideal of political self-determination as it had been articulated by the opponents of fascism during the War. But the realization of independence from Europe was rarely marked by a new dawn of economic success and cultural understanding. Quite the reverse was the case in many areas, as economic hardship and ethnic and religious strife made the challenges facing fledgling states almost intractable. One by-product of this instability was a dramatic rise in refugee crises after 1945.

The first significant overseas migration in Vietnamese history occurred as a direct result of French and American involvement in the affairs of South-East Asia. French colonial occupation of Vietnam began in the second half of the nineteenth century and continued until 1940 when the Japanese seized all of Indochina. At the close of the war in 1945 a Communist national resistance movement led by Ho Chi Minh declared Vietnam an independent state, but the French, with subsequent British and American support, refused to relinquish their colonial claims. A thirty-year military conflict ensued, with Communist forces effectively employing guerrilla tactics first against the French, and then, by the mid-1960s, against the Americans and their South Vietnamese surrogates. Before the fighting was concluded in 1975, upwards of 3 million North and South Vietnamese soldiers and civilians had died.

The initial Communist takeover of North Vietnam in 1945 had triggered the migration of almost 1 million people by the time that the country was officially partitioned in 1954. Most of those who journeyed south were Catholics escaping state-imposed land collectivization and religious persecution.[30] Subsequent United States involvement in the protracted military conflict with the North led to an enormous internal refugee crisis, with as many as 4 million peasants fleeing to the cities during the 1960s and early 1970s.

In the final days of the Vietnam war, as the government of the Republic of Vietnam collapsed and Communist forces pushed their way into the capital of Saigon, an estimated 135,000 Vietnamese, mostly military personnel and government officials and their families, desperately fled their homeland. The United States airlifted around 35,500, while the rest set off for American offshore naval vessels or to neighbouring countries in small and often unseaworthy boats.[31] Virtually all these initial refugees were eventually resettled in the United States. The less fortunate – some 1.5 million soldiers, police, and government officials of the now defunct South Vietnamese state, were sent to 're-education camps' by the victorious Communists, there to repent for their political errors under very harsh conditions.[32]

A centralized command economy was imposed on South Vietnam by the Communists, and coupled with an American economic embargo and the high cost of a military clashes with neighbouring China and Cambodia, unified Vietnam ranked as one of the poorest societies in the world during the late 1970s and early 1980s. Faced with rapidly deteriorating conditions, hundreds of thousands of additional Vietnamese peasants fled the country by boat, sailing long distances under terrible conditions in hopes of resettlement in a non-communist country. The exodus reached its height between the years 1978 and 1982. Travelling distances ranged from a few hundred to

5,000 miles in small, overcrowded, unsafe boats, and, facing attack from Vietnamese patrols and pirates at sea, thousands lost their lives before reaching asylum. The majority of the 'boat people' sailed directly to Hong Kong, the Philippines, Indonesia, Thailand and Malaysia. In some instances, the Thai and Malaysian authorities refused to allow the refugees to land, towing their boats back out into international waters. Those who did manage to disembark lingered in detention camps pending a final determination of their status.

In 1979, the United Nations High Commissioner for Refugees agreed a plan with the Vietnamese government for the orderly resettlement of boat people. The majority of these Vietnamese eventually found refuge in the United States, with smaller numbers accepted by Australia, Canada and Western European states. An additional 190,000 refugees from Laos and 130,000 from Cambodia also reached the camps and were accepted by the United States.[33] In 1987, the United States and Vietnam signed an agreement whereby former prisoners who had been confined to 'reeducation centres' for at least three years could emigrate to America and receive relocation assistance from the receiving country. Finally, in 1989, with receiving countries arguing that increasing numbers of Vietnamese asylum seekers were in fact economic migrants and not legitimate refugees, a United Nation Conference in Geneva established a more rigorous screening process and a programme of repatriation to Vietnam.

There were but a few thousand South-East Asians in the United States before 1975, but over the course of the next twenty years approximately 1.32 million persons from Vietnam, Cambodia and Laos (all areas impacted by America's military involvement in South-East Asia) came to live in the United States. Almost all of the Vietnamese settlers, some 700,000 out of 900,000, arrived as refugees who feared persecution for their political activities or affiliations prior to the Communist victory. Most of the refugees left everything behind, including friends and material possessions, and had no US destination in mind when they quickly left their homeland.

Reception in the United States was often inhospitable. As the nation principally responsible for the myriad hardships endured by the Vietnamese during the war, many Americans believed that the United States had a special responsibility to facilitate the transition of refugees to American life. Public assistance programmes were established which afforded the newcomers language and job training, health coverage and modest living expenses. But while many Americans believed that their country had a moral obligation to welcome the refugees, others resented these symbols of a failed foreign policy and an unpopular war which had claimed the lives of 58,000 American soldiers.[34] Upon their arrival in the United States at the end of the conflict, the government attempted to disperse the refugees across the country, as churches, families, and voluntary organizations led resettlement efforts. But eventually the overwhelming majority of the newcomers settled in California, with additional large communities resident in major cities like Washington, DC, Seattle, Houston and Chicago.

For the refugees, attachment to a new national home often involved conflicting sentiments. While grateful for their rescue, refugees often felt that their host country had abandoned the war effort, paving the way for the Communist takeover and the disastrous political and economic policies which ensued.[35] Refugee connections with kinsmen in Vietnam remain strong, despite the circumstances under which most people departed. One refugee recalled that while the United States offered material comforts, 'the joy and sentiment are not like we had in Vietnam. There . . . we had many relatives and friends to come to see us at home. Here in America, I only know what goes on in my home; my neighbour knows only what goes on in his home. . . .'[36] At the close of the twentieth century remittances from America to relatives still living in Vietnam total almost $1 billion annually.

In India, independence from Britain in August 1947 was followed by armed conflict and enormous human suffering in the north-east of the new country. Here Muslim nationalists declared a separate state of Pakistan, and the resulting communal violence was without precedent in the history of the subcontinent. Two provinces, Bengal in the north-east and Pubjab in the north-west, were divided between the two newly sovereign states, and as Muslims in India and Hindus in Pakistan fled to join their respective nations, over half a million were killed in 1948 alone. By the middle of that year, an estimated 5 million Hindu and Sikh refugees had arrived in India, and almost the same number of Muslims were seeking protection in Pakistan.

The refugees felt compelled to leave their homelands from fear of communal and religious violence; the very resort to cultural distinctiveness which Nehru and the secularist leaders of the Indian National Congress had hoped to erase. Again in 1971, as tensions between East and West Pakistan escalated, over 10 million refugees fled East Pakistan into India. The resulting refugee crisis was one factor contributing to the outbreak of war between India and Pakistan in that year. With the establishement of Bangladesh in the aftermath of the conflict, most of the refugees returned home, but only after placing enormous strains on the infrastructure of India's Bengal province.[37]

Like the Muslims of Pakistan and Jews of Israel, India's Sikh community often viewed itself as a nation, an ethnic group and a religious community deserving a separate national identity. Founded in the early sixteenth century by Guru Nanak (1469–1539), Sikhism represents a synthesis of the Hindu and Muslim traditions, rejecting caste and later adopting a martial component designed to protect the faithful in the face of Mughal persecution. Situated in the northern Punjab, Sikh leaders managed to establish a region of influence under declining Mughal hegemony until 1845, when British forces overwhelmed the defenders of the Punjab. In the aftermath many Sikh fighters were put into the employ of the British overseas forces, fighting in the service of the crown around the world. But their efforts, particularly on the Western Front during the First World War, were poorly rewarded. In 1919 in the Sikh capital at Amritsar, protests against new British taxes triggered mob violence against British interests. Crown forces responded by firing upon unarmed civilians trapped in the Golden Temple, the holiest of sites in the Sikh community. It was a bloody end to decades of fairly cooperative relations with the British crown.[38]

Since Indian Independence in 1948, Sikhs have sought to advance the call for a separate homeland (which they have named Khalistan) within the political arena, while simultaneously soliciting support from Sikh migrant communities in Britain, Canada and the United States. But when the leaders of a separatist movement were accused by the Indian government in 1984 of stockpiling weapons at the Golden Temple, the facility was stormed by Indian troops and 700 defenders were killed. Three months later, in a dramatic and tragic revenge attack, Sikh bodyguards assassinated the Indian Prime Minister, Mrs Indira Gandhi. Widespread communal violence and acts of terrorism resulted, including a June 1985 terrorist attack against an Air India jumbo jet which killed 329 passengers and crew off the south-west coast of Ireland.

The vast majority of Sikhs around the world were repulsed by such tactics, and in recent years political moderates have recommitted themselves to enhancing the common identity of Sikh communities around the world, all in an ongoing effort to win political recognition for a special territorial state in the Punjab. Should they eventually succeed in their efforts, Sikhs would be faced with reconciling the existence of a state where citizenship is predicated on descent in a territory where the majority of the indigenous population are not Sikhs. It would be a situation not unlike the dilemma confronting Israel in its dealings with the indigenous Palestinian population.

CRISES IN AFRICA

In 1990 there were an estimated 5 million refugees in sub-Saharan Africa, an enormous figure which, if accurate, placed 1 per cent of the entire population in a situation where flight from famine, civil war, ethnic conflict and/or authoritarian rule defined their immediate life situations.[39] There is not much question that Africa today is home to the world's largest refugee population; perhaps as many as every second refugee in the world today is displaced somewhere in an African country, and as often as not the refugee is in flight from one impoverished land to another.[40] During the final two decades of the century, for example, civil war and war-induced famine made refugees of 4 million Sudanese from the south of the country, but similar tragedies have affected others in the Horn of Africa.

Independent African states have struggled with very limited success to create stable democratic societies in the post-colonial era. Sweeping promises made by the first generation of democratically elected indigenous leaders could not be fulfilled in pre-industrial economies where population increases outstripped the ability of producers to maintain adequate supplies of food. State-controlled economies (a reaction against the 'capitalism' of colonial rulers) and the focus on single cash crops for export placed many sub-Saharan economies at the mercy of an unpredictable international market. As economies slumped in the 1980s, foreign investment shrank and debt multiplied. By 1990 Africa had experienced at least seventy military coups, but the trend towards strong-man military rule and dictatorship did little to improve the material conditions of the citizenry. Sadly, the decades of bi-polar Cold War encouraged the rise to power of client dictators like Mobutu Sese Seko of Congo and Samuel Doe of Liberia, grasping tyrants who enjoyed the backing of the United States prior to 1990. Endemic poverty, low life expectancy, illiteracy, and more recently the ravages of the AIDs epidemic all combined to forward cross-border migration throughout the continent.

During the near half-century Cold War, 'development' assistance to poor countries in Africa often meant little more than a boon for the military and political elites, while military involvement in surrogate conflicts at the behest of the Cold War principals guaranteed continued poverty and political instability for the inhabitants of 'receiving' nations. Instead of economic assistance aimed at enhancing the material circumstances of the indigenous population, the Cold War policies of the Soviets and Americans actually stimulated migration outflow, often in the form of unskilled and impoverished refugees. Africa is home to one-tenth of the world's population but as many as half its total refugee population. Most African migrants have fled their place of birth due to political and ethnic conflicts which often have their roots in the colonial experience.

Incapable of establishing diverse and stable economies due to continued Western domination of trade, more than a few fragile post-colonial democracies in Africa have over the past fifty years degenerated into military regimes. Those refugees fortunate enough to escape make their way, not surprisingly, to the former colonial powers: Zairians to Belgium, Senegalese to France and Nigerians to Britain.[41] With the advent of commercial air transport, many of the asylum seekers are able to present themselves before immigration officials very soon after crises emerge in their home countries. Not a few arrive on tourist or other forms of temporary visas.

But admission standards often remain tied to political and foreign policy agendas, and Africa's lack of strategic importance to the developed Western powers meant that relatively few asylum seekers were admitted. In the United States, the Immigration and Nationality Act of 1965 had failed to address the problem of refugees and asylum seekers, leaving this issue to the Executive branch of government in general and to the United States Attorney General in particular. The result was that the awarding of refugee status became closely linked to foreign policy priorities. During the Cold War, for example, refugee status was generously awarded to Cubans, Nicaraguans and Vietnamese who were anti-communists, but denied to those fleeing civil conflict during the 1980s in places like El Salvador and Guatemala, where the US government unflinchingly backed autocratic anti-communist regimes irrespective of their human rights records.

DIASPORA AT CENTURY'S CLOSE

The word 'diaspora' has in recent decades taken on a negative and sinister connotation, one very far removed from the ancient Greek idea of simple migration and colonization. Today the plight of Palestinian and African refugees is linked with the earlier banishment of Armenians from Ottoman Turkey, black slaves sold into bondage and destined for the Americas, and, in the ancient world, the forcible removal of Jews from their Promised Land in 586 BCE. Diaspora does not connote volition on the part of migrants; these communities are involuntary formations, victims of some larger moral infraction, often unwelcome additions to one of the almost 200 member states of the United Nations.[42] Cut off from their ethnic and territorial roots, their sense of self-identity could only be preserved through the careful maintenance of an intellectual and cultural tradition.

In Africa, in the Balkans, and in Afghanistan, refugee disasters born of national, linguistic, ethnic and religious hatred seem to have returned the global community to the ideological climate of the century which defined the beginning of this survey. The sixteenth-century wars of religion in Western Europe, the Sikh-Muslim conflict in India, the unilateralist attitude of *conquistadores* toward the native peoples of the Americas, the inter-ethnic wars of acephalous African tribes during the pre-colonial era – all resonated at the close of the twentieth century in the terrible bifurcation of peoples into categorical absolutes, into exclusive communities animated by an intense disdain for differences.

Data from the late twentieth century was deeply disturbing. During the 1950s and 1960s, around 2.5 million people qualified as refugees under the standards set by the United Nations. This figure increased to 15 million in 1989 and exceeded 23 million in 1994. Eighty per cent of these refugees were women and children. And at the end of the century, the main precipitant to involuntary relocation was conflict-related. In 1995 alone, for example, nineteen of the twenty biggest refugee sending countries were experiencing some form of armed civil disturbance. Over 90 per cent of all war-related deaths during the 1990s involved civilian non-combatants, often children.[43] Poorer nations in which the internal political, economic and social fabric had broken down, and where civil war resulted, were the most likely sending areas, while the typical response of developed nations was to better secure their own borders against unwanted migrants.

In sub-Saharan Africa, the stain of ethnic cleansing, genocidal murder, and a refugee crisis on a scale not seen since the Nazi holocaust took place in the tiny twin states of Rwanda and Burundi in the spring of 1994. As in so many crises of the late twentieth century, a background of overpopulation combined with land and resource depletion, provided ample opportunity for 'scapegoating' and military conflict. Tiny Rwanda, which had secured its independence from Belgium in 1962, was the most densely populated country in Africa by the early 1990s. The partition of farmland had reached a point where average farm size was insufficient to maintain cattle and feed a growing population. The resulting economic hardships were used by political elites to focus the animosity of the country's majority Hutu population against the Tutsi ruling elite.

Inter-ethnic differences between the two peoples were long-standing. In the first two years of independence, for example, ethnic clashes had led to the flight of over 60,000 Tutsi into neighbouring Burundi, while in 1988 Tutsi reprisals against Hutu attacks had led to the transit of some 100,000 Hutus into Rwanda and Zaire.[44] When a plane carrying the presidents of Rwanda and Burundi was shot down in April 1994 as they were returning from a peace conference in Tanzania, Hutu members of the presidential guard began indiscriminate attacks on Tutsis and Hutu moderates. A Hutu-controlled radio station encouraged the violence with racist propaganda, and before the genocide had ended, more than 800,000 Tutsi residents: men, women, children and infants, were dead. When the Tutsi eventually prevailed in the subsequent fighting, over 2 million Hutus were forced into exile in neighbouring Zaire.[45] Repatriation began in 1997, but not before Tutsi citizens of Zaire, resentful at the influx of Hutu refugees into their country, toppled their own dictator, President Mobutu Sese Seko. The inaction of the international community during this tragedy led to charges of indifference to massive human suffering when it involved people of colour who were poor. Perhaps the charge was unjust, especially given Europe's halting response to comparable behaviour on the Balkan peninsula.[46]

With the break-up of Yugoslavia in the early 1990s, the six successor states rejected the multi-ethnic compromise achieved after the Second World War under Josip Broz Tito and instead struggled to create culturally homogeneous territories. Internal labour migration had been promoted under the Tito regime, with the result that a good deal of ethnic and residential mixing had taken place within Bosnia-Herzegovina, Croatia, Macedonia, Montenegro, Serbia and Slovenia. All this was reversed in a few short years as the Communist regime imploded and the forces of ethnic nationalism took centre stage.

Slovenia was the first province to win its independence, but when Croatia followed this precedent in 1992, the Serb-dominated federal army of Yugoslavia intervened in order to protect the Serb minority living in the region. 130,000 Serbs eventually fled Croatian-controlled lands, while over 300,000 Croatians departed from their homes in Serb-dominated sectors before a UN-brokered ceasefire was established. Croatia eventually succeeded in its quest, but in 1992, when tiny Bosnia-Herzegovia declared independence from the shrinking Yugoslav state, resistance to the action by the minority (33 per cent) Serb population took on a brutal character and inaugurated the bloodiest conflict in Europe since the end of the Second World War.

While Muslims and Croats were in the majority in Bosnia-Herzegovina, the respective Serb, Muslim and Croat populations were largely mixed in a patchwork of neighbouring communities. After the independence declaration, Serbs – with the assistance of Serb-dominated Yugoslavia – called for their own government and began a process of 'ethnic cleansing' in an effort to create a secure territory. The authoritarian Serbian President, Slobodan Milosevic, endorsed this vicious campaign, which culminated in the bombing of Sarajevo and the massacre of 6,000 Bosnians (mostly Muslims) in the town of Srebrenica in 1995. Three years later, and this time within Serbia itself, over 850,000 ethnic Albanians in the Kosovo region were forced to flee their homes in the wake of another Milosevic-inspired 'ethnic cleansing' campaign.[47] Throughout the course of the 1990s hundreds of thousands of refugees flooded out of the war-torn region, creating a significant resettlement crisis and also raising disturbing doubts about the ability of Europe and the United States to act collectively in the face of massive war crimes.

For the first time in its history the UNHCR was asked to provide humanitarian assistance within a country accused of persecuting its own citizens. In theory, refugees were now to be protected before they fled their homeland. In the end, close to 4 million people were forced from their homes as a result of the wide-ranging and bloody conflict, and almost half of these became refugees in Western Europe. Tragically, ethnic and religious conflict plunged south-eastern Europe into the largest refugee crisis since the end of the Second World War, and the legacy of hatred and bitterness created by the atrocities of the 1990s boded ill for the future of the region. When the Kosovar Albanians returned to their homes afer a 79-day NATO bombing campaign against Serbia forced Milosevic to remove his troops, they immediately took revenge on the Kosovar Serbs who had once been their neighbours.

In Central Asia, the Afghan experience reinforced the strong connection between Cold War politics and the refugee phenomenon. It is estimated that in the wake of the 1979 Soviet invasion of Afghanistan, over 6 million inhabitants (one-third of the country's total population) fled, with the majority of displaced persons taking up residence in neighbouring Pakistan. For many the experience of exile woud last up to ten years. United States military aid to Pakistan increased sharply at this point, and Afghan guerrilla fighters used the refugee camps as bases for recruitment and training. With the Russian withdrawal in 1992, however, aid to the refugees evaporated, and the massive problem of repatriation was left without solution. The rise to power of the fundamentalist Taliban in the mid-1990s triggered another great outpouring of refugees from the country. By the end of the century, Afghanistan claimed the distinction of being the principal refugee sending state, with most of the 2.5 million who fled in 1999 finding refuge in India, Pakistan and Iran. An American and British bombing campaign against the Taliban in late 2001 compounded the already desperate situation of the civilian population.

Since its inception in 1950, the Office of the United Nations High Commissioner for Refugees sought first to enable refugees to return to their homeland under conditions which would allow them freedom from fear of persecution. This was a practical mandate so long as the Commission's charge involved Europeans displaced during the course of the Second World War. But as the ambit of the agency's duties widened during the 1960s, and as Cold War rivalries made repatriation more difficult, alternative models emerged. In particular, the practice of settling refugees in neighbouring states, or countries of 'first asylum', has been employed both for reasons of economy and in hopes that the host populations will share linguistic or cultural traditions with the newcomers.

The most expensive and logistically most difficult option involved relocation to a third country, where the refugee faced a range of impediments to assimilation and success. At the end of the century, however, most refugees around the world had at best secured temporary or provisional rights to settlement outside their homeland. In the year 2000, the United Nations High Commissioner for Refugees listed over 22 million persons of concern to the international community, up from 15 million one decade earlier, and projected to rise again in the immediate future.

Forced return of refugees had been prohibited under the 1950 Convention, but the problem of resettlement in a world of nation states with restrictive immigration regimes guaranteed that the work of the international community would remain both frustrating and, in some cases, futile. The admonition in Exodus 22:21: 'Do not mistreat or oppress a foreigner, remember that you were foreigners in Egypt' had failed to trump the nationalist imperatives of the territorial state. While the non-binding United Nations Universal Declaration of Human Rights states that every person 'has the right to seek and to enjoy in other countries asylum from persecution', the granting remained within the purview of each individual member state.

Some critics have argued that the Bosnian precedent, where the United Nations High Commissioner for Refugees attempted to provide relief assistance before a refugee situation unfolded, actually signalled the unwillingness of UN member nations to accept potential victims of persecution. Supporters of the initiative, on the other hand, argued in favour of the policy's foward-looking attempt to address injustices before persons are forced to flee, in the process securing the triumph of the internationalist agenda on human rights over the traditional sovereignty claims of the nation state. Neither position has satisfied the victims of forced removal, whose dilemma at the start of a new century dwarfed all previous refugee experiences.

CONCLUSION

Emerging Patterns in a New Century

A number of broad generalizations can be made about international migration flows at the start of the new century. As one observer has recently noted, there appear to be four distinct features of current migration. The first involves the role of communications and transport. Images – often distorted – of affluent societies are now accessed instantaneously by residents of developing states, while relatively cheap long-distance transport makes the lure of the modern urban lifestyle difficult to resist. Regular transatlantic jet services only began in 1958, but by 1970, with the introduction of jumbo commercial aircraft, relatively low-cost movement across international borders transformed patterns of personal mobility.[1] The second feature is associated with the drawing down of legal and bureaucratic impediments to international travel in lands formerly under the control of the massive Soviet Empire. As many as 450 million people in the old Eastern Bloc are now potential international migrants, and the number could grow exponentially should China begin to relax its controls over travel. A third factor influencing migration is the power of atavistic nationalism and ethnic exclusivism in some newly formed states. The multiple tragedies related to the 'ethnic cleansing' of the 1990s in the former Yugoslavia represent the most gruesome illustration of this development. Finally, the prominence of 'rights language' in many democratic and affluent receiving nations in the West has spurred the emergence of influential lobbies on behalf of particular migrant and refugee populations, directing the issue of movement across international borders on to the international humanitarian and human rights stage.[2]

AN AGGREGATE PERSPECTIVE

Given the enormous social and economic disparities between sending and receiving countries today, the actual size of international migration flows is still quite modest. Despite alarmist views of migration patterns at the start of the new century, total international migration in the early 1990s was quite small, about 2 per cent, in relation to the world's population.[3] And where movement across borders does occur, it remains largely a regional affair. The vast majority of the 9 million former Soviet citizens who have relocated since 1989, for example, have done so within the borders of the former Soviet state, and the same pattern of regional movement can be observed in Africa and Latin America.[4] And where there is international migration, most of it involves nations which are either contiguous or comparatively close to one another. The United States takes in migrants from around the world, but this model is still the exception.

More people move longer distances today than at any time in the past, but this must be understood within the context of modern transport combined with the knowledge that the world's population is larger. The fact remains that most persons remain fixed in the lands of their birth; international migration remains an exceptional option for most of the world's population. To date, there has been no uncontrolled outflow of persons from the poorest parts of the world to the richest. This is due largely to ever more restrictive immigration regimes established by receiving states, and without these formal interdictions the movements would doubtless be much greater.[5] Whether or not these regimes can be maintained into the next century, especially given demographic trends in the developing world and the current expansion in refugee situations, is very much an open question.

RICH AND POOR

Despite the devastating impact of two world wars on the Western Enlightenment ideal of material progress and human betterment, there has remained a large reservoir of confidence in the potential

216

for improving the human condition through the twin engines of advanced technology and global economic development. The last fifty years has been an era of rising levels of education, income and life span for the inhabitants of developed industrial countries. And these better educated, better fed and healthier humans have increasingly congregated in large metropolitan areas. After the Second World War about one-quarter of the earth's population lived in cities, but by 1990 this percentage had increased to just under a half of the total. Western urban civilization has in many respects been a story of material success since the defeat of totalitarianism in 1945, but that success is not unrelated to costs absorbed by peoples who were once subject to direct or indirect Western colonial rule.

For millions of mostly rural people in developing nations, wrenching poverty and a decreasing standard of living have been the norm for decades. And their flight to nearby domestic urban centres, most of which lack the infrastructure and public resources to handle the influx, has only exacerbated the myriad problems. In 1990 the World Bank estimated that over one billion people, or one-fifth of the globe's total population, lived in poverty. There are now more poor people on the planet than at any previous era, beginning with 1500. And demographic projections for the first half of the twenty-first century suggest that while the populations of Europe and North America will continue to stagnate thanks largely to the introduction of family planning and birth control measures, in the developing world fragile economies will struggle to support numbers which are now doubling every twenty-five years or even less.

Sending countries, as we have seen, tend to be places with rapidly expanding populations and comparatively low levels of economic development and job creation. And while public health measures have sharply reduced mortality rates in many poor sending states, concomitant internal social and economic trends of the type likely to lower fertility rates have not taken hold. Demographic boom areas in Africa, South Asia and Latin America now face the almost insuperable task of providing meaningful employment for their citizenry under conditions where available capital for infrastructure and physical plant is extremely limited.

Not surprisingly, nations with the highest level of economic development are also the principal target destinations for international migrants. North America, Europe, Australasia and Japan share a number of similarities; all are highly urbanized, all are governed in a democratic fashion, and all are characterized by low mortality and fertility levels.[6]

It is difficult to see how current trends in economic globalization will serve to alter migration patterns, particularly in the area of unskilled migrants seeking steady employment. Between 1995 and 2025, it is projected that the labour force in poor and developing countries will grow from 1.4 billion to 2.2 billion. Even robust trade with and economic development in these nations, were it to occur, is unlikely to accommodate the needs of the total workforce. Unfortunately, at present the vast bulk of globalization is focused on nations already far ahead in the development race. The least developed countries, home to 10 per cent of the world's population, enjoy a mere 0.3 per cent of current global trade. And 70 per cent of the world's population receives but 10 per cent of total global investment. The result has been a further widening of the gap between incomes in advanced and poor nations.

Thus far, globalization has done little to address widespread economic disparities, suggesting that migration pressures will only increase in the immediate future.[7] At present there are no large-scale international development projects designed specifically to provide basic needs satisfaction to the inhabitants of the world's poorest countries or, much less, any structural changes in the current world market system designed to advantage developing states.[8] We are left with a situation where, in the absence of serious international effort to insure basic material needs worldwide, continued international migration, often illegal migration, offers the only plausible prospect for individuals to improve their economic status.

CHEERIER FORECASTS

To be fair, the scenario outlined here has not gone unchallenged. Many free-market economists believe that as the global market extends its sway, economic conditions will improve in every nation where capitalist and internationalist market principles have taken root; that a convergence of material standards will be the end result of the emerging world economy.[9] If true, this would certainly be welcome news to Chinese authorities, as one recent estimate suggested that China has 200 million more workers than it can productively employ, and for political leaders in Indonesia, where the workforce faces an unemployment rate of around 40 per cent.[10]

The solution to unbalanced wealth and resources, these observers claim, is to accelerate the drawing down of national borders on the technological, manufacturing and financial fronts. Continue the flow of capital, plant, knowledge and money across international frontiers – everything but labour. The labour problem will sort itself out once the appropriate economic correctives are applied. Neoclassical economics tends to emphasize differences in wage rates between sending and receiving countries, looking especially at individual decisions to relocate on the basis of potential income and lifestyle improvements. According to these economists, the solution to high levels of international migration rests with the elimination of these great wage differentials through further development and freer trade.

WORLD SYSTEMS THEORY

A less confident theoretical perspective has emerged more recently and focuses attention on macro-level structural changes which accompany a particular nation's entry into the global market. So-called 'world systems theory' emphasizes the unequal terms of trade between developed and post-colonial developing countries around the world. It argues that the penetration of capitalism into pre-market societies creates a mobile, and underemployed, population which is then obliged to migrate to more developed centres.

World systems theorists emphasize the role of non-governmental agencies, such as banks and international corporations, in advancing the flow of international migration. As capitalists enter poorer countries in search of greater economies in terms of labour, materials and land, political elites in the target nations offer these

219

resources on attractive terms in hopes of pushing their states down the path of economic maturity. And as landholdings are consolidated, production mechanized, minerals extracted and crops produced for a wider market, traditional land tenure practices are upset and workers are made redundant. A mobile labour force then begins the process of movement first to urban areas at home and, finding little prospect of meaningful employment there, to foreign destinations where unskilled labour is in much greater demand. This transfer is facilitated by capitalist penetration of these states in the form of communications and transportation infrastructure, designed initially to move product, but also useful in the movement of displaced people.

World systems theory also links the growth of the military in core developed nations, particularly in the United States, with a larger objective of preserving the capitalist system as it penetrates new markets. Military intervention, both during the decades of the Cold War, and more recently in a multipolar world, is often linked to the preservation of political regimes that embrace the capitalist development paradigm. And the many links which the military establishes with political elites in these states, together with personal relationships and commercial bonds, also contribute to the migration flow into the dominant core country. The migration of South Vietnamese to the United States during the mid-1970s is an example of this type of linkage.

One prominent feature of world systems theory is its claim that migration is most likely to originate in areas already in the early stages of modernization and the development of market economies. This was the situation in Europe during the age of the 'Great Migration' in the late nineteenth century. Origin states are not those which are isolated from the main lines of global trade and communication, and where inhabitants are poor labourers who choose to relocate absent any external penetration of their traditional means of production. It is development, not the absence of it, that propels international migration in the contemporary world. The theory offers compelling empirical evidence from a number of regions around the globe, and if correct it suggests that the very process of extending global capitalism and market mechanisms results in more, not less, international migration, and especially migration by unskilled labourers.

CULTURES AND MIGRATION

It is perhaps useful to consider a wider range of variables when attempting to understand international migration over the past half century, and into the next. Individual calculations about a better lifestyle, household decisions to allow certain members to migrate with the goal of assisting those back home (a form of insurance in countries where there are no state-backed unemployment and insurance schemes), fear or direct experience of persecution at the hands of intolerant regimes, responses to famine, and capitalist market penetration into previously stable agricultural societies – all undoubtedly play some role in the current complicated migration phenomenon.

Whatever the relevant combination of factors, the movement of peoples across international borders will continue to redefine host cultures. Sadly, the Western view of international migration at the start of the twenty-first century is generally a negative one. Destination countries are no longer the land-rich, sparsely populated regions which served as an outlet for Western Europeans throughout the nineteenth century. North America, Europe, the Gulf States, parts of Asia, and the southern cone of South America are now the key destination points, but labour demands in these areas often compete with nativist arguments against diversity. Since the overwhelming majority of trans-state migrants are unskilled and poorly educated persons seeking employment in labour-intensive and service industries, popular opinion in democratic countries largely disparages the potential contributions of new migrants; this despite the obvious fact that immigrants often take up positions in the very sectors of the economy where natives are loath to engage. The same bifurcated outlook can be witnessed in Muslim Gulf State monarchies, where authoritarian rulers emphatically deny migrant workers any right to permanent resident status.

Funds, information and goods moved ever more freely across international borders at the start of the new century, but the relocation of people remained the one notable exception to globalization. Rather than make provision for the free transfer of peoples to centres of employment, international business brought physical manufacturing plant to the source of labour. The fact that the cost of labour was substantially lower in most potential sending areas meant that there existed a huge political incentive for maintaining stringent immigration regimes in the developed West. Poverty in distant lands was preferable to facing higher labour costs at home.

Undoubtedly some of the most difficult and poignant migration challenges occur in contiguous nation states with sharply unequal income levels. Whenever developed nations share a common border, an 'interface region' with a poor neighbour, forceful migration control regimes are erected. And whenever the economic imbalance is coupled with a cultural, religious and linguistic divide, as in the case of Mexico and the United States, the proclivity for distrust and misunderstanding is compounded. The adoption of the North American Free Trade Agreement in 1994 clearly facilitated the movement of capital and manufacture within the Canadian, Mexican and United States zones, and a robust North American economy during the 1990s greatly accelerated the migration levels of Mexican nationals into the United States, but these developments have done little to assuage a widespread perception among North Americans that a greater inclusion of Latinos is no more than a necessary evil.

Fear of the outsider, especially as it has recently manifested itself in the old, Europe-inspired receiving nations like the United States, too often serves to obscure the many demonstrated positives of increased international migration flows. Not the least of these benefits is the undoubted vigour and new ideas which recent arrivals bring to their host culture. The historian William McNeill has written that the contrast between cultures is the main drive wheel of history because new ideas and new techniques – often the result of cultural interaction – enable people to change and better adapt to their environment. Cultural diffusion, meetings between strangers, enliven and enrich the human journey.[11] As the twenty-first century unfolds, the ability of humans to preserve both the planet and themselves may indeed hinge upon negotiating difference, learning from and adapting to 'the other'. Forging institutional mechanisms whereby the process of human relocation might continue on the basis of choice rather than compulsion will not be easy, but the effort might best be looked upon as a simple survival strategy, an exercise in civilized behaviour.

Notes

Introduction

1. L.S. Stavrianos, *Lifelines from Our Past: A New World History* (Armonk, NY, 1997), p. 19, argues that early kinship societies were largely cooperative and communal, and that food production and consumption was based on reciprocity.
2. E.L. Jones, *The European Miracle* (Cambridge, 1987), pp. 229–31.
3. Mike Parnwell, *Population Movements and the Third World* (New York, 1993), p. 49.
4. Douglas S. Massey, *et al.*, *Worlds in Motion: Understanding International Migration at the End of the Millennium* (Oxford, 1998).
5. Immanuel Wallerstein, *The Modern World System: Capitalist Agriculture and the Origins of the European World-Economy in the Sixteenth Century* (New York, 1974), p. 15.
6. University of Leiden History of International Migration Site (www.let.leidenuniv.nl/history/migration/chapter3.html)
7. Robin Cohen, ed., *The Cambridge Survey of World Migration* (Cambridge, 1995), p. 3.
8. Alfred Crosby, *Germs, Seeds and Animals: Studies in Ecological History* (Armonk, NY, 1994), pp. 29, 30.
9. Massey, *et al.*, *Worlds in Motion*, pp. 1–2.
10. Ronald Skeldon, *Migration and Development: A Global Perspective* (Harlow, Essex, 1997), ix.

Part One

1. William Woodruff, *A Concise History of the Modern World* (London, 1998), pp. 1–3.
2. Columbus, *Journal*, quoted in C. Ho, S. Sawin, and W.M. Spellman, eds, *The Medieval and Renaissance World* (Asheville, NC, 1999), pp. 373.
3. Quoting Han Fe Tzu (*c*. 280–223 BCE) in Donald S. Gochberg, *et al.*, *World Literature and Thought: The Ancient Worlds* (Fort Worth, TX, 1997), p. 504. For the medieval Christian perspective, see R.H. Tawney, *Religion and the Rise of Capitalism*.

Notes

Chapter One

1. J.M. Roberts, *History of the World* (Harmondsworth, 1997), p. 510.
2. Peter Musgrave, *The Early Modern European Economy* (New York, 1999), p. 165.
3. Jerry H. Bentley, *Old World Encounters: Cross Cultural Contacts and Exchanges in Pre-Modern Times* (Oxford, 1993), pp. 168–70.
4. Musgrave, *Early Modern European Economy*, p. 39. See also Leslie Page Moch, *Moving Europeans: Migration in Western Europe since 1650* (Bloomington, 1992).
5. Semour Phillips, 'The Medieval Background' in Nicholas Canny, ed., *Europeans on the Move: Studies on European Migration, 1500–1800* (Oxford, 1994), pp. 9–25.
6. Roberts, *History of the World*, p. 513.
7. On new naval technologies and Spanish expansion, see Peter Biaxial, *A History of Latin America* (Oxford, 1997), pp. 40–1.
8. P.C. Elmer and E. Van Den Badgered, 'Colonialism and Migration: an Overview' in Elmer, ed., *Colonialism and Migration: Indentured Labour before and after Slavery* (Dordrecht, 1986), p. 3.
9. G.V. Scammell, *The First Imperial Age: European Overseas Expansion c. 1400–1750* (London, 1989), pp. 170–1.
10. William H. McNeill, 'The Great Frontier: Freedom and Hierarchy' in David J. Weber and Jane M. Rausch, eds, *Where Cultures Meet: Frontiers in Latin American History* (Wilmington, DE, 1994), p. 65.
11. Ibid.
12. Roberts, *History of the World*, p. 532.
13. Darwin, quoted in Alfred Crosby, *Germs, Seeds and Animals*, p. 12.
14. David Northrup, *Indentured Labour in the Age of Imperialism, 1834–1922* (New York, 1995), p. 4.
15. Magnus Morner, *Adventurers and Proletarians: The Story of Migrants in Latin America* (Pittsburgh, 1985), p. 9; Nicholas Sanchez-Albornoz, 'The First Transatlantic Transfer: Spanish Migration to the New World, 1493–1810' in Canny, ed., *Europeans on the Move*, pp. 27–8, 33.
16. Sanchez-Albornoz in Canny, ed., *Europeans on the Move*, p. 31.
17. Ida Altman, 'Spanish Migration to the Americas' in Robin Cohen, ed., *The Cambridge Survey of World Migration* (Cambridge, 1995), p. 28. [All subsequent references to this text will be abbreviated *CSWM*]
18. Morner, *Adventurers*, p. 12.
19. Philip D. Curtin, 'Migration in the Tropical World' in Virginia Yans-McLaughlin, *Immigration Reconsidered: History, Sociology and Politics* (New York, 1990), p. 28.
20. Asuncion Lavrin, 'Women in Spanish American colonial society' in Leslie

226

Bethell, ed., *The Cambridge History of Latin America*, 8 vols (Cambridge, 1986), 2:322.

21. Ibid., p. 323.
22. Peter Biaxial, *A History of Latin America* (Oxford, 1997), pp. 158–9.
23. Magnus Morner, 'Spanish Migration to the New World Prior to 1810' in Fredi Chiappelli, ed., *First Images of America: The Impact of the New World on the Old*, 2 vols (Berkeley, 1976), 2:753.
24. Mark Burkholder and Lyman Johnson, *Colonial Latin America* (New York, 1998), p. 114.
25. Altman in Cohen, ed., *CSWM*, p. 29.
26. Burkholder and Johnson, *Colonial Latin America*, p. 113; Morner, *Adventurers*, p. 10.
27. Maria Luiza Marcillo, 'The Population of Colonial Brazil' in *Cambridge History of Latin America*, pp. 48–9.
28. Ibid., pp. 42–3.
29. Burkholder and Johnson, *Colonial Latin America*, p. 128.
30. See Crosby, *Germs, Seeds and Animals*, p. 84; Nicholas Sanchez-Albornoz, 'The population of colonial Spanish America' in *The Cambridge History of Latin America*, 1:5–7, provides a breakdown for each region of the Spanish and Portuguese empires. Burkholder and Johnson, *Colonial Latin America*, p. 108, estimate that the total population for the Americas was between 35 and 45 million, but they acknowledge that scholars continue to disagree. See also William M. Denevan, ed., *The Native Population of the Americas in 1492* (Madison, WI, 1992), xxvii.
31. Burkholder and Johnson, *Colonial Latin America*, p. 2.
32. Cortez quoted in Biaxial, *A History*, p. 20.
33. Sanchez-Albornoz in Canny, ed., *Europeans on the Move*, 15.
34. Musgrave, *Early Modern European Economy*, p. 168.
35. Herbert S. Klein, *The Atlantic Slave Trade* (Cambridge, 1999), p. 18.
36. Biaxial, *A History*, p. 154; Burkholder and Johnson, *Colonial Latin America*, p. 117.
37. Sanchez-Albornoz in Canny, p. 4.
38. Bernard Waites, *Europe and the Third World: From Colonization to Decolonisation, c. 1500–1998* (New York, 1999), p. 34.
39. Scammell, *First Imperial Age*, p. 173.
40. David Hacket Fisher, *Albion's Seed: Four British Folkways in America* (New York, 1989), p. 16.
41. Bernard Bailyn, *The Peopling of British North America* (New York, 1988), pp. 9–14.
42. Marianne S. Wokeck, *Trade in Strangers: The Beginnings of Mass Migration to North America* (University Park, PA, 1999), describes the nature of the changes in migration patterns and transportation networks after 1700.

43. Bailyn, *The Peopling*, p. 16.
44. Richard S. Dunn, 'Servants and Slaves: the Recruitment and Employment of Labour' in Jack P. Green and J.R. Pole, eds, *Colonial British America* (Baltimore, 1984), p. 171.
45. Franklin quoted in John Isbister, *The Immigration Debate: Remaking America* (West Hartford, CT, 1998), p. 7.
46. Dunn in Green and Pole, p. 159.
47. Richard Middleton, *Colonial America: A History, 1585–1776* (Oxford, 1996), p. 12.
48. Burkholder and Johnson, *Colonial Latin America*, p. 127.
49. Edmund Morgan, *The Puritan Dilemma* (Boston, 1958), pp. 34–44.
50. K.G. Davies, *The North Atlantic World in the Seventeenth Century* (Minneapolis, 1974), p. 63.
51. Carl Ubbelohde, *The American Colonies and the British Empire, 1607–1763* (New York, 1968), p. 2.
52. Davies, *The North Atlantic World*, p. 63.
53. Stephen Saunders Webb, *1676: The End of American Independence* (New York, 1984).
54. Davies, *The North Atlantic World*, p. 66.
55. Roberts, *History of the World*, p. 513.
56. Scammell, *First Imperial Age*, p. 44.
57. Richard Middleton, *Colonial America, 1585–1776* (Oxford, 1996), p. 32.
58. Neal Salisbury, 'Native People and European Settlers in Eastern North America, 1600–1783' in Bruce Trigger and Wilcomb E. Washburn, eds, *The Cambridge History of the Native Peoples of the Americas*, 2 vols (Cambridge, 1996), 1:402–3.
59. Francis Jennings, *The Invasion of America: Indians, Colonialism, and the Cant of Conquest* (Chapel Hill, 1975), p. 30.
60. Cotton and Winthrop quoted in Noble David Cook, *Born to Die: Disease and New World Conquest, 1492–1650* (Cambridge, 1998), p. 199.
61. Amherst quoted in Russell Thornton, *American Indian Holocaust and Survival: A Population History Since 1492* (Norman, OK, 1987), p. 79.
62. James Axtell, *Natives and Newcomers: The Cultural Origins of North America* (Oxford, 2001), pp. 285, 290–1.

Chapter Two

1. Curtin, in Yans-McLaughlin, *Migration*, p. 21.
2. Bill Freund, *The Making of Contemporary Africa*, 2nd edition (Boulder, CO, 1998), pp. 27–8. See also Thomas Spear, 'Bantu Migrations' in Robert O. Collins, ed., *Problems in African History: the Precolonial Times* (New York, 1993), p. 95.

3. J. Vansina, 'Population movements and the emergence of new socio-political forms in Africa' in B.A. Ogot, ed., UNESCO *General History of Africa: Africa from the Sixteenth to the Eighteenth Century* (Berkeley, CA, 1992), p. 46.

4. David Brion Davis, *Slavery and Human Progress* (New York, 1984), p. 47.

5. Paul Bohannan and Philip Curtin, *Africa and Africans* (Prospect Heights, IL, 1988), p. 286.

6. William D. Phillips, Jr., *Slavery from Roman Times to the Early Transatlantic Trade* (Minneapolis, 1985), p. 121.

7. Phillips, *Slavery*, p. 140; Robert W. July, *A History of the African People* (Prospect Heights, IL, 1992), p. 50.

8. Phillips, *Slavery*, p. 87.

9. Ibn Khaldun quoted, and slave trade figures cited in Davis, *Slavery*, p. 45.

10. Davis, *Slavery*, pp. 38–9.

11. Irwin, ed., *Africans Abroad: A Documentary History of the Black Diaspora in Asia, Latin America, and the Caribbean During the Age of Slavery* (New York, 1977), p. 58.

12. Phillips, *Slavery*, p. 125.

13. Irwin, ed., *Africans Abroad*, pp. 138, 141.

14. J.E. Inikori, ed., *Forced Migration: The Impact of the Export Slave Trade on African Societies* (New York, 1982), p. 83.

15. J.E. Harris, 'The African diaspora in the Old and New Worlds' in UNESCO *General History of Africa: Africa in the Nineteenth Century until the 1880s*, 7 vols (Berkeley, CA, 1989), 5:113.

16. Phillips, *Slavery*, p. 158.

17. Ibid., p. 161.

18. Harris, 'The African Diaspora', pp. 113–14.

19. F.W. Knight, 'The African Diaspora' in UNESCO *General History of Africa: Africa in the Nineteenth Century until the 1880s*, 5:751.

20. Ibid., p. 759.

21. Phillips, *Slavery*, p. 151.

22. Peter Bakewell, *A History of Latin America* (Oxford, 1997), p. 156.

23. Philip D. Curtin, *The Atlantic Slave Trade: A Census* (Madison, WI, 1969), p. 87; Burkholder and Johnson, *Colonial Latin America*, p. 127.

24. Klein, *Atlantic Slave Trade*, p. 24; Davis, *Slavery*, xiii.

25. Curtin, *Atlantic Slave Trade*, p. 21; John Iliffe, *Africans: the History of a Continent*, (Cambridge, 1995), p. 131.

26. Quoting Crosby, p. 89.

27. Phillips, *Slavery*, p. 215; Burkholder and Johnson, *Colonial Latin America*, pp. 130–1.

28. Iliffe, *Africans*, p. 129.

29. Ibid., p. 131.

30. Bohannan and Curtin, *Africa and Africans*, p. 291.

31. Knight, 'African Diaspora', pp. 751, 760.
32. Dudley Baines, *Emigration from Europe, 1815–1930* (London, 1991), p. 11.
33. Inikori, *Forced Migration*, pp. 103–4, 108–9.
34. Richard Ligon, 'A True & Exact History of the Island of Barbados' in Irwin, ed., *Africans Abroad*, p. 187.
35. Hans Sloane, *A Voyage to the Islands Madera, Barbados, Nieves, S. Christophers and Jamaica* in Irwin, *Africans Abroad*, ed., pp. 195–6.
36. July, *A History*, p. 227.
37. Ibid.
38. Ibid., p. 227.
39. Christopher Fyfe, 'Freed Colonies in West Africa' in J.D. Fage and Roland Oliver, eds, *The Cambridge History of Africa*, vol. 5 (Cambridge, 1976), 5:181.
40. Clay quoted in Fyfe, 'Freed Colonies', p. 189.
41. J. Gus Liebenow, *Liberia: The Quest for Democracy* (Bloomington, IN, 1987), pp. 12–13.
42. Cohen in *CSWM*, p. 37.
43. Aderanti Adepoju, 'Migration in Africa: an overview' in Jonathan Baker and Tade Akin Aina, eds, *The Migration Experience in Africa* (Sweden np. 1995), p. 99.

Part Two

1. *CSWM*, p. 11.

Chapter Three

1. William Woodruff, *A Concise History of the World, 1500 to the Present*, 3rd edn (London, 1998), p. 74.
2. Ronald Skeldon, *Migrational Development: A Global Perspective* (London, 1997), pp. 63–4.
3. Roger Daniels, *Coming to America: A History of Immigration and Ethnicity in American Life* (New York, 1990), p. 24.
4. Baines, *Emigration*, pp. 8, 28.
5. Ibid., p. 12.
6. Daniels, *Coming to America*, p. 27.
7. Walter T.K. Nugent, *Crossings: The Great Transatlantic Migration, 1870–1914* (Bloomington, IN, 1992), p. 35.
8. Ibid., p. 35.
9. Baines, *Emigration*, p. 42; Daniels, *Coming to America*, p. 183.
10. Baines, *Emigration*, p. 44.
11. Daniels, *Coming to America*, pp. 27–8.

12. Ibid., pp. 25, 124.

13. Ibid., p. 266.

14. Ibid., p. 274.

15. Ibid., p. 168.

16. Alvin Jackson, *Ireland, 1798–1998* (Oxford, 1999), p. 83.

17. Donald M. MacRaild, *Irish Migrants in Modern Britain, 1750–1922* (New York, 1999), p. 9.

18. I.M. Cullen, 'The Irish Diaspora of the Seventeenth and Eighteenth Centuries' in Canny, ed., *Europeans on the Move*, p. 113.

19. Kirby Miller, *Emigrants and Exiles: Ireland and the Irish Exodus to North America* (Oxford, 1985), pp. 137, 143.

20. Ibid., pp. 103, 138.

21. Cormac O'Grada, 'Poverty, Population, and Agriculture, 1801–1845' in W.E. Vaughan, ed., *A New History of Ireland*, 10 vols (Oxford, 1989), 5: p. 120.

22. Ibid., 5:120–1.

23. Kirby Miller, *Emigrants and Exiles: Ireland and the Irish Exodus to North America* (New York, 1985), p. 102.

24. MacRaild, *Irish Migrants*, pp. 3, 15.

25. R.F. Foster, *Modern Ireland, 1600–1972* (London, 1988), pp. 367–8.

26. O'Grada in Vaughan, p. 121; MaCraild, p. 33.

27. Foster, *Modern Ireland*, p. 355.

28. Ibid., p. 350.

29. James S. Donnelly, 'Excess Mortality and Emigration' in *New History of Ireland*, 5:356.

30. Dermot Keogh, *Twentieth-Century Ireland: Nation and State* (New York, 1995), p. 61.

31. Ibid., pp. 89, 164, 165.

32. Ibid., p. 217.

33. Charles Townsend, *Ireland: The 20th Century* (London, 1998), pp. 168–9.

34. Robert Hughs, *The Fatal Shore* (New York, 1987), pp. 2–3. Transportation officially ended in New South Wales in 1840; it continued on the island of Tasmania until 1852.

35. Jeffrey Grey, *A Military History of Australia* (Cambridge, 1999), p. 5.

36. Ibid., p. 29.

37. Brian Murphy, *The Other Australia: Experiences of Migration* (Cambridge, 1993), p. 14. The full story of women prisoners is treated in Deborah Oxley, *Convict Maids: The Forced Migration of Women to Australia* (Cambridge, 1996).

38. Murphy, *Other Australia*, pp. 9–10.

39. Murphy, *Other Australia*, p. 18; Jan Kociumbus, *The Oxford History of Australia, 1770–1860* vol. 2 (Oxford, 1992), p. 313.

40. Kociumbas, *The Oxford History of Australia, 1770–1860* vol. 2 (Oxford, 1992), p. 297.

41. Ibid., p. 311.
42. Beverly Kingston, *The Oxford History of Australia, 1860–1900* vol. 3 (Oxford, 1988), p. 108.
43. Ibid., p. 112.
44. Charles Wilson, *Australia, 1788–1988* (Totawa, NJ, 1988), p. 127.
45. Andrew Markus, *Australian Race Relations* (St Leonards, Australia, 1994), p. 111.
46. Murphy, *Other Australia*, p. 30.
47. Markus, *Australian Race Relations*, p. 141.
48. Ibid., pp. 141, 151.
49. Ibid., p. 152.
50. Snedden quoted in Geoffrey Bolton, *The Oxford History of Australia* vol. 5 (Oxford, 1990), pp. 106–7.
51. Bolton, *Oxford History*, p. 53.
52. Murphy, *Other Australia*, p. 10; Bolton, *Oxford History*, p. 106.
53. Murphy, *Other Australia*, p. 172.
54. Hew R. Jones, 'Immigration Policy and the New World Order: the case of Australia' in W.T.S. Gould and A.M. Findlay, eds, *Population Migration and the New World Order* (New York, 1994), pp. 163, 165.
55. Grassby quoted in Markus, *Australian Race Relations*, p. 182.
56. Murphy, *Other Australia*, p. 221.
57. Sanchez-Albornoz, 'The population of Latin America, 1850–1930' in *The Cambridge History of Latin America*, 4:121.
58. Morner, *Adventurers*, pp. 23, 26.
59. Henry Finch, 'Uruguayan Migration' in *CSWM*, p. 205.
60. Albornoz in *Cambridge History*, p. 126; Morner, *Adventurers*, p. 25.
61. Bakewell, *History of Latin America*, pp. 410–11.
62. Morner, *Adventurers*, p. 38.
63. Albornoz in *Cambridge History*, p. 123.
64. Morner, *Adventurers*, pp. 55, 77; Albornoz in *Cambridge History*, p. 129.
65. Bakewell, *History of Latin America*, p. 415.
66. Cohen in *CSWM*, p. 203; Jeremy Adelman, 'European Migration to Argentina, 1880–1930' *CSWM*, p. 216; Albornoz in *Cambridge History*, p. 135.
67. Herbert Klein, 'European and Asian Migration to Brazil' in *CSWM*, p. 209.
68. Stavrianos, *Lifelines*, pp. 116, 117.

Chapter Four

1. Alan Wood, ed., *The History of Siberia: From Russian Conquest to Revolution* (London, 1991), p. 3. On Yermak, see Valentin Rasputin, *Siberia, Siberia* trans. Margaret Winchell and Gerald Mikkelson (Evanston, IL, 1991), pp. 39–44.
2. Stephen Kotkin and David Wolff, eds, *Rediscovering Russia in Asia* (Armonk, NY, 1995), p. 3.

3. Donald W. Treadgold, *The Great Siberian Migration* (Princeton, 1957), p. 19.

4. Victor L. Mote, *Siberia: Worlds Apart* (Boulder, CO, 1998), p. 2.

5. David N. Collins, 'Subjugation and settlement in seventeenth and eighteenth-century Siberia' in Wood, ed., *History of Siberia*, p. 38.

6. Collins in Wood, ed., *History of Siberia*, p. 39.

7. Treadgold, *Siberia Migration*, p. 20.

8. J.L. Black, 'Opening Up Siberia: Russia's Window on the East' in Wood, ed., p. 59.

9. James Forsyth, 'The Siberian native peoples before and after the Russian conquest' in Wood, ed., *History of Siberia*, pp. 82–3.

10. Rasputin, *Siberia, Siberia*, p. 49.

11. Wood, 'Russia's Wild East: exile, vagrancy and crime in nineteenth-century Siberia' in Wood, ed., *History of Siberia*, p. 118.

12. Mote, *Worlds Apart*, pp. 45, 61.

13. Leonid M Goryuskin, 'Migration, settlement and the rural economy of Siberia, 1861–1914' in Wood, ed., *History of Siberia*, pp. 140, 143. See also Steven G. Maks, 'Conquering the Great East' in Kotkin and Wolff, *Rediscovering Russia*, p. 23.

14. Goryuskin 14. For a description of life in newly constructed migrat villages, see Treadgold, *Siberia Migration*, pp. 132–40.

15. John Channon, 'Siberia in revolution and civil war, 1917–1921' in Wood, ed., *History of Siberia*, p. 159.

16. John Forsyth, *A History of the Peoples of Siberia: Russia's North Asian Colony, 1581–1990* (Cambridge, 1991), p. 292; Mote, *Worlds Apart*, pp. 93–4.

17. Forsyth, *Peoples of Siberia*, p. 363.

18. Rasputin, *Siberia, Siberia*, p. 372.

19. David Northrup, *Indentured Labour in the Age of Imperialism* (New York, 1995), pp. 8–9.

20. Ceri Peach, 'Three Phases of South Asian Emigration' in Judith M. Brown and Rosmary Foot, eds, *Migration: The Asian Experience* (Houndmills, 1994), p. 38.

21. Thomas Sowell, *Migrations and Culture* (New York, 1996), p. 312; Hugh Tinker, *The Banyan Tree: Overseas Emigrants from India, Pakistan, and Bangladesh* (Oxford, 1977), p. 11; Peach in Brown and Foot, *Migration*, p. 38.

22. Stanley Wolpert, *A New History of India* (New York, 2000), p. 136.

23. Ibid., pp. 143–4.

24. P.J. Marshall, 'British Immigration into India in the Nineteenth Century' in P.C. Emmer and M. Morner, eds, *European Expansion and Migration: Essays on the Intercontinental Migration from Africa, Asia, and Europe* (New York, 1992), pp. 183–9.

25. Madhavi Kale, *Fragments of Empire: Capital, Slavery, and Indian Indentured Labor Migration in the British Caribbean* (Philadelphia, 1998), sees the process

of labour migration as part of a larger and deliberate imperial labour reallocation in the wake of slavery's collapse.

26. Russell in Northrup, *Indentured Labour*, p. 62.
27. Ravinder K. Thiara, 'Indian Indentured Workers in Mauritius, Natal and Fiji' in *CSWM*, p. 63.
28. Stavrianos, *Lifelines*, p. 192.
29. Hugh Tinker, *A New System of Slavery: The Export of Indian Labour Overseas, 1830–1920* (Oxford, 1974), chapter 6, provides coverage of the plantation system.
30. Thiara in *CSWM*, pp. 66–7.
31. Thomas R. Metcalf, *Ideologies of the Raj* (Cambridge, 1994), p. 216.
32. Steven Vertovec, 'Indian Indentured Migration to the Caribbean' in *CSWM*, pp. 57–61.
33. Sowell, *Migrations*, p. 367.
34. Ibid., p. 314.
35. Tinker, *The Banyan Tree*, p. 2.
36. Sowell, *Migrations*, p. 314; Peach in Brown and Foot, p. 40.
37. J.S. Mangat, *A History of the Asians in East Africa, 1896–1965* (Oxford, 1969), p. 39.
38. Quoted in Metcalf, *Ideologies*, p. 219.
39. Sowell, *Migrations*, p. 323.
40. Ibid., pp. 321–2, 328.
41. Tinker, *The Banyan Tree*, p. 150; Peach in Brown and Foot, *Migration*, p. 46.
42. Peach in Brown and Foot, *Migration*, pp. 48, 50.
43. Lynn Pan, *Sons of the Yellow Emperor: A History of the Chinese Diaspora* (New York, 1994), p. 6.
44. Ibid., pp. 25, 48–9.
45. Ibid., p. 8.
46. Evelyn Hu-Dehart, 'The Chinese of Peru, Cuba and Mexico' in *CSWM*, p. 220.
47. Marianne Bastid-Bruguière, 'Currents of Social Change' in Denis Twitchett and John K. Fairbank, eds, *The Cambridge History of China* (Cambridge, 1980), 2:582.
48. Walter Look Lai in Pan, *Yellow Emperor*, p. 52; Sowell, *Migrations*, pp. 175, 183, 192.
49. On the Chinese self-perception in 1800, see Olivier Bernier, *The World in 1800* (New York, 2000), pp. 293–7.
50. Bastid-Bruguière in Twitchett and Fairbank, *Cambridge History*, p. 582.
51. Lynn Pan, ed., *The Encyclopedia of the Chinese Overseas* (Cambridge, MA, 1999), p. 61.
52. Bastid-Bruguière in Twitchett and Fairbank, *Cambridge History*, 2:584–5.
53. Jonathan Spence, *The Search for Modern China* (New York, 1999), p. 210.
54. Pan, ed., *Chinese Overseas*, p. 58.

55. Pan, *Yellow Emperor*, p. 21; Spence, *Modern China*, p. 209.

56. Sowell, *Migrations*, p. 185; Wang Gungwu, 'China's Policies Towards Overseas Chinese' in Pan, ed., *Chinese Overseas*, p. 99.

57. Spence, *Modern China*, pp. 210–11.

58. Ibid., p. 364.

59. Him Mark Lai, 'Immigration on An Equal Basis: after 1945' in Pan, ed., *Chinese Overseas*, p. 267.

60. Sowell, *Migrations*, p. 226.

61. James L. Tigner, 'Japanese Immigration into Latin America' in *Journal of Interamerican Studies and World Affairs* 23 (no. 4) 1981, p. 458.

62. Duncan McCargo, *Contemporary Japan* (New York, 2000), p. 19.

63. Tigner, 'Japanese Immigration', pp. 459, 462.

64. Sowell, *Migrations*, p. 107.

65. Gary Y. Okihiro, *Cane Fires: The Anti-Japanese Movement in Hawaii, 1865–1945* (Philadelphia, 1991), provides the best coverage of developments both before and after American involvement in the islands.

66. Tigner, 'Japanese Immigration', pp. 460, 463.

67. Mitsuru Shimpo, 'Indentured Migrants from Japan', *CSWM*, pp. 48–9.

68. Mark R. Peattie, 'The Japanese Colonial Empire, 1895–1945' in John W. Hall, *et al., The Cambridge History of Japan* 6 vols (Cambridge, 1988), 6:261–2.

69. Ibid., p. 262

70. Helmut Loiskandl, 'Illegal Migrant Workers in Japan' in *CSWM*, p. 371.

71. Michael Weiner, *Race and Migration in Imperial Japan* (New York, 1994), p. 214.

72. McCargo, *Contemporary Japan*, p. 70; Loiskandl in *CSWM*, p. 372.

73. McCargo, *Contemporary Japan*, p. 72; Peter Stalker, *Workers without Frontiers: The Impact of Globalization on International Migration* (Boulder, CO, 2000), p. 30.

Chapter Five

1. William H. McNeill, 'Demography and Urbanization' in *The Oxford History of the Twentieth Century* (Oxford, 1998), p. 8.

2. Alan Ryan, 'The Growth of a Global Culture' in *Oxford History*, p. 64.

3. Stalker, *Workers*, p. 14.

4. Skeldon, *Migrations*, p. 43.

5. George J. Borjas, *Heaven's Door: Immigration Policy and the American Economy* (Princeton, 1999), p. 4.

6. Skeldon, *Migrations*, p. 75.

7. Ibid., 77.

8. Robert Skidelsky, 'The Growth of a World Economy', in *Oxford History*, p. 57.

9. Stalker, *Workers*, p. 29.

10. Sabri Sayari, 'Migration Policies of Sending Countries: Perspectives on the Turkish Experience' in *The Annals of the America Academy of Political and Social Science*, vol. 485 (May 1986), p. 93.

11. Stephen Castles and Mark J. Miller, *The Age of Migration: International Population Movements in the Modern World* (New York, 1993), pp. 65–70.

12. Russell King, 'European International Migration, 1945–1990: a statistical and geographical overview' in King, ed., *Mass Migration in Europe: The Legacy and the Future* (London, 1993), p. 29.

13. Castles and Miller, *Age of Migration*, p. 79; Atalik and Beeley, p. 165.

14. Saskia Sassen, *Losing Control?: Sovereignty in the Age of Globalization* (New York, 1996), p. 80; Castles and Miller, *Age of Migration*, pp. 71–3.

15. Panikos Panayi, *The Impact of Immigration: A Documentary History of the Effects and Experiences of Immigrants in Britain Since 1945* (Manchester, 1999), p. 15.

16. Ibid., p. 28.

17. Mike Parnwell, *Population Movements and the Third World* (London, 1993), p. 61.

18. Atalik and Beeley, p. 166; Massey, pp. 134–5.

19. Massey, p. 138; Sergio DellaPergola, 'The Global Context of Migration to Israel' in Elazar Leshem and Judith T. Shuval, eds, *Immigration to Israel: Sociological Perspectives* (London, 1998), p. 65.

20. Nicholas Van Hear, *New Diasporas: The Mass Exodus, Dispersal and Regrouping of Migrant Communities* (Seattle, WA, 1998), p. 80.

21. Massey, p. 168.

22. Castles and Miller, *Age of Migration*, pp. 146–52.

23. Louis Desipio and Rudolfo O. De la Garza, *Making Americans, Remaking America* (Boulder, CO, 1998) p. 53.

24. Massey, *Worlds in Motion*, p. 203.

25. Desipio and De la Garza, *Making Americans*, p. 38.

26. Ibid., 40.

27. Massey, *Worlds in Motion*, p. 64.

28. Desipio and De la Garza, *Making Americans*, p. 49.

29. Borjas, *Heaven's Door*, p. 9. This figure actually exceeds the annual total for the period of the 'Great Migration', but since the country is much more populous today, the percentage of foreign-born residents in the overall population is much smaller (15 per cent in 1910 and 10 per cent in 1998).

30. John Isbister, *The Immigration Debate: Remaking America* (West Hartford, CT, 1998), pp. 2, 5.

31. Anthony Fielding, 'Migrations, institutions and politics: the evolution of European migration policies' in King, *Mass Migration in Europe*, p. 41.

32. Sassen, *Losing Control?*, pp. 72–3.

33. Anthony Fielding, 'Migrations, institutions and politics: the evolution of

European migration policies', p. 44.
34. Van Hear, *New Diasporas*, p. 25; Stalker, *Workers*, p. 95.
35. Stalker, *Workers*, p. 97.
36. Castles and Miller, *Age of Migration*, p. 269.
37. Skidelsky, 'The Growth of a World Economy' in *Oxford History*, p. 50.
38. Sassen, *Losing Control?*, pp. 59–60.

Chapter Six

1. Russell King, 'European International Migration, 1945–90: a statistical and geographical overview' in King, ed., *Mass Migration in Europe: The Legacy and the Future* (London, 1993), pp. 20–2.
2. Skeldon, *Migrations*, pp. 42–3.
3. Castles and Miller, *Age of Migration*, p. 9; Sassen, *Losing Control?*, p. 63.
4. Hannah Arendt, *The Origins of Totalitarianism* (Cleveland, 1969), p. 293.
5. Quoted in Valerie O'Conner Sutter, *The Indochinese Refugee Dilemma* (Baton Rouge, 1990), p. 1.
6. Michael R. Marrus, *The Unwanted: European Refugees in the Twentieth Century* (Oxford, 1985), pp. 6–7.
7. Ibid., pp. 14–18. See also the Website of the US Committee for Refugees at http://www.refugees.org
8. Ibid., pp. 18–23.
9. Robin Cohen, *Global Diasporas: An Introduction* (Seattle, WA, 1997), pp. 45–6.
10. Marrus, *Unwanted*, pp. 74–81.
11. Ibid., p. 92.
12. Cecil Roth, *A History of the Jews* (New York, 1970), pp. 149–68; Robert Chazan, 'The History of Medieval Jewry' in Burton Visotzky and David Fishman, eds, *From Mesopotamia to Modernity* (Boulder, CO, 1999), pp. 106–23.
13. Sowell, *Migrations*, p. 246.
14. Cohen, *Global Diasporas*, p. 9, and, more generally, Norman Roth, *Conversos, Inquisition, and the Expulsion of the Jews from Spain* (Madison, WI, 1995) and Jane Gerber, *The Jews of Spain: A History of the Sephardic Experience* (New York, 1992), pp. 115–44.
15. David Fishman, 'Modern Jewish History' in *From Mesopotamia to Modernity*, pp. 183–7; Sowell, *Migrations*, p. 258.
16. Tony Kushner and Katherine Knox, *Refugees in an Age of Genocide: Global, National and Local Perspectives during the Twentieth Century* (London, 1999), p. 149.
17. Sowell, *Migrations*, p. 265; Zvi Gitelman, 'From a Northern Country': Russian and Soviet Jewish Immigration to America and Israel in Historical Perspective'

237

in Noah Lewin-Epstein, Yaacov Ro'iand Paul Ritterband, eds, *Russian Jews on Three Continents* (London, 1997), pp. 23–5.

18. Sergio DellaPergola, 'The Global Context of Migration to Israel' in Elazar Leshem and Judith T. Shuval eds, *Immigration to Israel: Sociological Perspectives* (London, 1998), p. 55.

19. Cohen, *Global Diasporas*, pp. 13–14.

20. Ibid., p. 116. On early Zionism see Jacques Kornberg, Theodore Herzl (Bloomington, IN, 1993) and Anita Shapira, *Land and Power: The Zionist Resort to Force, 1881–1948* (Stanford, 1992), chapter 1.

21. The literature on the founding of the State of Israel is vast. Howard M. Sacher, *A History of Israel: From the Rise of Zionism to Our Time* (New York, 1979), offers a good starting point. See also Yossi Beilin, *Israel: A Concise Political History* (New York, 1992).

22. Ibid., p. 123.

23. Sowell, *Migrations*, pp. 234–5.

24. DellaPergola in Leshem and Shuval, eds, p. 63.

25. Ibid., p. 51.

26. Majid Al-Haj, 'Soviet Immigration as Viewed by Jews and Arabs: Divided Attitudes in a Divided Country' in Leshem and Shuval, eds, p. 212.

27. Mike Parnwell, *Population Movements and the Third World* (New York, 1993), p. 41.

28. Ibid., p. 52.

29. US Committee for Refugees Home Page http//www.refugees.org

30. John Chr. Knudsen, 'When Trust is on Trial: Negotiating Refugee Narratives' in E. Valentine Daniel and John Chr. Knedson, *Mistrusting Refugees* (Berkeley, CA, 1995), p. 14.

31. Arnold R. Isaacs, *Vietnam Shadows: The War, Its Ghosts, and Its Legacy* (Baltimore, 1995), p. 150.

32. James M. Freeman, *Changing Identities: Vietnamese Americans, 1975–1995* (Boston, 1995), p. 2.

33. Isaacs, *Vietnam Shadows*, p. 155.

34. James W. Tollefson, 'Indochinese Refugees: a Challenge to America's Memory of Vietnam' in D. Michael Shafer, ed., *The Legacy: The Vietnam War in the American Imagination* (Boston, 1990), p. 264.

35. Isaacs, *Vietnam Shadows*, p. 160.

36. Quoted in Isaacs, *Vietnam Shadows*, p. 149.

37. Stanley Wolpert, *A New History of India* (Oxford, 1999); Larry Collins and Dominique Lapierre, *Freedom at Midnight* (New York, 1975), provide good coverage of early refugee crises in the post-independence era.

38. Hugh McLeod, *Sikhism* (New York, 1997), offers a good analysis of Sikh culture and politics.

39. William T.S. Gould, 'Population movements and the changing world order' in

W.T.S. Gould and A.M. Findlay, eds, *Population Migration and the Changing World Order* (Chichester, 1994), p. 4.

40. Adepoju in Baker and Tede Akin Aina, eds, p. 101.
41. Castles and Miller, *Age of Migration*, p. 140.
42. Cohen, *Global Diasporas*, ix–x.
43. Hal Kane, *The Hour of Departure: Forces that Create Refugees and Migrants* (Washington, DC, 1995), pp. 18, 21.
44. Anthony Clayton, *Frontiersmen: Warfare in Africa since 1950* (London, 1999), p. 184.
45. Dallaire, *Hard Choices*, p. 78; Clayton, *Frontiersman*, p. 186; Kane, *Hour of Departure*, pp. 14, 21.
46. Samantha Power, 'Bystanders to Genocide' *Atlantic Monthly* (Sept 2001), pp. 84–108.
47. William R. Keylor, *The Twentieth-Century World* (New York, 2001), pp. 480–3; Robert F. Gorman, *Historical Dictionary of Refugee and Disaster Relief Organizations* (London, 2000), p. 250.

Conclusion

1. Skeldon, *Migrations*, p. 67.
2. Van Hear, *New Diasporas*, p. 3.
3. Ibid., p. 260.
4. Skeldon, *Migrations*, p. 202.
5. Skeldon, *Migrations*, p. 4; Massey, pp. 6–7.
6. Skeldon, *Migrations*, p. 77; Massey, p. 277.
7. Stalker, *Workers*, pp. 139–40.
8. Johan Galtung, 'Global Migration: A Thousand Years' Perspective' in Nicholas Polunin, ed., *Population and Global Security* (Cambridge, 1998), p. 174.
9. Matthew Connelly and Paul Kennedy, 'Must It Be the West Against the Rest?' *Atlantic Monthly* (1994), pp. 96–114.
10. Massey, p. 166.
11. William H. McNeill, *A History of the Human Community* (Englewood Cliffs, NJ, 1993), xiii.

Index

241